PLAYING THE SUPPORTING ROLE

Strip Club Managers and Other Third Parties

Strippers may be the main attraction of strip clubs, but their work is bolstered by people who are rarely meaningfully considered: those who organize, supervise, manage, or coordinate the labour of erotic dancers, including managers, bouncers, and disc jockeys. *Playing the Supporting Role* contends it is essential to explore the managerial layer in order to have a comprehensive understanding of the power relations and working conditions in the erotic dance sector – and, consequently, distinguish banal or beneficial from unfair or exploitative sex-industry labour practices.

Focusing primarily on third parties in the erotic dance sector, this book examines who these individuals are; how they manage clients, workers, security, and stigma; the services and resources they provide; and, in turn, strippers' experiences and perceptions of these practices. Through qualitative interview data with third parties and strippers from two Ontario cities, *Playing the Supporting Role* ultimately advances an understanding of third-party work as gendered, classed, and racialized occupational performance in a stigmatized labour sector that is simultaneously over- and under-regulated.

TUULIA LAW is an assistant professor of criminology at York University.

Playing the Supporting Role

Strip Club Managers and Other Third Parties

TUULIA LAW

UNIVERSITY OF TORONTO PRESS
Toronto Buffalo London

© University of Toronto Press 2023
Toronto Buffalo London
utorontopress.com

ISBN 978-1-4875-4894-0 (cloth)   ISBN 978-1-4875-5113-1 (EPUB)
ISBN 978-1-4875-4979-4 (paper)   ISBN 978-1-4875-5040-0 (PDF)

Library and Archives Canada Cataloguing in Publication

Title: Playing the supporting role : strip club managers and other third parties / Tuulia Law.
Names: Law, Tuulia, author.
Description: Includes bibliographical references and index.
Identifiers: Canadiana (print) 20230200338 | Canadiana (ebook) 20230200486 | ISBN 9781487548940 (cloth) | ISBN 9781487549794 (paper) | ISBN 9781487550400 (PDF) | ISBN 9781487551131 (EPUB)
Subjects: LCSH: Sex industry – Ontario. | LCSH: Sex industry – Ontario – Management. | LCSH: Sex industry – Ontario – Employees. | LCSH: Stripteasers – Ontario.
Classification: LCC HQ127.S77 L39 2023 | DDC 338.4/7306709713 – dc23

Cover design: Liz Harasymczuk
Cover image: Rene Böhmer/Unsplash

We wish to acknowledge the land on which the University of Toronto Press operates. This land is the traditional territory of the Wendat, the Anishnaabeg, the Haudenosaunee, the Métis, and the Mississaugas of the Credit First Nation.

This book has been published with the help of a grant from the Social Sciences and Humanities Research Council of Canada, through an institutional Knowledge Mobilization Grant.

The author and publisher would like to thank the Faculty of Liberal Arts & Professional Studies, York University, Toronto, Canada, for the financial support it provided to this work.

University of Toronto Press acknowledges the financial support of the Government of Canada, the Canada Council for the Arts, and the Ontario Arts Council, an agency of the Government of Ontario, for its publishing activities.

   Canada Council   Conseil des Arts
     for the Arts   du Canada

*To Chris Bruckert, who has accompanied my journey into academia, from the pages of her book, to supervising my graduate work, to writing together as peers:
I could not have gotten here without you.*

Contents

Acknowledgments ix

Introduction: Looking Beyond the Stage to See the Workplace 1

1 Who Are Third Parties? Managers, DJs, Bouncers, and Others 13

2 Is It Exploitation? A Closer Look at the Employment Relationship 33

3 Backstage: A Divided Workplace 54

4 Frontstage: Impression Management in a "Party" Environment 72

5 Safety and Security: Unpacking Danger, Mitigating Risks 94

6 Stigma, Stereotypes, and Solidarity 115

Conclusion: The Good, the Bad, and the Future of Strip Club Management 130

Appendix: Methodology 149

Notes 153

References 159

Index 183

Acknowledgments

This book would not have been possible without the help, participation, and encouragement of many people. First and foremost, thanks go to those who volunteered to participate in interviews and share their time and stories with me and other team members in the Rethinking Management in the Adult and Sex Industry Project. I am grateful to have been included in the project by its investigators, Drs Chris Bruckert, Colette Parent, Lesley Jeffrey, Maria Nengeh Mensah, and Patrice Corriveau, and to have worked alongside the community researchers and members of the community advisory group who facilitated the project's success. That project and my doctoral research, which together furnish the data used in this book, were funded through grants from the Social Sciences and Humanities Research Council of Canada.

Thanks also to the members of my thesis committee and examiners, Drs Samia Chreim, Steve Bittle, and Becki Ross, whose insightful comments informed this final iteration of my research on the erotic dance sector. And thanks to my informal key informants and friends, J and K, for keeping me accountable to the community. Thanks as well to my friend and comrade Dr Laura Kwak, who made the process of writing this book – from proposal drafting to editing again and again – seem more manageable, social, and important, in so many book-writing sessions over coffee or beer. Finally, thanks to the anonymous reviewers, whose perspective and meticulous attention made this a better book, and to everyone who contributed to its production at the University of Toronto Press, especially Jodi Lewchuk, who smoothly and calmly guided me through the whole process.

Introduction

Looking Beyond the Stage to See the Workplace

From the marquees and neon signs to the dimly lit, sexually charged ambiance of the club, to the skimpy outfits and seductive athleticism of the stage shows, it is clear that the strippers are the main attraction of the strip club. Looking beyond the veneer of spectacle, however, reveals the strip club to be a workplace and an environment curated and maintained by managers and other supporting workers – social actors who are rarely meaningfully considered. Understandably, for patrons enjoying an evening of erotically charged leisure, managers and other fully clothed staff sequestered in the back office, the DJ booth, and other margins of the club occasion little concern. Conversely, local residents and politicians opposed to strip clubs on moral grounds – of whom many (but probably not all) may never have set foot in a strip club – harbour considerable concern about management, whom they imagine to be exploiters, abusers, criminals, and even traffickers (Weitzer, 2012). Both of these framings overlook the practice and implications of management, and have shaped regulation that is overly restrictive of the services provided at strip clubs and negligent of occupational health and safety and workplace equity – issues that strippers themselves have decried time and again. This book seeks to address this paucity of knowledge through the perspectives of these supporting actors, put in conversation with strippers. In so doing, the book contends that it is essential to look at what managerial individuals do in order to thoroughly understand power relations and working conditions in the sex industry and, in turn, differentiate between violence, economic exploitation, and good employment practices (see Bruckert & Law, 2013; Bruckert & Parent, 2018).

Public understanding of sex industry working conditions has long been limited by stigmatic, misleading, and incomplete media and popular culture representations. Indeed, as Hallgrimsdottir et al. argue, "it is through the media that most of us, including academics and policy makers, acquire much of our knowledge of sex work" (2008, p. 120). That said, while, over the past twenty years, Canadian newspapers have wavered between representing strip clubs as tolerable local establishments and sites of exploitation and trafficking (Mensah, 2018, p. 24), generally speaking, news coverage reflects the dominant perception of strip clubs as relatively tame, compared to other sex industry businesses (e.g., erotic massage parlours) insofar as "strip club management appeared to be granted the most legitimacy as a sex industry source" (p. 29). Strippers have also occasionally been featured speaking for themselves in the news – more often when they have aligned with popular framings of lap dancing as demeaning, although some more recent coverage has featured strippers talking about unfair labour practices (see Law, 2015).

Entertainment media also exercise an important influence on popular understandings of stripping. Strippers populate the lyrics and videos of rap and hip hop, bolstering the pimp persona of "some of the biggest names in hip-hip culture, such as Jay-Z, 50 Cent, Snoop Dogg and Ice-T, ... even if these artists have never been pimps or on the streets themselves" (Benson, 2012, p. 430), or in narratives characterizing strippers as formidable self-made entrepreneurs (e.g., Megan Thee Stallion, Missy Elliott, Drake). Perhaps the most important and refreshing voice in this regard is rapper Cardi B, who, in her songs and press interviews, unashamedly references her career arc from stripper to musician, and who has risen to significant influence at a time when other celebrities have also begun to talk about their previous careers as strippers (e.g., Blac Chyna, Amber Rose). While their insistence that stripping/sex work is work is important, issues like employment relations and problematic managerial demands are largely absent from their narratives.

Strippers are also visible in contemporary television and movies, albeit more often in problematic depictions of stripping as a terrible fate from which women need to be rescued (*Afternoon Delight*, 2013), or in which they are killed – whether in tired tragic tropes (*I Know Who Killed Me*, 2007; several episodes of *Law and Order: SVU*) or jokes (*Rough Night*, 2017; *Unbreakable Kimmy Schmidt*, season 4, episode 1, 2018). When stripping is represented as a job, strippers are shown to be exciting and entrepreneurial (*Magic Mike XXL*, 2015; *Hustlers*, 2019), or the audience is given a brief glimpse of troubling management practices (*Magic Mike*, 2013; *We're the Millers*, 2013; Lee Daniels' *Star*, 2016). As this book endeavours to show, paying more attention to management reveals that stripping can involve both. When analysed using a labour framing and business terminology in place of the salacious imagery monetized in gangsta rap and mobilized in regulatory efforts to repress stripping and other forms of sex work, management and managers become relatively banal.

Moving from Sex Work to Labour Relations: Scholarly Perspectives

Like news media and pop culture narratives, academic scholarship has featured diverging framings of stripping and other commercialized sexual services, and these framings have evolved over time. Following radical feminist theorizations of gender relations centring men's "virtually transhistorical" domination and leaving little room for women's resistance or social change (Valverde, 1989, p. 239), some scholars view stripping, pornography, and prostitution as inherently violent, harmful, and degrading to women (e.g., MacKinnon, 1987; Dworkin, 1985; Holsopple, 1998). From this perspective, clients and managers, invariably assumed to be men, are seen as exercising and facilitating physical and sexual violence against women, who are characterized as victims or, in rare acknowledgments that some women do decide for themselves to sell sexual services, as desperate, falsely conscious, or ultimately harmed (e.g., Raymond, 2003; Day, 2008).

Conversely, scholars adhering to the opposing perspective examine involvement in the sex industry as labour. In so doing, they employ the term *sex work*, a description coined in 1980 by sex worker activist Carol Leigh (1997, p. 230), who, feeling objectified by the aforementioned feminists' focus on *men's use of prostitutes* wanted to redirect attention toward *what women do*. Academics who view sex work as stigmatized, precarious, and/or marginalized labour understand erotic dancers as skilled workers exercising agency in an environment that can be both empowering and constraining (examples of Canadian studies include Bouclin (2009), Bruckert, Parent, & Robitaille (2003), J. Lewis & Shaver (2006), Maticka-Tyndale (2004), and Ross (2000; 2009)). Research in this area has so far generally focused on, interviewed, and attended to the concerns of strippers, examining their relationship to the work, money, and clients, and highlighting their experiential knowledge.

Further nuancing this labour framework, some recent strip club research has attended to power relations and their impact on working conditions. Althorp (2013) and Bradley-Engen and Hobbs (2010) have studied the regulation and organization of labour in the erotic dance sector; Egan (2004), Lavin (2013), and Murphy (2003) have examined managerial surveillance and social control in strip clubs; Maticka-Tyndale et al. (2000) and Lewis and Shaver (2006) have identified lacunae in occupational health and safety; while Bouclin (2004; 2006; 2009),

Bruckert (2002), Egan (2006b), and Lewis (2006) have drawn attention to dancers' resistance amid problematic working conditions. Such studies have generally examined the management of strip clubs from the perspective of dancers, although some include information garnered from (usually one or two) managerial individuals as a secondary focus to dancers' work and experiences.[1] Only DeMichele and Tewksbury (2004) focus explicitly on the perspective and role of strip club bouncers. In contrast, this book contributes to the erotic dance and sex work literature by featuring the narratives of strippers as well as those of third parties – the people who organize, supervise, manage, or coordinate their labour. In so doing, it demonstrates that bringing third parties to the foreground – examining who they are and what they do, as well as the services and supports they provide – is necessary for a fulsome understanding of the conditions and challenges faced by erotic dancers. Moreover, by including the perspectives of an equal number of strippers and third parties (fifteen of each), the research contributes a more expansive view of third parties' tasks, experiences, and perspectives than previous studies have done.

Socio-Legal Context: Putting Ontario's Erotic Dance Sector in Perspective

In featuring third parties' perspectives and experiences alongside those of strippers, this book brings to life a sector of the sex industry that is, in spite of regional variation, generally more integrated into mainstream nightlife and less stigmatized and criminalized than other forms of sex work. As the book draws on data from Toronto and Ottawa, Ontario, Canada, the following socio-legal context puts strip clubs in historical and regional perspective while highlighting some cross-cutting issues shaping worker-manager relations.

While Ontario strip clubs have featured full nudity since the 1970s, contemporary clubs offer lap dancing, which involves a dancer sitting between a customer's legs or directly on, or hovering above, their lap, and dancing against and about the customer. In Ontario, strip clubs are legally permissible insofar as they are licensed by the province as liquor establishments and by the municipality as adult entertainment purveyors. However federal morality laws pertaining to bawdy houses, indecency, and trafficking have historically been used to police strip clubs, though they have not consistently culminated in convictions (Bruckert & Dufresne, 2002; Law, 2015).

As Lewis has observed, the introduction of physical contact with lap dancing in the mid-1990s "resulted in a blurring of the boundaries between stripping and prostitution," leading to "the defining of lap dancing as a social problem" (J. Lewis, 2000, p. 203). Newspaper coverage, local residents, and municipal politicians framed lap dancing as prostitution, demeaning to women, and criminogenic, characterizations that slowly relaxed as the practice became more institutionalized and tolerated, with cries of immorality and surveillance turning instead toward erotic massage parlours in the mid- to late 2000s (Law, 2015). Even some strippers objected to lap dancing in its early days, calling the practice divisive and referring to those who engaged in it as "Dirty Girls" (DERA, 2002, p. 8). While the dancers who participated in this study did not hierarchically differentiate "Dirty Girls" from "Good Girls," they remain concerned about financial competition with regard to the extent of sensual/sexual services offered in strip clubs.

The regulation of lap dancing has similarly been the subject of considerable debate. Supreme Court justices have wavered, at first ruling that the touching occurring in lap dances was indecent (in *R v Mara*, 1997), and subsequently, amid some dissention, that touching between dancer and patron is not indecent as long as it is out of public view (*R v Pelletier*, 1999). After the Supreme Court of Canada fell short of prohibiting lap dancing, local authorities stepped in, with most Ontario municipalities introducing bylaws against physical and/or sexual contact between dancers and customers. However the practice continued unabated, becoming established as the norm, and, over time, bylaw enforcement waned alongside moralistic zeal. Indeed, Toronto municipal officials admitted in 2002 that strip club bylaws were "generally violated,"[2] but the city did not review its adult entertainment parlour regulations until 2012, in a process culminating in a slight relaxation of the touching prohibition (Law, 2015). Thus, there remains a tension between Ontario's strip club bylaws and practices.

Compared to other Canadian jurisdictions, Ontario strip clubs are perhaps most similar to those in Quebec. Indeed, the club that occasioned the *Pelletier* decision was in Quebec, a province long known for its liberal attitudes toward strip clubs. Although a 2009 provincial court decision rendered the practice punishable under the bawdy-house provision of the *Criminal Code* (see *Alexandre c R*, 2009), lap dancing in Quebec continues to include touching, but clubs are subject to police scrutiny. By contrast, lap dancing is not as prominent a practice in other parts of the country. In Alberta and British Columbia, stage shows are the main attraction, and lap dancing occurs in only some clubs. Other provinces are even more conservative: for example, contact is not allowed in Nova Scotia, where the province's last strip club closed in 2018, along with the lone remaining club in Prince Edward

Island (Hanlon, 2014; Hayes, 2018), and the few businesses in Saskatchewan that have attempted to circumvent provincial regulations prohibiting full frontal nudity in establishments serving liquor have not lasted (Giles, 2014; Melnychuk, 2019; Teitel, 2015). In short, stripping in Canada is informed by local social norms and is subject to provincial and municipal regulation, and occasionally federal criminal laws, all of which may be applied (or ignored) to varying extents, depending on the city and the club.

Internationally, it appears that stripping is a Western cultural phenomenon.[3] Although erotic dance varies considerably across the United States (from peep shows, to topless only bars, to clubs with physical contact), scholars report significant workplace inequities and managerial control over dancers (Barton, 2006; Bradley-Engen & Ulmer, 2009; Brooks, 2010; Egan, 2006b), issues that have also been noted in Canada, Australia, and the United Kingdom. Lap dancing arrived later in the United Kingdom than in North America – according to Hubbard (2009), the practice was introduced when a Toronto chain opened a location in London – and municipalities responded with the imposition of strict regulations (Hubbard & Colosi, 2012). Lap dances are also offered in Australia, and some clubs even arrange dates outside the club, but, as with Canadian jurisdictions where lap dancing is allowed, no genital touching, penetration, or oral sex is permitted in licensed strip clubs (Jeffries & Lynch, 2007).

At the same time as they are relatively permissive, compared to their counterparts in other provinces and countries, Ontario strip clubs are subject to regulations that are similar to other jurisdictions, insofar as they derive from moral concerns and neglect occupational concerns (Bruckert & Dufresne, 2002). In this context, club operators across Canada, the United States, and the United Kingdom have taken advantage of a dearth of labour oversight to offer sub-par working conditions and limit dancers' access to labour rights. These factors shape the relationship between management and dancers that this book seeks to examine.

Research Approach and Participants

Endeavouring to preserve people's presence as subjects and to acknowledge that "their experiences are a very important resource" (Kearney et al., 2018, p. 295), this book draws from individual interviews and focus groups with people who work or worked as, or, in various capacities, organize or organized the labour of, strippers. In so doing, it weaves together participants' partial perspectives and situated knowledges garnered through qualitative, semi-structured interviews, understood as narratives of experiences and reflections captured at a particular moment in time (Hill Collins, 2000; Fontana & Frey, 2005). The book is also informed by institutional ethnography, insofar as it engages with participants' narratives in order to examine social relations and organizational systems, procedures, and discourses (see D.E. Smith, 2005). In this respect, it also includes some document-based research of city bylaws, city meeting minutes and reports, legal decisions, and documents produced by stripper rights groups and an organization representing strip club owners (see Law, 2015 for a more expansive analysis of these regulatory texts). In methodological terms, the book draws from symbolic interactionism and institutional ethnography to map organizational relationships, roles, and work practices in a sector in which there is little reliance on locally produced texts (strip clubs do not generally produce reports or memos) but where other regulatory texts (especially bylaws) inform the production and enforcement of unwritten rules and norms (see Turner, 2006).

Interview data were collected through two interconnected research projects that consulted with community members and key informants in order to be respectful of and useful to strippers and other sex workers rather than merely voyeuristic. (See the appendix for a description of the methodology for the Rethinking Management in the Adult and Sex Industry Project and the doctoral research underpinning this book.) In this respect, another commonality this research shares with institutional ethnography is its aim to identify "possible 'levers' or targets for activist intervention" as a project that has been shaped by concerns arising from community stakeholders (DeVault & McCoy, 2006, p. 19). Project findings also informed the design of various sector-specific community research products, including in-kind contributions to a Toronto-based stripper-led advocacy group called Work Safe Twerk Safe. In addition, while the literature employs the term *erotic/exotic dancer* more often than *stripper*, this book uses both terms interchangeably, including *dancer* as a short form, to reflect participants' self-identification with both terms (see also *WSTS v Ontario*, 2021a).

Against a backdrop of pervasive misconceptions about people working in the erotic dance sector, this book endeavours to humanize the research participants by featuring quotes expressing their personalities and life experiences, comparing stripping and its management to other kinds of jobs, and using accessible language to appeal to readers of various educational backgrounds and levels of knowledge about the sex industry. To this end, the more academically rigorous legal and theoretical details are available in the endnotes for readers so inclined, and a more expansive description of methodological considerations and research methods used to gather the data featured in the book is available in the appendix.

To protect participants' anonymity, the names used throughout the book are pseudonyms. While a few third parties were assigned a pseudonym because they declined to choose one, three others enthusiastically selected full names – Jimmy Popsicle, Fuzzy Pickle, and Studley Hungwell. For consistency, their (pseudo) surnames will not be used in the rest of the book. Readers will also notice that no city appears beside participants' names, and that interviewees' pseudonyms are omitted where they are talking about a specific city. In addition to protecting participants' identities, this is also to accommodate dancers' mobility; although most had worked primarily in the city where they were interviewed, a considerable number of dancers spoke of working in more than one municipality, and some had worked in both Toronto and Ottawa.

In total, interview data from thirty participants who work or had worked in the erotic dance sector in Ontario – fifteen third parties and fifteen dancers – are featured in this book. In terms of demographics, all except one of the fifteen third parties are men; the one woman third party was also the only bartender in the study. At the time of the interviews, the third-party participants were between twenty years old and their mid-60s. One third party identified as Asian Canadian, and two identified as Black; the rest were white. With one exception, all identified Canadian as their nationality. They came from mixed socio-economic backgrounds: the majority (eight) were from the middle class; four were from the lower middle class; two were working class; and one hailed from the upper middle class. Six third parties worked or had worked in Ottawa, and the other nine in Toronto (including one who had worked a few months in Ottawa).

Most of the stripper participants identified as women, save for one, who embraced a gender-neutral identity but for whom a feminine pronoun was acceptable. Aged between twenty and fifty years old, all had spent a significant amount of time in the industry, ranging from three to eighteen years, with an average of 7.5 years of experience. Eight were working as dancers at the time of the interview; the remaining seven had moved on to other work. All were Canadian citizens, but two were born in Eastern Europe. Most of the participants were white; however, one was Asian, and another identified as Indigenous. Five of the women had worked solely as dancers; five others had occasionally provided private (i.e., outside the club) services to select clients, ranging from dinner dates or stripping only (no sex) to escorting; and the remaining five participants had worked in various other sectors providing sexual services in addition to stripping (including escorting, erotic massage, and street-based sex work).

Prelude: A Dramaturgical Perspective on Gendered Labour Relations

Since this book relies primarily on interviews, it adopts a theoretical lens suitable to the interpersonal scale of the experiences, performances, and relationships participants discussed, as well as the organizational scale of workplace practices: a mix of symbolic interactionism and critical management studies. The latter attends to workplace relationships and power relations, organizational culture, and policies; the former allows for an examination of the meanings expressed and interpreted in interactions between strippers and third parties, and with clients; both are attuned to the intersectional gendered elements of strip club work and management.

In particular, the book is informed by Goffman's dramaturgical approach, which he applied to make sense of how individuals perform particular expressions of themselves to foster impressions that define the social situation for other individuals in their presence (Goffman, 1959). Enacted repeatedly, these pre-established patterns of action – performed individually or collaboratively with others – foster social relationships between the performer(s) and the audience. At strip clubs, gender features significantly in workers' occupational performances, more obviously for strippers but, as this book argues, also for third parties.[4] At the same time as dancers' and third parties' occupational roles are informed by normative classed, abled, and racialized notions of beauty, strength, and professionalism, the particular iterations of gender performed at strip clubs are also specific – one would not go to a strip club expecting the women and men who work there to act like women or men working in a bank or a hospital. To accommodate all these attributes, I employ Crenshaw's concept of intersectionality (1989) to highlight their interplay in shaping people's performances and the ways they are perceived as normal, subversive, or suspect.

Like other sex industry spaces and actors, strip clubs and their workers are subject to stigma. Interpersonally, stigma occurs in an interaction when an individual is perceived by another as possessing a failing or a shortcoming on the basis of one discrediting attribute (Goffman, 1963), and can further lead to labelling, stereotyping, differentiation, status loss, and discrimination (Link & Phelan, 2001; see also Jones et al., 1984). Embedded structurally – for example, in the municipal bylaws described above – stigma can precipitate disproportionate state surveillance or policies to manage the risks a particular population is presumed to pose (Hannem, 2012; Bruckert & Hannem, 2013a).

Of course, occupational roles at strip clubs are not only gendered, racialized, classed, and stigmatized in particular ways; they are also informed by organizational structure and occupational title. This book draws from critical management studies (CMS) to consider questions of managerial power and control raised in the erotic dance and sex work literatures. CMS looks beyond conventional theorizations of conflicting interests between management and workers (Knights, 2004), to examine the ways in which workers (inclusive of managers below the level of ownership) misbehave, resist, and conform – sometimes simultaneously – to make the best of their position in the organization and in capitalist relations of production (Burawoy, 1979; Hodson, 1991; Willmott, 1997).

Synopsis

As Willmott (1997) argues, managerial workers "do not 'just' operate or supervise the physical and organizational means of production in ways dictated by the imperatives of capitalism" (p. 1354); they are also human subjects who struggle with existential questions and job-related anxieties. Chapter 1 endeavours to address the paucity of research focusing on managerial actors from their own perspective by introducing the third parties who participated in the research. In so doing, it provides empirical data that belie popular assumptions and generalizations, including, for example, that managerial individuals in the sex industry make disproportionately large amounts of money (they don't), and that they are distinct from and more nefarious than managers in other labour market sectors (they aren't). The chapter examines pathways in and out of third-party work, as well as its enjoyable and off-putting aspects, many of which are comparable to other kinds of jobs. The chapter also sketches the roles and daily tasks of third parties who are formally affiliated with (employed by) strip clubs, as well as those who are unaffiliated (involved in direct fee-for-service relationships with strippers). As unaffiliated third parties are not part of, and are thus unable to speak to, the workplace relations and organizational practices at strip clubs, Eric, a driver and security provider and the only unaffiliated participant in my research, appears only in chapter 1.

The next four chapters examine the workings of strip clubs from the perspective of club-affiliated third parties and strippers. Chapter 2 situates strip clubs in contemporary labour market trends, drawing on CMS scholarship to consider dancers and third parties (who are not owners) as workers who inhabit different employment relationships to the club. Furthering scholars' problematization of club operators' classification of strippers as independent contractors – which, among other things, denies them access to labour protections and facilitates discriminatory hiring and dismissal practices (Althorp, 2013; Bouclin, 2004; Brooks, 2010; Bruckert, 2002; Couto, 2006; Egan, 2004; Maticka-Tyndale, 2004) – it argues that strip clubs are made up of two parallel organizational structures: the club infrastructure that employs managers, bouncers, DJs, servers, and other support staff; and the agglomeration of entrepreneurs that dancers constitute. In exploring their implications, the chapter highlights the ways in which these parallel structures can be frustrating and confusing but also can challenge conventional assumptions of hierarchy, managerial control, and exploitation in organizations in general and the sex industry in particular.

Chapters 3 and 4 focus on how the parallel structures inform strippers' and third parties' performances for each other and for strip club customers. Drawing on Goffman's theorization of how people perform frontstage and relinquish their roles backstage, respectively (Goffman, 1959), these two chapters examines how third parties and dancers follow and subvert organizational rules and policies, negotiate shared and conflicting interests and goals, and work around and manipulate each other. Chapter 3 showcases how dancers' and third parties' "back regions" are disparate in significant respects, and how this informs training, oversight, and surveillance, and the ways dancers meet each other's needs when third parties do not. Chapter 4 turns to the "front region," to explore how third parties perform gender, class, and race, even in their supporting roles vis-à-vis the strippers. It considers how dancers' and third parties' respective gendered performances impact their expectations of and interactions with each other. The chapter also discusses how the onus to continually perform in view of customers can impede professionalism in ways that are comparable to and distinct from, but not necessarily worse or less manageable than, workplace sexual harassment in mainstream organizations.

Chapter 5 examines questions of risk and security at strip clubs, beginning with dancers' and third parties' perceptions of the risks each faces and how these impressions depart from and reproduce gender norms and popular assumptions about the sex industry. Although participants worried less about violence than stereotypes of customers suggest, and were more concerned about financial and legal risks, strippers' and third parties' performances together create an atmosphere of relaxed, heteronormative sexual expression tolerant of customer misbehaviour. In this contrived "party" environment, dancers, who are responsibilized to manage their own safety, and third parties – particularly bouncers and managers juggling their responsibilities for protecting the club and the dancers – instrumentally enact gendered and other situated strategies to prevent and respond to risks.

Turning to consider the manifestations and effects of stigma, chapter 6 begins by looking at the moments and reasons third parties are discredited in interpersonal interactions – with strangers, romantic interests, or partners, and among co-workers. In examining these scenarios, the chapter complements and builds on scholarly observations about how strippers and other sex workers confront and manage stigma in ways that contest and reproduce respectability politics and normative judgment (e.g., Bruckert, 2012; Scambler, 2007; Trautner & Collett, 2010), as well as how stigma affects and circulates through organizations (Devers et al., 2009; Hudson & Okhuysen, 2009). Integrating dancers' experiences of stigma from, and stigmatizing perceptions of, third parties, the chapter further shows that strip club workers sometimes reject stigma – for example, by talking back or refraining from making assumptions about their counterparts – but also at times reproduce hierarchical characterizations of stripping as less immoral and more respectable than prostitution.

The concluding chapter of the book brings together the salient workplace issues arising from the six substantive chapters, summarizing good and bad managerial practices in the erotic dance sector to propose policy alternatives that respond to the concerns of participants in the research, with a view toward combatting particular forms of exploitation, violence, and harassment in ways that neither patronize nor further marginalize strippers. Reflecting on recent changes in the erotic dance sector in Canada and their implications, the book's conclusion situates stripping in overlapping broader contexts of contemporary precarious labour and sex work, their regulation and conditions, and worker organizing and resistance.

Chapter One

Who Are Third Parties? Managers, DJs, Bouncers, and Others

As sex worker activists (e.g., Leigh, 1997; Sterry & Martin, 2009) and scholars (e.g., Brewis & Linstead, 2000; Jeffrey & MacDonald, 2006a) have long asserted, people become involved in sex work for myriad reasons, which often relate to the availability and accessibility of adequate work – a point often made to support the argument that sex work is work. However, in order to fully rebuke the simplistic characterization of the sex industry as an engine of sexual victimization, such arguments need to extend to third parties, since for there to be a victim there must also be a victimizer. This chapter, then, introduces and endeavours to humanize the third parties who participated in this research, drawing from their interviews to narrate who they are, how they got into their work, and what they like and do not like about it. Their accounts demonstrate that third parties, too, come to work in adult entertainment for various reasons, which are also often related to the availability of employment. The chapter also highlights the tasks and skills involved in being a strip club manager, bouncer, or DJ – the main occupations discussed in the book – and presents other third parties who play relatively minor roles in strippers' labour (e.g., bartenders) or who are not directly employed by strip clubs (e.g., drivers, agents). Across these themes, this chapter considers the intersecting impacts of class, gender, and race on how third parties are perceived and how they perceive their own work. To begin, it elaborates on the demographic information collected in the study, which allows for a broad overview of third parties' personal and professional backgrounds before narrowing in on the particulars of their experiences and occupations.

Delving Deeper into Demographics: Class, Career, and Income

Although the majority of the third parties interviewed for this research identified as middle to working class, a few spoke of "rough" beginnings: a manager and head bouncer, Reverend "grew up on the streets and had to basically fight to survive at times" but later was able to complete some college courses, whereas George, a bouncer, had previously struggled with homelessness as well as drug addiction. In contrast to dominant perceptions of underclass criminality and concomitant assumptions of little to no education, third-party participants for this study had completed various levels of formal schooling: three had completed university; four had completed college; another four had some college education; two had their high school diploma; and the remaining two had not completed high school.

Many of these participants had enjoyed extensive careers working in strip clubs: five had done so for twenty years or more; four had worked almost as long, between fourteen and seventeen years; four others had worked for approximately four to five years. Of the remaining two, one had worked for two years, and the other had only six months experience at the time of the interview. Some interviewees had worked in only one third-party position: three were DJs; two were managers; two were bouncers; one identified himself as a driver/protection provider; and one was a bartender. The others spoke of simultaneous or successive roles: four were disc jockeys and managers, and two were bouncers and managers. To reflect this variety, third parties' self-described (and in the case of multiple positions, relevant) job title appears beside their pseudonyms throughout the book – a slash indicates combined roles (e.g., manager/DJ); distinct roles are listed separately (e.g., Dalton worked as a manager and a DJ at different clubs and spoke of his observations and experiences in and across both roles).

In contrast to managerial individuals in the incall/outcall sector (e.g., massage parlours, escort agencies), where scholars have observed that, after a few years as service providers, women can become managers or run their own business (Bruckert & Law, 2013; Goldstein, 1983; Heyl, 1977, 1979), none of the strip club third parties had themselves been erotic dancers or sex workers in other sectors. That only one of the third parties to participate in this research was a woman speaks to the gendered and heteronormative distribution of labour in strip clubs. Indeed, studies show that men predominantly occupy manager, bouncer, bartender, and DJ positions, with women working as waitresses, "shooter girls," and dancers (DeMichele & Tewksbury, 2004; J. Lewis, 2006; Price, 2008; Price-Glynn, 2010). Moreover, it appears that only the roles usually occupied by men are imbued with formal authority and opportunities for career advancement.[1] In spite of this apparent "gendered hierarchy" (DeMichele & Tewksbury, 2004, p. 545), academics argue that the power dynamics at strip clubs cannot simply be reduced to male management controlling female workers: some authors apply a Foucaultian lens to highlight the ways in which dancers challenge relations of power, while others focus on strippers' resistance to managerial gendered expectations (e.g., Bruckert, 2002; Egan, 2004; Frank, 2002a; Murphy, 2003; Ross & Greenwell, 2005).

Most of the third-party participants' experience in the sex industry was limited to the erotic dance sector; however, three had also worked as third parties in other sectors: as a driver and (temporarily) manager at an escort service; a manager of a sex chat website; and as a driver and provider of security services to escorts. Participants had a wide range of work experience outside the sex industry as well. Some of this experience was related to the jobs they did at strip clubs: three DJs had worked in radio, one of whom also had experience DJing at weddings and nightclubs as well as in recording studios; two bouncers had worked security in other businesses, and another had served in the military; one manager had managed a nightclub; and the bartender had experience in hotel management. In addition, participants had a variety of experience in unrelated jobs, which included: construction worker (6); sales clerk (3); cook (3); server (3); information technology expert (2); social worker (2); stock broker (1); factory worker (1); landscaper (1); lab technician (1); government worker (1); office worker (1); teacher (1); mechanic (1); and driver (1). The majority (11) had managerial experience outside of the sex industry, including four who had operated their own businesses. These varied experiences demonstrate that people who manage, supervise, or coordinate the work of strippers are not outside the mainstream labour market. Rather, the third parties featured in this book participated in conventional labour market sectors as well, either prior to, during, or after their time in the erotic dance sector. This overlap suggests that they were able to apply the skills they learned in the erotic dance sector to mainstream jobs, and vice versa.

When asked about their income in the most recent year they had worked in the erotic dance sector, some former third parties said it had been too long to remember. However of the twelve who answered, most (eight) reported earning in the $40,000 to $60,000 range; only one (notably, a manager) reported making $60,000 to $80,000; while another two had made $20,000 to $40,000; and one made less than $20,000. These salaries are certainly modest in comparison to the extravagant profits associated with the "pimps" and "traffickers" of popular imagination, reflected in estimates in news reports and accounts by some academics (see Hallgrimsdottir et al., 2006, and Jeffreys, 2008, respectively). Indeed, one article places such profits in the millions of dollars, or thirty times the earnings of one woman (Leidholdt, 1993). Other scholars have critiqued such claims as conflating trafficking with sex work and as significantly lacking in methodological rigour (Ham, 2011; Jahic & Finckenauer, 2005; O'Connell Davidson, 2006; Weitzer, 2012). Moreover, in the individual interviews conducted for this study, dancers reported making $300 to $700 per night or $40,000 to $100,000 per year,[2] thereby generally out-earning the third parties in this research, some of whom worked at the same clubs. This discrepancy further challenges popular assumptions about the financial exploitation of sex workers by third parties, and also reflects the seldom celebrated fact that "sex work [is] one of the few labour markets in which the gendered wage gap is reversed in women's favour" (Gillies et al., 2019, p. 362). Here it is worth noting that, as with the gendered wage gap in other industries, these earnings do not include the profits of business owners.

Becoming a Third Party: How They Got into the Work

Cutting across academic research,[3] popular culture, and strippers' everyday lives is a palpable fascination with why women (and, less so, men) do this *kind of work*. Often, albeit perhaps sometimes unintentionally, the question – *Why do you do it?* or *How did you get into it?* – is asked derisively, subtly implying that the woman's character, reputation, or psyche is irreparably damaged by sex work; moreover, sex workers are seen as at risk, even when they are also (or primarily) seen as risky (Bruckert, 2012; 2014). By contrast, and in keeping with dominant characterizations of sex industry managers as deviant, suspicious, dangerous, or immoral, we wonder less about how third parties come to be involved in the work. Indeed, if we accept these framings, the question unproblematically (if tautologically) answers itself: men (for, from this perspective, they are always men) pursue this deviant activity because they are immoral.

When real people answer this question, a considerably different picture emerges: as the following discussion shows, the various paths people take to becoming a third party are comparable to those taken by strippers (with the obvious exception of "tendency toward exhibitionistic behavior" [Forsyth & Deshotels, 1998, p. 82]), service industry workers, and those labouring in working-class occupations (Williams & Connell, 2016; Willis, 1977). Across participants' narratives, there emerged four pathways into third-party work: serendipity or chance; applying because they needed a job; getting the job through a contact; and – notably the only reason that could not describe why someone enters into any kind of occupation not requiring specific experience or educational credentials – wanting specifically to work at a strip club.

The underlying reasons participants took these paths can be contextualized in the dependence and compulsion of the neoliberal labour market (Westcott et al., 2006): financial need, and not being able to find a job in their field of study or experience.

Adam, Gilles, Kelly, and Eric all came to work in the erotic dance sector by chance. For Adam, an impromptu visit to a strip club led to a career spanning eighteen years, first as a bouncer, then as a DJ and manager:

> It was pretty early in the night. And the bar was pretty quiet. And a fight broke out between two people ... I just happened to open my mouth and talk to the waitress and asked her if that sort of thing happened very often. And she said, "Oh, don't worry about it; they're just regulars. They do this all the time." And I said, "Well, don't you guys have like a doorman to, something to, you know, keep them in line?" She's like, "No, we go through doormen like water. Do you want a job?" And, before I could say no, she was gone ... She came back five minutes later and said, "The manager will see you." My friends were like, "Go, go, go!" ... There was a seedy bald man sitting behind the desk. He says to me, "So, you want a job as a bouncer, uh?" And I'm like – I wanted to say no, but I said, "Sure, why not?" So, he handed me an application [and] says, "You know, bouncing in a strip club is a very prestigious job and there's a lot of applicants. If we need you, we'll give you a call." Which was really the answer I wanted to hear. Because I didn't really want the job in the first place ... Went to work the next day, got home, lay down for a nap, 4:30, my phone rings, ... "Well, we'd like to hire you. When can you start?" I'm like, you know, I think I'll do this once and then I'll just, you know, get it out of my system. I'm like, "When do you need me to start?" "Can you come in tonight for 8:00?" ... And I just stayed ... It was a cool interesting job. I had the time to do it. Girls were really nice. And I guess not long after that, they lost a DJ, and I became a DJ.

Gilles came from a career in the applied sciences in which he often worked alone. His desire to learn English provided the impetus for a career in strip club management in 1990: "That's a job I find by fluke, and I was manager, like, right away – no experience." Similarly Eric, a driver and security provider whose work is examined more closely toward the end of this chapter, said that "I was actually minding my own business and a young lady approached me."

Although Kelly also initially "got a job at a strip club by accident," it was because she needed the work: "I had applied for a job at a restaurant and they flipped my resume to the strip club, and they called me and I needed a job, so I went in." In this respect, Kelly's story combines all four pathways – after her first, short, stint as a waitress, she moved in and out of waitressing and bartending at strip clubs, a trajectory facilitated by contacts. Additionally, her bartending teacher had "pulled me aside and was like, 'If you wanna make good money, the adult entertainment industry is the way to go – you look like you could do well there' … So then she gave me the number of the manager at the [club], and then I got a job."

George, Jimmy, and Reverend all got their jobs through contacts. Reverend had asked an acquaintance for a job as a bouncer at one strip club and was later recruited back to strip club security, "probably because of my reputation, you know. I'm not a hothead; I don't grab people quickly and get physical with people." For George, getting hired was serendipitous: "I dated an ex-dancer. I went to the club a few times, made friends with the other doormen – just happened to go in there one day … and they needed a doorman, so I got the job." Similarly, Jimmy was informally recruited by a strip club manager to work as a DJ:

> I was in the middle of college … working this part-time job at a paintball place … I was a ref … during the game, you'd hear me … And one day this guy came up to me and he said, "Hey, you're pretty funny. Do you want to, you know, try the mic out at the club?" I'm like, "What club are you talking about?" He's like, "Oh, it's this strip club that I run." I'm like – I was eighteen at the time – so I'm like, "Uh, alright, I'm in for new experiences."

Among those driven by financial need, Chico and Tony both began DJing at strip clubs when they could not find work in broadcasting in spite of their considerable experience in the field. Chico had moved in and out of being a strip club DJ as his other music-related pursuits and income waxed and waned; after a hiatus he returned to work at a strip club when he needed to support his new family. Fuzzy, who had previous experience in radio, applied to a strip club through an ad in the newspaper. By contrast, Studley had absolutely no experience as a DJ:

> [It] was essentially just an ad in the paper. I was desperate for work. The girlfriend I had at the time pretty much told me, "Go and apply for this job" … I was eighteen. I wasn't even old enough to be in the bar yet, and I lied to them. I told them I was twenty-one, and I told them I had a couple years' experience. They told me to go and give it a shot. It was – the bar wasn't open yet. It took me about twenty-five minutes to figure out how to turn everything on, and finally, I did – I made a quick stage announcement,

and there was, in fact – the owner was there having coffee with a dancer ... I don't even know what I said on the mic, but it sounded horrible, and he asked her what she thought, and she said, "Give the kid a break. Give him a job," you know. So – and it was – basically, from that moment on, it was trial and error.

Sal and Marcus also needed work, but did not get the jobs they were expecting. Although he was applying as a bartender at various kinds of establishments after completing a bartending course, Marcus's imposing physique got him hired as a strip club bouncer instead. Sal, who like Chico and Tony, could not find work in his field, was surprised to find that the job advertised turned out to be at a strip club:

I was fresh out of college ... I was still living at home, and my mom was kinda on me about like, getting a job and moving out, being an adult. So I was, uh, looking through the newspaper one day and there was an advertisement for a DJ, and it didn't really specify anything else other than they were looking for a DJ, and uh I called and this funny little guy answered the phone and said, "Ok, well why don't you come down for an interview?" ... so I took the bus all the way out ... and I looked up and I was like, wow, this is a strip club. And I remember thinking for a split second like, you know what, maybe I should just turn around and go back home, like I'm not too sure if this is a good idea. And then I was like, you know what ... I'm gonna go in and see what he's got to say.

Although Sal would stay in the business and later become a manager, this initial impression highlights another element not considered in popular (mis)conceptions of sex industry third parties: that they share common perceptions about sex industry businesses and their operators as seedy, unsavoury, or untrustworthy.

Only two of the fifteen third-party participants pursued the job specifically because they wanted to work in a strip club. For Dalton, "the initial intrigue was probably voyeuristic ... I had been in the nightclub industry for a very long time as a DJ. And a job came up in the Toronto area to work as a DJ in a strip joint. And I just happened to get it." Like some of his counterparts included here, and, of course, the dancers, Dalton also appreciated the "cash on a daily basis." Scott's initial attraction to working as a strip club bouncer was informed by another popular perception of manual and sex industry work – also espoused by some aspiring dancers (Forsyth & Deshotels, 1998) – that it is easy: "I was a university student, but just looking for a little extra cash in the summer, took advantage of my security experience and my size to apply at clubs.

Figured it'd be easy work." Like Dalton, Scott also thought working at a strip club would be "an entertaining job." Thus, third parties' trajectories are informed not only by financial need and serendipitous contacts or timing, but also a sense of curiosity or adventure informed by dominant depictions of strip clubs as titillating and taboo.

The Benefits and Drawbacks of Being a Third Party

In keeping with this sense of adventure, many third parties enjoyed the job because it afforded them an opportunity to spend time in a highly social, entertainment-focused environment. Adam liked interacting with people as a manager: "It's a fun job ... The best part of the job is being around all the people. There are so many different interesting people that come and go, both staff and customers." As Tony (manager/DJ) succinctly put it, "my day is never boring." He added, "if you like music, ya know, you got music around you all day ... I enjoy going to work, I really do."

Participants also took pride in their work and responsibilities. For Chico, and most if not all of the other DJs interviewed in this research, contributing to the atmosphere of the club was both professionally important and personally rewarding: "On a good night, when you've got the right audience and you've got a couple of funny lines that come out of you and the whole crowd laughs and the girl laughs and everybody enjoys it ... That's like being on stage, you know? It's like I just sang three songs, and the crowd gave me a standing ovation." As a bouncer, Marcus highlighted the value of security and the essential role it plays in the success of the club and the work of his colleagues: "I liked the responsibility of being a protector ... just making sure that everything was normal and safe."

Jimmy (DJ) enjoyed being appreciated as a good worker:

> The number 1 thing I liked about that place is the confidence they had in me. I think out of all the other workplaces, you know, this was the one thing where they said, "You know what, that guy is really good at this, and he can handle the heavy nights, he can handle the girls, he can do this and he can do that." And that's really sometimes all you need.

Likewise, Dalton felt very successful as a DJ and manager, which he measured in praise he received from people with whom he had worked. This was a source of pride he described as "life affirming ... I was doing something really good and that I was performing in the field that I had chosen to do."

Many of the men who participated in the study spoke of initially enjoying the dancers' stage shows; however, this feeling usually waned over time:

> You get to see naked women all the time. I mean, I guess that's kind of a fringe benefit. For the most part, though, after a while … you're kind of immune to it. Um, I mean, you know, you see a new girl comes in, you watch her … make sure to see that she doesn't, like, kill herself or that she's capable [on stage]. (Adam, manager and DJ)

For some, it was not just their interest in the strippers that waned: their interest in the job and the lifestyle they initially associated with it also faded over time. For Chico (DJ), who eventually came to think of his alcohol use as problematic, this perspective was related to becoming sober. Similarly Studley (DJ/supervisor), for whom "probably 90 per cent of the sex that I had in my life probably came out of the club … that whole lifestyle that comes with that, you know – the sex, the drugs, the rock and roll … Now I don't think of it as a benefit; I think of it as a lot of wasted time." For others, the appeal had not faded as much; for example, Fuzzy (DJ) admitted, "I have a good time. … I mean let's face it. I look at naked women – you know, beautiful, naked women – all day, and I listen to music, and, you know, I laugh and make jokes." Dalton (DJ and manager) similarly described working in strip clubs as fun countless times in his interview.

Virtually all of the men insisted that their work in no way resembled the male fantasy associated with working in a strip club. Fuzzy described his job as a DJ as something that "most guys would call the best job in the world" but stated that it is, in practice, "very stressful work." Instead of basking in the attention of alluring seductresses, they found themselves frequently clashing with strongly opinionated women. This impacted Studley's personal life:

> I *constantly* argue with girls, and that I don't enjoy. It's a stress-out extremely and affects me outside of work. I leave work sometimes, it will put me in a bad mood for the rest of the night … sometimes for a day or two – which isn't fair to the people in my personal life, you know – my girlfriend, my children. It's made me a bitter person.

Reverend (manager/bouncer) even went so far as to compare his job to "being married to, like, forty women at once. Who all bitch, moan, nag, complain, tease the shit out of you but don't put out, and you know, you go home alone."

As with the good qualities of third-party work in the erotic dance sector, some of the difficult aspects of the job that participants described are germane to bar work and/or night shifts. Jimmy (DJ), for example, found the night schedule took a toll on his health and relationships with friends. This view was confirmed by Reverend: "You end up with no life pretty much." While Kelly found the schedule convenient, as a bartender she worried about overly inebriated strippers or customers getting into a car accident and was sometimes annoyed by intoxicated people "because I'm always sober and they're never sober, so it gets a little – on a good day I'm fine with it, but on a bad day, I'm just ready to leave ... But it's the same in any bar." Similarly, Marcus (bouncer) "didn't like the drugs" that he saw at his club.

Like many other types of workers, third parties were also critical of managerial styles, organizational hierarchy, and work under capitalism. Adam described the worst part of his job as a manager as "the owners ... because they're never around their bar and they have no clue what goes on ... But they always want you to do something that doesn't make any sense." Chico (DJ) echoed Adam's critique of owners, speaking to frustrations arising from the dual position of third parties as both employees and management (see also Willmott, 1997):

> The owners have this totalitarian mentality: "We own the club; you work for me," you know, "The hell with you; get out; you're banished." And I don't think an industry should be run that way in any way, shape, or form, and I think there's still too much of it. On the other side, I'd like to see girls [dancers] treat it more as a 9-to-5 job ... like what I'm trying to do, I guess, you know. I don't achieve it every day.

While the issues Chico names – authoritarian managerial styles, worker apathy, and poor employer-employee relations – are common to contemporary workplaces, they are additionally shaped by gendered scripts and stigma in strip clubs, as chapters 4 and 6 will elaborate.

Some third parties were troubled by things they witnessed or perceived as happening in clubs. These included an increase in "extras" (sexual services beyond lap dances), and social judgment and abuse of dancers by customers, romantic partners, or men they suspected to be pimps. Some managed these feelings by separating themselves from their work: "I really have to turn off a part of myself to deal with those [troubled] girls because if I don't, then it's going to haunt me" (Studley, DJ/supervisor). For others it was not so easy: Jimmy (DJ) found himself particularly affected, and came to feel "deep despair," which led to "drinking a lot [at work,] ... losing control," and eventually leaving the business.

Leaving the Club

Although eight participants were third parties at the time of their interview, seven men no longer worked in the erotic dance sector. As with dancers – and myriad other types and classes of workers (see Ebaugh, 1988) – many third parties who left the industry liked the work until they did not. For some, this meant soldiering on until they could no longer bear it or until they found another job; for Adam, increasing conflict with managers led to him being fired as a DJ and not returning to strip clubs. In addition to work-related tensions, as with their entry into the industry, these changes were also informed by timing, chance, and opportunity.

Notably, some third parties managed to leverage the skills they learned in strip clubs to their advantage in other jobs. On his résumé and in job interviews, Jimmy highlighted the managerial skills he had learned as a DJ, effectively transforming himself into a viable job candidate:

> I said, well, my job was essentially [a] management position without the paycheque. So I was running the shows, talking to the girls, and having to handle all of that ... And it did me wonders. People were saying, "Oh, well if you can handle that, and you could handle it nine hours straight, we could definitely put you somewhere to do something."

Similarly, although his connection to strip clubs had made Scott's application to the police force more difficult, he had "made connections that I needed to get [in]to the security fields" in his capacity as a strip club bouncer, and had been recruited by a private security firm. As the next section illuminates, some of the skills third parties use in their work are also relevant in other contexts. For Jimmy, working in the club had honed his social skills: "Before I started working there, I didn't know a whole lot about, you know, the social environment. And then after working there, I could schmooze anybody. I could get free drinks out of a man!"

What Do They Do? Third Party Roles, Tasks, and Skills

As some of the drawbacks enumerated above suggest, strip club third parties occupy a conflicted role: they provide services and support to dancers at the same time as they contribute to the overall atmosphere, maintenance, and profits of the club. These club-affiliated third parties take on principal (managers, bouncers, DJs), occasional (owners), or auxiliary (bartenders) responsibilities for organizing, supervising, managing, and/or coordinating strippers' labour. While some responsibilities are the purview of specific third parties (e.g., DJs are in charge of music), others are shared. The distribution of managerial responsibilities between bouncers, DJs, and bartenders depends on the size of the club: larger organizations have more third parties, with narrower job descriptions, while smaller businesses have fewer third parties, with more diverse responsibilities. Finally, there are third parties who are not employed by strip clubs but who provide representation, transportation (driving), and security services in direct fee-for-service relationships with dancers.

Owners

The only participant able to speak about strip club ownership from personal experience – albeit in a limited capacity – was Dalton, who at one point in his career had opened a new club as a manager who inhabited a close relationship with the owner and took the lead in developing the marketing plan and in staffing and opening the club. It appears Dalton's active involvement at the club emanated from this dual role as a leading operator and manager; otherwise, similar to the findings of other scholars (Bruckert, 2002; DeMichele & Tewksbury, 2004; Price, 2008), most other participants described owners as largely absent from and uninvolved with the daily operation of the business (see also Kraus, 2007; Lavin, 2013). For strippers, this means that "you don't really see them [owners]. You can work there for years and not know who they are" (Jenna, dancer).

Club owners do, however, involve themselves in broader business considerations, such as regulation. In Ontario, club owners have been active in lobbying to change bylaws and laws pertaining to strip clubs – sometimes individually but often under the auspices of the Adult Entertainment Association of Canada (AEAC), a "business stakeholder organization" focused on "assisting adult entertainment clubs to become more prosperous" (AEAC, 2013, n.p.), which represented as many as fifty-four Ontario strip clubs (Taylor, 2008). Although the organization folded amid internal strife in 2016 (Kolanko, 2017), it nevertheless made important marks on Ontario's erotic dance sector during its tenure. AEAC statements and members were quoted in Toronto and Ottawa newspapers; the organization also challenged municipal bylaws pertaining to strip clubs and advocated for more restrictions on erotic massage parlours; and soon after their requests for Toronto to revise its adult entertainment bylaws finally culminated in a review in

2012, the AEAC was found to have interfered with surveys meant to be completed by dancers. AEAC representatives also voiced club owners' objections to restrictions on immigration regulations for erotic dancers (alongside sex worker rights groups who argued that the restrictions would exacerbate risks faced by migrants). In addition, the AEAC participated in the consultations leading up to Canada's most recent prostitution laws, introduced in the *Protection of Communities and Exploited Persons Act* of 2014, arguing (unsuccessfully) that strip club operators should, on the basis of their experience supporting strippers' health and safety, be permitted to operate brothels adjacent to strip clubs (Lambrinos, 2014). Notably, this suggestion was not supported by over 60 per cent of dancers in a report the AEAC commissioned (Czekalla, 2014); nor (as chapter 6 elaborates) does it appear most third parties who participated in my research would be supportive of integrating strip clubs and brothels.

While owners' energies may be focused elsewhere, the decisions they make – for example, concerning aesthetic standards governing hiring, or club rules – impact both third parties' and dancers' labour. Moreover, some participants reported owners providing helpful services to dancers. For example Bobby (dancer) mentioned an owner who helped her save money by "let[ting] me put money in the safe every night ... He'd bend over backwards for the girls." Marie (dancer) had also "heard of the owner doing nice things for other dancers. Like let's say they're in trouble, they don't want to strip anymore, well he would hire them as waitresses instead or bartenders." Thus, it appears that some owners are involved with their club and the people who work there, while others leave its operation to third parties they have hired.

Managers

As other scholars studying strip clubs in various jurisdictions have found (Bruckert, 2002; Kraus, 2007; Murphy, 2003), strip club managers, like managers in other occupations, oversee the operation of the business on a day-to-day basis. An important part of this is hiring and supervising the other third parties and support staff. Sal (manager) explained his relationship to his staff using a sports analogy: "So, like, I'm the coach, and then that's my team, right, and so I'm there to try to like – to try to motivate them, and to try to get them to do their job to the best of their ability." Gilles, another manager, emphasized the importance of keeping "harmony ... between staff." As in other types of nightclubs, bars, and restaurants, strip club managers are also responsible for distributing salaries, counting money, and/or taking care of banking, doing inventory, and ordering supplies (e.g., liquor). Additionally, they organize the schedules of the staff, and often, the dancers – a task that Adam and Dalton, who had both worked as managers, described as involving communication with and understanding and flexibility toward workers.

In order to attend to all of their responsibilities (and to ensure that other workers are doing the same), managers are perpetually moving around the bar. As Dalton declared, "I would never allow myself to be in the office, except at the beginning of the night and at the end of the night. And the rest of the time, I was just travelling around, making sure that – not just making sure that my staff is doing their job, but also watching for hot spots." Some managers, like Adam, for whom the social aspect was a significant part of the appeal of the job, also include customer relations in their rounds: "The best part of the job is being Johnny handshake – knowing the customers, knowing who they are, knowing what they spend, knowing what they drink."

Attending to these organizational and surveillance responsibilities means that managers seldom spend extended time with dancers. Moreover, because strippers are self-motivated contractors who generate income from customers directly through the sale of lap dances, there is little need for interaction between dancers and managers unless a problem occurs. Not surprisingly, then, Monica (dancer) recalled that most of her interaction with managers occurred when she was first hired. Managers may also monitor customers' and dancers' conduct for the purposes of security and legality, but this is not their primary focus.

Bouncers

Security is, predictably, the principal role of bouncers – something Marcus (bouncer) took very seriously: "My number one goal was to protect the people working there, make sure that no harm came to any of the dancers, and also monitor the clients to make sure they weren't too drunk or weren't acting up. Just making sure that everybody was playing nice." This responsibility sometimes extends outside the confines of the club. As in DeMichele and Tewksbury's (2004) research, some participants noted that bouncers walk dancers to their car or a taxi. For the most part, dancers' interactions with bouncers centre on conflicts with customers. In addition, bouncers are responsible – "with instruction [from the manager] as to ... what should be allowed and shouldn't be allowed" (Adam, manager) – for ensuring that dancers' and customers' conduct does not violate municipal and/or club standards; at some clubs, managers participate in this surveillance as well. Otherwise, bouncers are responsible for duties germane to bar security, such as screening and monitoring who enters the club (bouncers also referred to themselves as doormen but, for consistency and to reflect that this is only one of their responsibilities, they are described as bouncers in this book), and "making sure [customers] were legally of age to enter" (Marcus). Occasionally, they are also tasked with other duties, like helping to stock the bar (see DeMichele & Tewksbury, 2004).

Although bouncers echoed DeMichele and Tewksbury's finding that violence is a potential but not necessarily routine aspect of strip club security (2004, p. 539), they espoused varying attitudes toward the use of force (see also Hobbs et al. 2005). For example, Marcus (bouncer) employed what he referred to as a non-violent strategy, preferring to "restrain people if they're getting a little bit too rowdy. I have a black belt in Jujitsu, so it's like a non-violent sort of martial art. Basically you get people in a lock so they're incapacitated." By contrast, Scott (bouncer and manager) argued that, "any police officer or martial or specialist trainer in that field will tell you, 'You know, leg lock, ankle lock, all that fancy stuff ... you can't do in a bar.' I mean, because it's excessive use of force." In light of discrepant viewpoints on, and tendencies toward, violence, senior bouncers endeavour to "make sure the other doormen didn't take things too far, whether by physical force or just ... be[ing] an asshole" (Scott). Such remarks reflect DeMichele and Tewsbury's insistence that bouncers must regulate customers' behaviour in the least intrusive manner in order to "quickly return a setting back to one facilitating alcohol consumption and normal business practices" (2004, p. 540; see also Hobbs et al., 2005).

Bartenders

The only bartender, and also the only woman third party, to participate in this study was Kelly. While the other bartenders at Kelly's workplace are men, a few participants had worked with a woman manager. It appears some strip clubs prefer to hire men as bartenders, but others prefer women. For example, when Dalton was hiring bartenders as a manager, he chose "really sexy" men to "keep the girls [dancers] happy."

Kelly reported that most of her duties, unsurprisingly, revolved around the operation of the bar, but a few of her responsibilities related to dancers' labour, making her a third party as well. She is "in charge of giving cash advances to [the] customer to pay the dancer" and handles the entry fee for the VIP section. Although it is not officially part of her job, Kelly also endeavours to resolve payment disputes between dancers and patrons before the bouncers get involved. She additionally recommends strippers to customers whose requests she perceives as legitimate, and will inform dancers if a customer is waiting for them.

Echoing the findings of Bruckert (2002) and Price (Price, 2008; Price-Glynn, 2010), some dancers described bartenders as having limited or occasional managerial responsibilities. For example at Jenna's workplace, both bartenders and managers (and, according to other dancers, sometimes also waitresses) explain the hourly rates to customers before they begin their time in the champagne rooms. Donna (dancer) had worked at a club where "the barmaid signed people in, and she had the authority to hire people if a manager was not there," while Shane (dancer) had been hired by a bartender in one club and a DJ at another.

DJs

As their job title evinces, disc jockeys are in charge of the music and the stage shows, which are key to the atmosphere of the club: "You're the control centre of the entire place, so keep it going. Without you, there is no party. You are the party, you know? And you have to be the part of the party that is invisible; it just keeps everything running" (Fuzzy, DJ). Because the stage is central to "running the party" at a strip club, the stage roster is a key component of DJing. Although the order is, in principle, organized on a "first come, first serve" basis (Chico, DJ), DJs must be prepared to rearrange the stage show roster for numerous reasons, including, as discussed in chapter 2, race-based aesthetic restrictions:

> If two husky blondes come in, I'm going to try not to put those two girls next to each other. Black girls – I'm not supposed to put Black girls next to each other. If I find that, you know, the girls have a similar frame and hair colour, I won't put them together – or similar names ... because then, you're just asking for confusion. (Fuzzy, DJ)

The way DJs organize and communicate the roster may differ significantly from club to club. As Brigitte (dancer) explained,

> I've worked at clubs where ... I sign up for a show, and I know what time it's at, and I love that, and I've worked at clubs where I know I'm going to be on two times, and ... know exactly how many girls [until my show], and I don't mind that either. And I've worked at clubs where I have no idea when I'm going to be onstage.

Brigitte's fellow focus group participants agreed with her dislike of the last arrangement. Charlene added, "it can be *extremely* stressful dealing with a DJ who is disorganized or otherwise incompetent." Acknowledging these challenges, DJs emphasized the importance of multitasking. As Studley (DJ/supervisor) described it,

> On a busy night, I might have thirty girls ... and every ten minutes, I've got a different girl in there changing her music, changing her mind, changing her lights ... So you have to be a juggler in that sense; you have to be able to please several different people at once and do it on the fly while you're trying to do something else.

Because DJs' responsibilities in regard to dancers revolve around shows, their involvement in rule enforcement is largely limited to the stage: "Don't be late for [the] stage, stay up there for three minutes a song, get naked" (Studley, DJ/supervisor). Although strippers can choose their own music, DJs must ensure it is appropriate in both length (at least three minutes) and style. In order not to disrupt the continuity of stage shows, dancers must also inform or seek permission from DJs if they are arriving late, missing a shift, or leaving early. Some DJs noted additional managerial duties: at one club, Adam had collected the house fee and made the weekly schedule for the dancers; at another, Studley had made the schedule for other DJs, supervised them, and taken care of the sound equipment as the head DJ.

Drivers, Agents, and Associates

In addition to the above-mentioned third parties who are formally affiliated with strip clubs through employment or ownership, there are peripheral third parties who offer supplemental services to dancers. One such third party in the erotic dance sector is the agent, whose role is similar to that of a modelling agent. Although Marie (dancer) had recently worked through an agent in rural Quebec, and agents remain key players in western Canada (Althorp, 2013) and the rural United States (Price-Glynn, 2010), only two participants had had direct experience with these third parties in Ontario – a sign of the agent's decline as the erotic dance sector shifted from revolving feature shows to lap dancing. Gilles (manager) had helped a friend start an agency in the 1990s, and Bobby, a forty-eight-year-old dancer who had been in the business seventeen years, had "had agents over the years ... They can find you good clubs or get you into a club you're trying to get into ... That was way back in the day."

Some participants mentioned providing driving services for strippers, usually operating as unlicensed taxis advertised through word of mouth (see also Bruckert, 2002). When transportation is combined with other elements of work facilitation (such as security, negotiation, or arranging), these peripheral third parties can be characterized as *associates* – individuals who organize or facilitate the labour of sex workers, in an occasional or informal relationship, and who charge a fee for service or take a portion of worker earnings (Bruckert & Law, 2013). Two third parties participating in this research fit this description: Marcus and Eric.

As an offshoot of his work as a strip club bouncer, Marcus "sometimes arranged stag parties." He kept this secret from club management because "it just didn't seem like a good idea to tell the club that I was making money with their dancers, somewhere else, that they weren't getting a piece of [laughs]." For these private parties, which he arranged at the request of a dancer or a club customer, Marcus drove the dancers to the venue (usually a private home) and provided security, including hiring other security personnel as necessary. Although Marcus did not usually allow customers to initiate touching – "You do not get to touch the girls; if they want to touch you, they will touch you … You get one warning, you do it again, the show's over and you lose your money" – he accommodated dancers who wanted to provide additional services, but he insisted that they do so with only one party guest, inspected the room for cameras, and stood guard at the door.

The only third party in the research not formally affiliated with a strip club, Eric similarly drove dancers to and from work but also provided supplementary services, including moral support. In addition to driving the dancer with whom he primarily worked to the club, he "would look out for her. And I would sit in the club and I would watch certain things; she'd always ask me to like, not let certain guys go talk to her, or to show certain guys that I am there so that they wouldn't." Eric further asserted the importance of his "treat[ing] her right":

> You have to invest in your commodity, so her gear – her clothes, her heels, her nails, her hair, her skin. Basically trying to treat her right is the key of all because basically once you put too much stress on the woman it shows, it shows in her appearance, it shows in her desire to get up and walk to work. I don't think dudes understand that, more than they need to beat the shit out of her … No, your money, treat your money like you love your money, so I'm gonna love my money, I'm going to love my girl.

Eric's use of possessive language and his description of their relationship resemble elements of the stereotypical "pimp"; his rejection of violence, however, is a significant departure. As a Black man who drives dancers to work and sits in the club watching, Eric also conformed to the purported characteristics of a pimp enumerated by other third parties and some dancers interviewed in this research (though it is worth noting that none identified as a pimp or as having had relationships with pimps themselves; see Law, 2020). At the same time, dancers did not perceive unlicensed taxis, or bouncers providing transportation and security to dancers offering sexual services outside the club, as problematic. This discrepancy speaks to hierarchical divisions in the sex industry informed by mutually constitutive racialized, classed, and gendered tropes – notably the categorization of strip clubs as "classy," relative to the underclass, racialized context of street-based sex work that pimps are popularly imagined to occupy.

An alternative avenue through which to make sense of Eric's occupational role is through a labour lens, comparing agent fee-for-service arrangements. Eric described an informal, almost tip-like, financial arrangement: "She'd make like, five, six bills [$500–$600] certain nights, and I wouldn't ask her for anything but at the end of the night she'd give me two bills." This is a more informal arrangement than that of Marcus, who would pay himself and other security personnel $50 per hour, charged directly to the client, leaving the dancers to establish their own hourly rate – "They'd usually get 300 an hour" – which he would collect in advance. Eric's portion of one-third is more than the (at most) one-sixth portion Marcus charged to stag party customers for security, and, as well, is more than the fees demanded by the club (house fee) and affiliated third parties (tips), or those of other drivers (whose rates dancers described as similar to or cheaper than taxi fare). However Eric's informal rate is comparable to or less than the cut of up to 50 per cent usually taken by escort agencies providing transportation (outcall) or a workplace (incall) as well as screening and booking (Bruckert & Law, 2013).

Concluding Remarks: Ordinary People in an Unconventional Workplace

As this chapter has shown, looking to third parties' own narratives and understandings of their work furnishes a more human and more ordinary portrait of jobs – and people – that supply necessary supports to strippers, including a venue and staff infrastructure, security, booking, and transportation. Coupled with their pathways into the work, the variety of skills it involves demonstrates that, in contrast to popular representations and assumptions, third parties in the erotic dance sector are no more a *type* of person than any other worker; rather, save for the fact that they do not mind working in an unconventional workplace, they are often merely a person who wants a job. Also like other workers, third parties enjoy some aspects of their work but not others, and some like the work more than others. At the same time, third parties' humanity does not mean that all are fair or proficient at delivering the services dancers require, nor does it guarantee that they provide, or wield enough organizational authority to support, decent working conditions. Rather, it means that third parties with managerial responsibilities in the erotic dance sector are like other managers: criminologists, economists, and sociologists have argued that inequity and managerial apathy emanating from both personal and structural factors and culminating in unpaid labour, worker injury, and demoralizing conditions are certainly present, if not pervasive, in mainstream labour market sectors (e.g., Bittle, 2012; Noack & Vosko, 2011; Snider, 2001; Westcott et al., 2006; Willmott, 1997). Such arguments suggest that strip clubs are, in important ways, like other workplaces, as the coming chapter will show by putting third parties' accounts in conversation with those of dancers, as well as sectoral and labour market trends.

Chapter Two

Is It Exploitation? A Closer Look at the Employment Relationship

While there continues to be disagreement about whether stripping is empowering or exploitative – a question that Frank (2007) argues has been exhaustively reiterated by academics (see also Rambo et al., 2006), including by those who frame stripping as labour – for third parties, the question takes on a rather different meaning. The acceptance (or, rather, rejection) of sex industry third-party work *as work* pivots on assumptions of exploitation that feature prominently in criminal laws prohibiting advertising and profiting from the sale of sexual services (e.g., *Protection of Communities and Exploited Persons Act*, 2014) and more subtly in characterizations of strip clubs as risky and immoral (Hubbard, 2009). Even from a labour perspective, managerial actors are generally positioned as having opposing interests to those of sex workers (e.g., Bouclin, 2004; Chapkis, 2000). This is, of course, understandable, since managers in any labour market sector are in a position to discipline and discriminate against workers and, in turn, are frequently the subject of workers' complaints and a source of their frustration. However, such characterizations do not take into account the fact that, save for owners, most strip club third parties are also employees, in addition to having some degree of organizational authority over strippers, and that the strippers do not really work *for* third parties in the sense of a conventional employment relationship.

This chapter, then, seeks to unpack the question of exploitation by putting the voices and experiences of strippers in conversation with those of third parties, and contextualizing both more broadly in what Dorothy Smith calls the "ruling relations" – "that extraordinary yet ordinary complex of relations that are textually mediated, that connect us across space and time and organize our everyday lives" (2005, p. 10) and include interconnected bureaucratic, discursive, organizational, and translocal relations and processes (DeVault & McCoy, 2006). In the erotic dance sector, the regulatory texts that permeate social relations and workplace practices comprise both the conventional kinds of texts commonly applied to and in mainstream institutions – contracts, legal conventions and decisions, laws and bylaws – and less formal, often unwritten texts that nevertheless mediate and inform what people (can) do at strip clubs (see DeVault & McCoy, 2006), namely, rules applied (or not) by, as well as to, third parties.

This exploration of workplace and ruling relations is informed by critical management scholars' rejection of dichotomous framings of organizational relationships that either romanticize and exaggerate worker resistance or characterize it as ineffectual against managerial control (Mumby, 2005), or cast managers as uniquely concerned with controlling workers (Willmott, 1997). It also attends to the impacts and intersections of gender, race, and class. Interspersed with comparisons to labour relations in fields both similar and dissimilar to erotic dance, this chapter sheds light on the organizational and employment relationships at strip clubs, and on club-affiliated third parties' contradictory position as workers with managerial responsibilities navigating a workplace subject to both too much (moralistic) and not enough (labour) regulation.

Situating Third Parties in Neoliberal Capitalist Workplace Relations

Just as activist Carol Leigh (1997) coined the term *sex work* in 1980 to draw attention away from assumptions of dominance and violence and toward the work women do, the research project from which this book draws applied the term *third party* in order to include managers, agents, drivers, security providers, and others who facilitate or organize the labour of sex workers, both to highlight the work these social actors do and to break from stereotype-laden terms like *pimp* and *procurer* (see Bruckert & Law, 2013; Bruckert & Parent, 2018). In short, the term *third party* is a tool to unpack and nuance assumptions of capitalist as well as gendered exploitation.

In contrast to small owner-operated businesses in the incall/outcall sector, strip clubs are usually larger operations in which owners have few third-party responsibilities – in other words, owners seldom actively participate in managing, overseeing, or facilitating the labour of erotic dancers on a daily basis; instead the other third parties they employ, like managers, DJs, bouncers, and sometimes bartenders, attend to these responsibilities. Willmott describes workers in such positions below the ownership or executive level of an organization as grappling with their "contradictory and precarious positioning with[in] capitalist relations of production" (1997, p. 1353). Simultaneously exploitative agents of capital and subjugated workers – at once charged with and targets of surveillance – club-affiliated third parties must exert control over workers but cannot exercise control over the organization. Like other workers, managers may fear the authority of the club owner: "When they're there ... you would see a lot less of some of the bullshit, because everybody was afraid for their jobs a little bit" (Kristen, dancer). Thus, subject to the owner's surveillance, other third parties endeavour to deliver their best performance. Such behaviour reflects Willmott's argument that middle managers feel pressured to mitigate the precarity of their contradictory position by justifying their continued relevance as workers (1997, p. 1353) and demonstrates that, like other workers, third parties are compelled by the socio-economic necessity of work that belies the neoliberal rhetoric of freedom, choice, and self-reliance (Westcott et al., 2006).

Like strippers, third parties are engaged in non-standard work – temporary or precarious rather than permanent or secure; part-time or poorly paid; non-unionized; and/or without a pension plan or benefits (Ontario Federation of Labour, 2016; Noack & Vosko, 2011; Vosko & Clark, 2009). In this regard, Fuzzy compared his working conditions as a DJ to those of other service industry workers: "No benefits. You know, I don't have health coverage. There's no pension plan ... You might be making a little bit more than the guy who's working at McDonald's."

The Organization of Labour in Ontario's Erotic Dance Sector

Stripping was not always precarious in the way it is today; prior to the 1970s, strip tease consisted of elaborate stage shows featuring contracted and salaried performers, though "salaries varied wildly" and working conditions were worse than those of other entertainers (Shteir, 2004, p. 158; see also Ross, 2009). The introduction of table dancing, a personal performance delivered to individual customers for $5 to $10 on a small, portable wooden stage – which Frank (2002a, p. xxv) situates as part of late capitalist consumer culture's preoccupation with spectacle, experience, and individualized services – effectively transformed stripping from entertainment to service work in the early 1980s (Bruckert, 2002, p. 12; Tracey, 1997). Table dances provided dancers with income that management (erroneously) characterized as tips, and on this basis reduced dancers' wages to $30 to $40 per eight-hour shift (i.e., approximately minimum wage) and began charging them a house fee of $10 (Bruckert, Parent, & Robitaille, 2003, p. 31). The 1990s saw the introduction of lap dancing and "champagne rooms" (private rooms for lap dancing). In return for this more personal service – which, at $20 per song cost double the price of a table dance – customers were allowed to touch dancers for the first time. As lap dancing became the industry norm, it exerted a significant impact on dancers' relationship to management. Alongside declining wages and increasing precarity in service industry jobs during a national recession, salaries in the erotic dance sector atrophied, and lap dances became the sole source of income for most dancers (Bruckert, 2002; Bruckert, Parent, & Robitaille, 2003).

Through these incremental changes, club operators came to consider dancers as *independent contractors*, a status that allows owners to charge house fees in exchange for use of club space (e.g., bar, stage, change room), services (e.g., security, music, drinks) and customers (Bouclin, 2004; Bruckert, 2002). House fees have been critiqued by scholars and strippers as inconsistent across clubs, unreasonably high, and a source of income that incentivized owners to expand dancer rosters, sometimes beyond what their club's clientele could support, thereby reducing potential income among dancers and increasing their likelihood of engaging in riskier activities like fellatio or penetrative sex, referred to in the erotic dance sector as "extras" (DERA, 2002; Maticka-Tyndale, 2004). Furthermore, as independent contractors rather than employees, dancers are not entitled to benefits, employment insurance, pensions, or the protection of most labour legislation, nor do they qualify to join unions (Althorp, 2013; CUPE, 2005). LeRoy compares the conditions strippers are subject to as independent contractors to those of Uber drivers, noting that "[strip] clubs and other companies use individual entrepreneurship to shift their business expenses to workers" (2017, p. 252). Yet dancers resemble employees insofar as they must comply with certain rules and expectations dictated by club management (Althorp, 2013; Bruckert, 2002; Couto, 2006; Fischer, 1996; Fogel & Quinlan, 2011).

Although they are treated in many ways like employees, erotic dancers were legally classified as independent contractors as early as 1940 in the United States, and, since that time, the label has been applied across many jurisdictions (Gall, 2016). A 1981 Ontario Labour Relations Board (OLRB) decision on a case brought by a collective of dancers called the Canadian Association of Burlesque Entertainers (CABE) against Toronto strip clubs for barring entry to known labour organizers, *Canadian Labour Congress (Canadian Association of Burlesque Entertainers, Local Union No. 1689) v Algonquin Tavern (CABE v Algonquin Tavern)*, remains influential in Canadian labour law. The OLRB distinguished between freelancers, who, as long as they met the tavern's four-hour minimum requirement, were able to control their own schedule and were thereby deemed independent contractors, and "house dancers," who, because they received a wage in return for working full (six- or eight-hour) shifts, were deemed dependent contractors, a classification recognizing their employee-like status. As Bouclin (2009) notes, although the latter designation was a partial victory, dancers were never able to collectively organize to compel the tavern to abide by provincial labour law and, for example, provide vacation or overtime pay to dependent contractors. In effect, then, only the former aspect of *CABE v Algonquin Tavern* affected dancers, who in practice continue to be treated as independent contractors by clubs even if they are "house dancers."

Speaking to the prevalence of precarious and inferior working conditions across labour market sectors in Canada (Fudge et al., 2003; Vosko, 2010) and, with it, the increasingly nebulous distinction between employees and self-employed workers (P. Lewis et al., 2003; Vosko, Zukewich & Cranford, 2003), the OLRB continues to use the factors enumerated in the *Algonquin Tavern* decision to determine if an individual is an independent contractor (freelance worker) or dependent contractor (Couto, 2006) – and, in turn, if workers can organize into collective bargaining units (see *Milk and Bread Drivers et al. v Canada Bread Company*, 2017 [*Milk and Bread*]). In this respect, dancers' relationship to strip clubs resembles that of independent contractors in other sectors – such as taxi drivers and some truck drivers (*Milk and Bread*) and hairstylists (Sanders et al., 2013) – whom Fudge et al. (2003, p. 193) describe as, paradoxically, categorized as self-employed yet dependent on the sale of their labour and subject to inferior working conditions. Thus, although *employment relationship* does not quite apply to strippers in a strictly legal sense, this book follows Lewis et al. (2003) in using the term to describe both dancers' and third parties' economic, social, psychological, and political relationship with each other and with club operators.

Employment-like Practices and Employee-like Obligations

In spite of strippers' de facto status as independent contractors, third parties exercise considerable control over their access to the club through hiring and scheduling policies, rules, and obligations, in order to ensure continual, quality (as defined by the club) entertainment for customers. Dancers must first seek permission to work at the club by the hiring third party, most often the manager. Consistent with practices across different areas and eras, hiring at strip clubs in Toronto and Ottawa largely conforms to a heteronormative, Eurocentric beauty ideal.[1] Studley (DJ/supervisor) described the hiring policy at his club:

You don't have to be 101 pounds, blonde, and wafer-thin to be beautiful, but we do expect you to take care of yourself, you know – put some effort into trying to look your best ... At the same time, like, to be blunt, you have to be discriminatory to run a business successfully ... because your reputation as a business is based upon the entertainment that you provide, so if you can't provide the entertainment that the clientele wants, they'll go somewhere that does.

Scott (bouncer and manager) connected this selectivity to purported market demand: "The customers wanted usually the stereotypical white, blonde, big-breasted bimbo or other variety of girls, Asian girls, brunette girls, redhead girls, but only so many Blacks." While Studley's comment suggests that there is some openness to variety, both remarks demonstrate that third parties responsible for hiring serve as gatekeepers whose decisions, based on their own or club owners' perception of beauty and client desires, impact dancers' access to work. Although requirements vary somewhat from club to club, the normative strip club aesthetic favours youth, femininity, thinness, and whiteness. In practice, this often results in discrimination, most especially against Black women. Indeed, most participants reported limitations on the number of Black dancers allowed per shift, which ranged from two to five at clubs hosting approximately thirty to eighty or more dancers on average per night. Speaking to how racially informed staffing restrictions are "a prejudice" in the industry that "runs very deep," Dalton (manager and DJ) found himself in a conflicted position as a Black man having to discriminate against Black women:

If you're Black and heavy, you're certainly not getting in. If you're Black, you may get in, but you better be real good looking, you know. And you better be not an instigator, right. And – yes, so, that was a real contradiction for me, you know, being Black and having to tell Black women, "No, you can't work here" ... Very, very difficult.

The roster of dancers contributes significantly to the club's image, and the hiring practices of "upscale" clubs align more closely with a Eurocentric beauty ideal, restricting opportunities for women who do not conform to it (see also Bradley-Engen & Ulmer, 2009; Egan, 2006b). Only two of thirty participants worked at clubs without racial limitations; notably, these were working-class establishments in "bad" neighbourhoods. As Ross and Greenwell (2005, p. 158) argue, the discrepancy between working-class clubs, which are more accepting of racialized dancers, and "classy" clubs attempting to attract wealthy, white patrons discursively and geographically reproduces class and racial divides between affluent and impoverished neighbourhoods (see also Bradley-Engen & Ulmer, 2009; Brooks, 2010).

Maintaining the club's aesthetic standard extends beyond hiring dancers. Sal (manager), like some of the incall/outcall third parties interviewed in the larger research project that this study draws on (Bruckert & Law, 2013), was troubled by having to enforce his club's aesthetic guidelines but also admitted it is sometimes necessary:

> I also feel really uncomfortable having to tell someone ... "I'm sorry, we're letting you go because like, you've put on weight," or something, right. You sound like the biggest asshole in the world when you say that to someone. So I try to word it in as gentle a way as possible ... A lot of times when we're letting girls go or telling them we're not hiring them, they'll say, "Why?" ... I use the word "suitable" [chuckle], I'm like, "Well, you know, we don't think that you're suitable anymore" ... If it gets to a boiling point, I have to be like, "Listen, the owner and the management just don't think you're good-looking enough to work here, like, I'm sorry." And it's only come to that a couple times, and I really hate that.

Notwithstanding occasional signs in the change rooms – "you know, 'The holidays are coming and we should all look our best. Do your hair and makeup and your nails'" (Jenna, dancer) – it appears that clubs maintain their aesthetic standards largely by punitive and exclusionary means. Dancers observed third parties giving warnings to, firing, or not hiring women who fail to embody or maintain a normatively attractive body size and aesthetic.

While these aesthetic requirements are certainly problematic and facilitate discrimination against racialized and plus-sized women, they are not exclusive to the erotic dance sector. Third parties in other sex industry businesses, including escort agencies and erotic massage parlours, often abide by similar aesthetic standards (Bruckert & Law, 2013; 2018a). Comparable gendered appearance-related requirements have been noted in service industry occupations, including flight attendant (Hochschild, 1983), retail worker (Williams & Connell, 2016), and of course waitress (Spradley & Mann, 1975). The Ontario Human Rights Commission (OHRC) took particular issue with restaurant service work, noting that,

> Despite legal protections, sexualized and gender-specific dress codes appear to be common in the food service industry, particularly in table service ... Women have raised concerns about being required or pressured to

conform to gender-based and sexualized expectations, such as being told to wear high heels, makeup, jewelry, particular hair styles, short skirts, and uncomfortable, tight or otherwise revealing clothing. (2017, p. 4)

In sex industry and service industry jobs alike, these aesthetic requirements often mean fewer employment options, lower income, and less negotiating power for women who are racialized or who otherwise do not conform to normative femininity (Ontario Human Rights Commission, 2017; Bruckert & Parent, 2018). As several studies have highlighted, this does not mean that racialized women do not resist or cannot be successful in the erotic dance sector (Ross & Greenwell, 2005; Brooks, 2010; see also Miller-Young, 2014); however, it does mean that they may be more likely to enjoy success and reasonable working conditions as independents (e.g., self-employed escorts) (Raguparan, 2017).

Once strippers are deemed to fit a club's aesthetic requirements, the hiring and intake process is cursory. In Ottawa, where there are no entertainer licences, it can be as brief as a third party "tak[ing] two pieces of ID and photocopy[ing] them" (dancer). In Toronto, strippers must additionally show a valid municipal licence, which the manager photocopies to keep on file. These files are often used to remind dancers to renew their licences, a matter about which third parties (especially managers) appear considerably concerned. Although some Toronto dancers suspected that this was primarily for the club's protection, one recalled that her club had provided a lawyer who got her fine reduced after she was caught with an expired licence. One Toronto third party also worked at a club that supported new dancers by facilitating the purchase of costly municipal licences: "They'll get you your licence, you can work it off on schedule." Some clubs also have a "dancer contract" that details "some guidelines and rules and stuff, of the club" (Sal, manager). It focuses on dancers' obligations to the club, and not the reverse – as in some other jurisdictions, including British Columbia, dancer contracts set out the rules, fees, expectations, and disciplinary measures to which strippers are subject but offer them little in return (Althorp, 2013; see also Colosi, 2010a). For the legal protection of the club, these contracts sometimes include clauses forbidding dancers from providing "extras" or even doing lap dances.

Although auditions are not the norm in either Ottawa or Toronto,[2] Dalton (DJ and manager) had a special process for vetting inexperienced dancers, which was part audition and part training (or screening):

You have the girl come in and she says, "Well, I want to be a dancer." And here she is, a hot girl, great, she's got everything you need. Right? And I go, ... "Well, what makes you think that you're going to be able to take your clothes of in front of, you know, 200 guys?" "Well, I can" ... I'd say to them, you know, "Bra, panties, now, go walk around the room 10 times." You know, half of them couldn't do it.

In contrast to Price-Glynn's (2010) suggestion that club managers pressure waitresses to become dancers, the third parties in this study acknowledged, like Dalton, that being a stripper is not a job that just anyone would feel comfortable doing. That said, Reverend (manager/bouncer) explained that sometimes it was unclear whether women wanted to work as waitresses or dancers: "The worst is when girls come in ... to be a server or something like that but didn't specify. So when you ... start to talk to her about everything ... she gets very upset. And I'm like, 'No, I wasn't trying to be a pig, but the majority of the girls who come to see me want to dance. You did not state your intentions.'" Despite the distinction between the expectations for strippers and wait staff, servers may use their sexuality to their advantage to boost their tips. Indeed, Scott (bouncer and manager) noted he had to make sure that the waitresses and shooter girls did not go too far when flirting with customers – in particular, by allowing customers to touch them, which not only competes with dancers but also contravenes municipal bylaws.

Once hired, dancers may be subject to limits on when and for how long they may conduct their business – for example, some clubs impose a five-hour minimum work period (e.g., to ensure an adequate supply of strippers before midnight), while others do not let dancers leave the premises once they have signed in (e.g., to prevent them from leaving with customers to perform sexual services). All dancers must pay a daily house fee of $10 to $60, which varies depending on the club and the time. Although the demands made on strippers by clubs in Ottawa and Toronto are similar in many respects, the scheduling requirements differ considerably. In Toronto, they can elect to be a scheduled "house dancer," or "housegirl," for which they receive a salary, or to freelance and work the hours of their choosing; in Ottawa, all dancers are effectively required to be scheduled, but are not paid by the club. According to participants working in Ottawa, dancers are obliged to work three shifts per week, including a slower shift, such as during the day or Sunday evening. Comparing this policy to those noted by Bouclin (2006) and Bruckert (2002), it appears that mandatory unpaid scheduling has become prevalent in Ottawa in recent years: while one dancer recalled, "I had so much freedom ... There was no schedule," when she worked in Ottawa from 2007 to 2009, another, having danced in Ottawa since 2011, had experienced only the mandatory scheduling policy.

In Toronto, by contrast, scheduled dancers are compensated (more or less at minimum wage) but are significantly outnumbered by freelancers. As a result, it appears that Toronto clubs have little means of ensuring a consistently adequate number of dancers – a problem that Ottawa clubs seem to have somewhat resolved by instituting mandatory scheduling (although some Ottawa dancers maintained that they were able to bend or flout the scheduling requirements). A Toronto manager described this challenge as

> a very vicious difficult circle ... There are some days where you have a lot of girls and you don't have enough customers to service the girls. In which case then you've got a lot of bitter women who think, "Oh, well, this is going to be a shitty week." And then, they take the next day off. And then, the next day rolls around and there are a lot of customers and there aren't enough girls. And then, the customers leave because there's not enough girls to service the customers. There's no way to fix it. There's nothing you can do. You can promote the bar all you like, you can hire as many dancers as you want, but who shows up on a day-to-day basis is completely random.

The unpredictability of a majority freelancer workforce has created leeway for scheduled dancers to subtly resist managerial expectations (see Murphy, 2003). In regard to unpopular (e.g., afternoon) shifts, for example, one Toronto dancer explained that she was frequently "20 minutes or half an hour late, and – it didn't really matter." Of course, this leeway is not unlimited: another Toronto stripper noted that management would stop scheduling dancers if they missed too many shifts but would still allow them to work as freelancers, while yet another recalled feeling she had to gradually reduce her scheduled shifts rather than suddenly switch to freelancing, fearing she would otherwise be dismissed. To mitigate the unreliability of freelancers, Toronto clubs offer house fee reductions or reimbursements for stage shows (usually $10 to $20), as well as cheaper house fees for dancers who arrive earlier (e.g., before 9:00 pm). Although some Toronto dancers said they would rather forego the extra $30 to $80 (salaries vary by club and shift) to decide their own schedule and not be required to do three stage shows, one woman was of the opinion that being on the schedule "motivates you to go to work," while, for another, "it's a principle thing; I don't want to pay the club to work there ... even though it's really bad pay."

It is worth noting that these expectations and wages (or lack thereof) are comparable to or better than those in other sex industry sectors. In the incall/outcall sector, for example, agencies or brothels, which are often smaller organizations than strip clubs, with only one or two third parties (e.g., a manager/operator only; a manager and a driver; or an owner/operator, security, and administrative assistant), do not usually offer wages for shifts. Additionally, smaller agencies like erotic massage parlours may expect workers to do several shifts per week in which they may also have to perform unpaid labour such as laundry or administration, even if they do not get any customers. Moreover, third parties at incall and outcall agencies take higher portions of service fees charged to customers which, at 30 to 50 per cent (Bruckert & Law, 2013),[3] are comparable to hair salons, which usually deduct 50 per cent from stylists' rates. By contrast, at most Ottawa and Toronto strip clubs, a dancer has to "pay [the house fee] up front or sometime during the course of the night to be allowed to work there. Other than that, all the money she makes is her own" (Scott, bouncer and manager).[4]

Discrepant Goals and Parallel Structures

As with sex workers in incall establishments, strippers are provided with a physical space to work by third parties. However, in contrast to outcall third parties like escort agency operators, strip club third parties do not *directly* organize the labour of dancers. They do not choose clients for dancers or vice versa (unless specifically requested by one of these parties); rather, they maintain the space, services (e.g., alcohol, food), and ambiance of the club, which facilitates dancers' interactions with customers. Instead of making money from a portion of sex workers' service fees, strip clubs are licensed liquor distributors whose "business plan is, in a nutshell, is to sell alcohol. That's the most important thing and that's how we make our money" (Sal, manager). Thus, for the most part, dancers and third parties are relatively uninvolved with each other's labour because they are busy trying to achieve different business goals. With the exception of the DJ who makes the stage roster and, for those on schedule, the manager, there is generally little reason for dancers to interact with third parties. In turn, dancers' goal is to earn money as entrepreneurs by selling dances, which may not necessarily help advance the club's goal of selling alcohol.

The *CABE v Algonquin Tavern* (1981) decision largely rests on these discrepant goals: the OLRB ultimately agreed with the tavern's argument that the entertainment provided by dancers is an "ancillary concern" and that the tavern's "principal business is the supply of food, beverages, or accommodation to the public. It is here that they make their profit" (para. 4). It should be noted that, at that time, strip *bars* were relatively new, having proliferated in the 1970s as taverns where strippers periodically performed (Bruckert & Dufresne, 2002). By comparison, dancers are central to the marketing and general appeal of today's strip clubs, making them integral to customer satisfaction and, in turn, the success of the club through alcohol sales. A 2014 Nevada Supreme Court decision rested squarely on this fact: the justices declared that, because the defendant, Sapphire Gentlemen's Club, "bills itself as the 'World's Largest Strip Club,' and not, say, a sports bar or nightclub, we are confident that the women strip-dancing there are useful and indeed necessary to its operation" (*Terry et al. v Sapphire Gentlemen's Club*, 2014, pp. 19–20), and therefore are employees who should be paid minimum wage. Other similar class action suits in the United States have also been successful. For example, a group of New York City dancers was awarded $10.8 million in back wages by a federal judge, who ruled that their club could not treat them as independent contractors and had to pay them minimum wage; and, in 2012, strippers who worked at Spearmint Rhino chain locations in California, Nevada, Florida, Texas, Idaho, and Kentucky were awarded a $13 million settlement (CBS News, 2014; Kandel, 2012). Canadian dancers have not brought forwards any such suits – which, it should be noted, are not a panacea. One reason for the popularity of this form of collective resistance in the United States may emanate from the fact that the erotic dance industry is larger and franchises are more common than in Canada; a class action suit is more feasible and worthwhile against a chain operation with many locations, or, alternatively, a very large operation, as only the defendant named in the suit is affected by the outcome. Thus, while they may be successful against a chain or stand-alone club, such suits do not precipitate sector-wide change. Moreover, a class action suit may not be desirable for dancers, because it transforms their legal status, and once they are classified as employees, they will have less flexible schedules than they would as freelancers (Gall, 2016) – at least in Toronto, where there remains a distinction between scheduled and freelance dancers. Given that Ottawa strippers are scheduled but not paid, they may be able to build a better case that they are de facto unpaid employees.

Of course, as workplace resistance is dialectical and embedded in ongoing relationships between workers and management characterized by power imbalances, such instances of collective action may not be entirely successful (Mumby, 2005). As Berg and Penley note in relation to another sector of the sex industry, "porn workers do not simply react to top-down management; just as often, changes in management style represent capital's desperate responses to workers manipulating the system in ways management never anticipated" (2016, p. 162). In this respect, dancers and researchers in the United States have found that when strippers win a class action suit, the defendant club finds new ways of exploiting workers, including taking a higher percentage of lap dance money or tips. Club operators are also known to fire dancers whom they discover are involved in collective action (Gall, 2016).

The independent contractor moniker has, nevertheless, shaped the ways third parties and dancers interact in the workplace, with implications for both. For third parties, this means attempting to ensure from a distance that dancers provide adequate service to customers. At the same time, it is in dancers' collective interest to give quality customer service, since poor service would hinder both their personal business and the success of the club, by attracting fewer customers and hampering dancers' earnings. In this respect, dancers and the club can be seen as inhabiting parallel structures – the organizational structure of the club, and the agglomeration of entrepreneurial workers that dancers collectively constitute – that are both dependent on and independent of each other. Although the notion of parallel structures refers to organizational structures, it is also used here to evoke the metaphor of twin buildings situated opposite each other: the two structures are close, the inhabitants of each can (often, but not always, as the next chapter will show) see their counterparts in the other, and, as a matching set, each structure helps to define the other.

Who's the Boss? The Employment Relationship in Practice

Although dancers and third parties can be said to inhabit an interdependent relationship that requires minimal interaction, their respective vantage points in the parallel structures can inform conflicting and nebulous professional relationships and expectations, disrupting conventional notions of organizational hierarchy. Scott (bouncer and manager) offered the following reflection in this regard:

> Some of the managers and doormen are of the state of mind that these girls work for us; they don't work with us. They're not fellow staff members. They come in, they make this bar money and then they go ... So, that whole "with" and "for" slash gets a little blurry when it comes to the dancers ... I mean, my job was to regulate them. But, without them, I'm not making money. So, in that sense, I kind of see them, you know, kind of almost equal. I have a little bit authority over them.

In addition to hiring and firing, this third-party authority includes rule enforcement, a practice undertaken largely by managers and bouncers, and usually, but not consistently or always logically, informed by municipal bylaws and federal (e.g., prostitution, drug) laws. Some rules are known to dancers and relatively commonly enforced – as Kristin (dancer) put it, "usually the only rules that are super enforced are rules that involve paying the club [i.e., paying the house fee] and rules that govern when you work and when you show up." Other rules are widely known but virtually never enforced (e.g., municipal prohibitions on touching); and still others are inconsistent in formulation, communication, and/or application. Club rules generally pertain to scheduling, performing on stage, dancers' behaviour (e.g., appropriate interactions with customers and other dancers, no overt intoxication), pricing (e.g., dances, time in champagne rooms), and legal and/or security concerns (e.g., no illicit drugs or sexual services, no potentially jealous and disruptive boyfriends). Additional expectations or guidelines vary by club and may include requiring dancers to maintain a certain level of weight/fitness, be continually present on the floor, or wear appropriately sexy clothing and shoes. To this end, and consistent with Carrie's and Marie's (dancers) experiences, Studley (DJ/supervisor) made an effort to "make sure if the girl is new to the bar – whether she's new to the business or not – that she understands our house rules, because they differ from club to club."

Third-party approaches to rule enforcement also vary with managerial styles. For example Sal (manager) "let [dancers] bend some of the rules a little bit and stuff," an approach he described as "firm but fair": "The girls know that if they step out of line, then they get pulled into the office and reprimanded. But no one's power tripping over it or anything." By contrast, Reverend (manager/bouncer) kept a record of dancers' rule infractions: "If it's a quiet shift and you don't show up, I will write that down because I will be looking to see if it becomes a behaviour pattern."

Penalties for rule infraction can range from verbal admonishment to suspension, termination, or a ban (i.e., firing with no chance of rehiring). Consistent with previous research in Ontario, British Columbia, and the United States (see Bruckert, 2002 and Bouclin, 2006; Althorp, 2013; and Egan, 2004, respectively), participants also mentioned fines for arriving late or leaving early, with respect to either the schedule or the stage, or for damaging club property. However, third parties seemed to favour other disciplinary techniques over fines, as Adam (DJ and manager) explained: "A night off, or a week off, or a couple of days off [is] way better than fining anybody. It's got more impact ... If you take $20 away from somebody who made $1000 ... they're going to laugh at you ... If you take their way of making a living away from them for a day, it hits home." That managers have the ability to cut off strippers' source of income speaks to the necessity of the club setting for dancers to conduct their business, and the importance of maintaining a peaceful relationship with third parties to ensure their continued access to it.

It appears that termination is exercised only as a response to egregious disregard of club rules and expectations; out of the fifteen dancers who participated in this study, the majority of whom had worked at numerous clubs, only four had been fired during their careers. Third parties' descriptions of their practices, similarly, suggest that they tend toward imposing short-term suspensions or merely reprimanding dancers (e.g., for unsanctioned contact/services during a lap dance or physical altercations). This finding is analogous to other studies noting few, occasional, or no repercussions for dancers for tardiness or absence (Barton, 2006; Bruckert, 2002; Fogel & Quinlan, 2011). At the same time, however, these studies tended to characterize third parties as capricious and micromanaging. Rather than being contradictory or misinterpretations, these observations highlight the inconsistency of rule enforcement at strip clubs (Bruckert, 2002; DeMichele & Tewksbury, 2004; Lavin, 2013).

Echoing the complexities faced by independent contractors and part-time and non-permanent workers in other labour market sectors (see Fudge et al., 2003; Vosko & Clark, 2009), several dancers expressed feeling precarious. Carrie (dancer) felt that third parties "have a lot of power ... There's a hierarchy... We're at the bottom." In one focus group, Charlene, Bobby, Leigh, Jen, and Brigitte together agreed that dancers are "disposable" (Bobby) because "they'll fire you and just hire somebody else" (Jen). In this context, as noted by several scholars (see Althorp, 2013; Bruckert, 2002; Colosi, 2010a; Egan, 2006b), dancers are for the most part unwilling to confront third parties regarding unfair labour practices: "There's nothing you *can* do, really" (Jenna, dancer; participant's emphasis). While quitting is an avenue of resistance to unreasonable demands by management (Bruckert, 2002), it is not necessarily an effective one, as Donna (dancer) explained: "When I eventually got fed up with all the BS at my club, I just quit ... So if you aren't happy at one, you can always try another, although I find that most clubs have the same rules." Donna's comment is a reminder that, although it may be personally satisfying, quitting a club does nothing to change the organizational or economic structures of the erotic dance sector, or dancers' need for employment. When quitting is not an option, dancers may merely "complain to each other and then we bite the bullet" (Kristen, dancer), or resist, manipulate, or negotiate with third parties.

Even as they described occasional, casual collective resistance strategies (from complaining to withholding tips or cuts), most dancers perceived collective action as unfeasible or futile, anticipating or having experienced hostile reactions from management (see also Althorp, 2013; Bouclin, 2004; Colosi, 2010a). For example, Shane (dancer) recalled that, "sometimes girls would share information about different things that were going on where dancers were trying to organize themselves and, like, the managers would take the information away and get really mad." Donna (dancer) once "attempted to get collective action, and ... they [her colleagues] weren't interested. They were just too scared of getting fired and losing their job. And I do know that managers ... will call other managers and report someone as a troublemaker." Tony (manager/DJ) spoke of getting just such a call. In Bouclin's research (2004; 2009), Ottawa dancers similarly described managers cooperating to "blacklist" labour agitators. Echoing Althorp's (2013) and Price-Glynn's (2010) observations of managerial unwillingness to improve working conditions, Leigh's demands were met with hostility by the club manager when she spoke up for her colleagues during staff meetings: "I'd be like, ... 'We were wondering if perhaps, you know, we could have different chairs in the change room,' or whatever – some kind of right, and then basically ... I'd be dismissed, 'I didn't come here for that. This is the end of this meeting.' And then he'd leave." Thus, not only do strippers feel precarious as workers, but the conditions of clubs suggest that third parties undervalue them.

Although (conventionally attractive) dancers may choose not to work at a poorly equipped club, many indicated that the amenities in strip clubs are often insufficient or inadequately maintained. A commonly noted problem was the size of change rooms. Speaking to the impacts of the shift to lap dancing, and increases in club rosters with the introduction of the house fee system (Maticka-Tyndale, 2004), dancers reported that some clubs have a single change room "for about fifty ladies and waitresses" (Jenna) that can get "pretty cramped. At the end of the night, it's a nightmare when everybody's in there trying to get changed" (Jill). As a result of overcrowding, there may be a shortage of secure places for dancers to store their valuables: "When you get there, if you're lucky, there's a locker available. If you're not, then tough luck for you" (Marie, dancer). For Monica (dancer), this situation had resulted in theft. Given that dancers must style their hair for work, electrical outlets can also be an issue: Tony (manager/DJ) recalled "work[ing] in clubs where there's one electrical plug in the whole change room, and you're trying to get 14 curling irons in there, you know?"

Monica and Marie (dancers) reported that their clubs were cleaned every day, while Ashley (dancer) thought that strip clubs were as "grimy" as other nightclubs where she had worked. Poor facility maintenance can affect dancers' morale as well as their safety. In Kristen's experience, third parties at some clubs did not clear the stage of safety hazards such as body oil between shows, "even if you make the request," making it "very dangerous to be walking in big heels." More than a lack of cleanliness, Jenna experienced these conditions as a lack of respect, noting they made her "feel small and very powerless": at one club, for example, "we're not trusted [i.e., supplied] with hand towels," while, in another, she noted that the change room had "two toilets, [in] one bathroom, and the partition between the two toilets is a goddamn shower curtain." Jenna's comments illustrate the asymmetries of organizational power relations (Hodson, 1999), and, indeed, dancers indicated that there was very little they could do as independent contractors to motivate management to improve workplace facilities or their upkeep.

At the same time, although they do not provide dancers with the entitlements and rights of employees, the parallel structures of the strip club allow dancers considerable agency to govern their own activities. Dancers appreciate that their work is self-directed and self-motivated, even if some simultaneously feel that third parties do not particularly care about them. Although she admitted that it did not cancel out her aforementioned feelings of powerlessness about the poorly maintained facilities, Jenna appreciated the relative freedom of the independent contractor relationship:

> I think, you know, bitching notwithstanding, we have a lot of freedom, in a way that, you know, you can get drunk or a little bit high, you can swear, there's no [specific] dress code really, and if you don't want to deal with someone, you can not deal with them, whereas in other work environments you have to. Like if you're doing sales, and you don't like your client, in a square job, you still have to deal with them. I don't have to deal with clients I don't like. So that's kind of nice.

As with incall/outcall workers (Bruckert & Law, 2013), strippers acknowledge that the infrastructure and services third parties provide allow them to come and go without worrying about the responsibilities germane to running a business, including advertising, pricing, and managing a workspace – as Studley (DJ/supervisor) put it, "we provide all the physical equipment you need to do the job with the exception of what you are wearing." Strippers and incall/outcall workers who choose to work for third parties also appreciate the freedom from the investment and time commitment that running a business requires (Bruckert & Law, 2013; Caradonna, 2018). As Ashley (dancer) put it:

> I felt very much in control of my own decisions in that environment ... You go there, you do what you wanna do, you work when you wanna work, you make your money, and then you leave, and you don't have any – you don't have to, like, prove to your company that you care about what you're doing, ... which was something that was really appealing to me about working at strip clubs.

Marie further commented: "You can just go in whenever, and if you don't go during a week or two weeks, like, nobody cares, cause, like, it doesn't matter." Thus, while strippers may depend on clubs and third parties for the stage, bar, and ambiance that makes their work possible, their work pace, tasks, and interactions with customers are largely self-governed.

Third-Party Misbehaviour

Although dancers enjoy a level of self-governance seen in few other work contexts, other kinds of occupations and organizations also contend with tensions arising from service oversight from afar. Bolton and Houlihan (2010) find similar separation between third parties and workers in the service sector, with particular implications for front-line managers, who must ensure but do not personally deliver quality service to customers while juggling their other responsibilities with handling customer complaints and respecting the directives of upper management. Moreover, relative to dancers, third parties below the ownership level are more conventional employees (albeit in a stigmatized labour market sector) who are also subject to organizational rules and policies. In short, third parties must balance their roles as managers and workers as they navigate what Bolton and Houlihan call the "worker-manager-customer triangle" of interactive service work. At each point of this triangle are different actors who are essential to the operation of service-based businesses – in this case strippers, (non-owner) third parties, and customers – each of whom have divergent interests and/or goals (2010), p. 378). While negotiating the tensions between company policies, customer satisfaction, and fair treatment of workers, strip club third parties, like their front-line counterparts in the service industry, may *misbehave*, a term management scholars apply to resistant acts that undermine the goals of the organization – and notably something not normally associated with managers in any field. Just as the "pimp" and unsavoury manager stereotypes leave no room to acknowledge sex industry third parties' frustrations, limitations, and resistance, Hadjisolomou (2019) notes that front-line service managers' actual and perceived instances of powerlessness and the misbehaviour they inspire have been subject to little scholarly attention.

Like dancers, third parties, as employees of the club, are subject to workplace rules; indeed Kelly (bartender) had received a lengthy employee manual from the owner of the club where she worked. As with dancers, although these rules are comparable in Toronto and Ottawa, it seems they are not consistently enforced or followed. Some rules are specific to individual third-party roles – for example, bouncers are discouraged from using excessive or unnecessary force. Like the bouncers in DeMichele and Tewksbury's (2004) and Lavin's (2013) studies, various third parties mentioned that they are not allowed to drink at work. Still, a few participants suggested that this rule is overlooked in practice, noting that there is little oversight in the "party atmosphere" (Jimmy, DJ). The next three chapters will reflect further on the influence of the strip-club environment on its organizational culture and practices, as well as on other instances of third-party rule-breaking and the implications for dancers. The remainder of this section elaborates some of the reasons strip club third parties engage in rule-breaking behaviour.

As noted in the job descriptions outlined in chapter 1, managers surveil the club and the people in it, including other third parties. But when these other third parties – such as DJs, bartenders, and bouncers – are out of view of the manager (or the owner), they occasionally misbehave. Third parties may break club rules for the benefit of dancers, out of frustration emanating from their lack of influence over organizational policies they perceive to be impractical or unjust, or because they feel undervalued as workers. For example, Kelly (bartender) elected not to follow certain rules she perceived as unfair to strippers – including a new policy dictating that they be charged 10 per cent when customers use gift cards. Showing similar sympathy for dancers, Fuzzy (DJ) took advantage of a manager's absence by cancelling a nightly promotional event they did not like: "It wasn't that busy, and I didn't want to interrupt the girls that were making some money to bring them out to do a free dance because at the end of the day, the more money the girls make, the better my night is going to be ... So I just skipped over it." Just as managers in mainstream labour sectors occasionally subvert organizational hierarchy (Willmott, 1997), Fuzzy resisted by making a decision beyond his level of authority, prioritizing the dancers' financial interests as well as his own (i.e., he was likely to receive more tips from happier dancers) over the putative interests of the organization.

Other examples from third-party participants demonstrate more sustained resistance emanating from frustration over a lack of control over the organization (Willmott, 1997). Even though he is a manager, Sal breaks the rules governing drug use at his club because he disagrees with the owner's policy: he allows dancers to smoke cannabis (still criminalized in Canada at the time of the interview) in the indoor smoking room when the owner is not on the premises. Ignoring the rules in this way prioritizes the dancers' safety – they can avoid going outside into the "pretty rough neighbourhood" surrounding the club – and helps ensure that those who prefer to indulge will be content and provide better service to customers. This reflects Bolton and Houlihan's (2010) "worker-manager-customer triangle" insofar as third parties sometimes disregard the directives of upper management in the interest of workers; in this particular example, Sal is also indirectly endeavouring to improve customers' experiences.

Strip club third parties also resist perceived injustices against themselves. For example, Kelly (bartender) disregarded some of the policies at her club because she felt underpaid:

> We're supposed to upsell. So if a regular thing like a bar shot is $8.50 ... we try and sell the $11.50, and ... as much as I'm supposed to do that, sometimes it's worse for me if I do. I know if I upsell this, and I sell this, then it's gonna come out to $20 even ... Nobody's really gonna dig in their pocket, or break another 20. ... And they pay me $8.90 an hour ... I want to do a good job, and I'm honest and stuff but like, if it comes down to, if you really want me to upsell against all odds, like, you better pay me more.

As with Marcus's side business as an agent (see chapter 1, p. 30), Kelly's strategy demonstrates that third parties sometimes break the rules in order to prioritize their own financial benefit over the club's profits.

Concluding Remarks: The Dialectics of Parallel Structures

As this chapter has shown, strip clubs are organizations in which there are two kinds of employment relationships. Whereas dancers are classified as independent contractors, all third parties below the level of ownership are, along with other staff like servers, employees in the conventional sense – they receive a wage from the club in exchange for their labour. Mixed organizational structures exist in other sectors as well – for example, in Canada's public service and the information technology industry, in which there may be a mix of permanent employees, temporary or casual workers, and consultants (independent contractors) working at any one time, precipitating tensions between workers occupying different organizational roles and strata (Gallagher & Sverke, 2005; Ilcan, Oliver, & O'Connor, 2007; Stecy-Hildebrand et al., 2018). Indeed Stecy-Hildebrand et al.'s (2018) description of the Canadian public sector as divided between permanent workers who can access the advantages garnered through public sector unions, and temporary workers who are excluded from coverage and disqualified from protections, is analogous to the parallel structures of strip clubs.

To return to the question of exploitation, this chapter has highlighted a number of problematic aspects of third parties' treatment of strippers – in particular, poor maintenance and facilities – in response to which dancers feel they have little to no recourse as independent contractors. At the same time, dancers enjoy the relative leeway they have to govern their own work pace, schedules (within limitations that vary between Ottawa and Toronto), and interactions with customers, and are able to negotiate, bend, or break club rules. Dancers found that some elements of this relationship liberated them from the constraints of the conventional employer-employee relationship, but they also recognized its unjust and exploitive aspects (see also Brooks, 2010; Bruckert, Parent, & Robitaille, 2003). For their part, third parties navigate their positions as stewards of the club space who are charged with overseeing some aspects of dancers' activities but who, in practice, cannot really control what dancers do. At the same time, they feel underappreciated and underpaid as employees, and selectively subvert the rules or shirk their responsibilities. Such behaviour, in turn, makes it difficult for dancers to tell when third parties will flex their authority. In these respects, the power relations between and among club-affiliated third parties and dancers are not strictly determined by organizational hierarchy but, rather, are an ongoing dialectic conditioned by their respective occupations and attendant freedoms, constraints, and legal statuses. In short, local organizational relations and practices in the erotic dance sector are connected to translocal neoliberal labour precarity and intersecting social norms and expectations; together, they inform the workplace interactions that are elaborated in the following chapters.

Chapter Three

Backstage: A Divided Workplace

A central claim of this book is that there is more going on at the strip club than the performances on the stage and in the champagne rooms. Because the strip club is an environment in which workers together endeavour to create an atmosphere for, and to evoke particular feelings and behaviour in, clients, both strippers and third parties can be described as *performing* occupational roles comprising particular iterations and clusters of gender, sexuality, class, and race. This and the following chapter use a dramaturgical lens to examine how third parties and dancers prepare for and perform their roles. This exploration begins backstage, in order to examine the spaces, preparations, and negotiations to which customers are not privy. More precisely, this chapter elaborates on the implications of the parallel structures by delineating the "back regions" of dancers and third parties, and reflecting on the extent and implications of their separateness. As part of this analysis, the chapter considers how the parallel structures, in concert with the physical layout of strip clubs, impact communication and cooperation between third parties and dancers, and third parties' oversight of dancers' activities (e.g., training, surveillance). As this discussion is grounded in Goffman's theoretical elaboration of performance, the chapter begins by introducing his perspective more fully.

Goffman (1959) developed what he called a "dramaturgical approach" to make sense of how individuals behave in the presence of others, and the meanings conveyed by, and interpreted from, these performances. Reflecting on the social interaction, he argued that individuals perform particular expressions of themselves in order to foster impressions that define the social situation for, and evoke appropriate behavioural responses from, other individuals in their presence (their audience). Enacted repeatedly, these expressions, which Goffman (1959, p. 16) refers to as pre-established patterns of action, parts, or routines, foster social relationships between the performer and the audience, in turn reflecting and affirming a particular social role. The performance of a social role occurs in, and is limited to, a place (and time) Goffman calls the "front region," where performers perpetually enact their roles, whether interacting directly with or merely in view of their audience (p. 107). It is in the "back region," out of sight of the audience, that performers may relax and "step out of character" (p. 112).

Of course, many roles are being performed simultaneously in a service industry organization in which people work together to attract, cater to, entertain, and regulate the behaviour of clients. Thus, Goffman (1959) suggests that performances are often carried out in a team, which he defines as "a set of individuals whose intimate co-operation is required ... in relation to an interaction or series of interactions in which the relevant definition of the situation is maintained" (p. 104). However, workers and managers are not necessarily members of a team simply by virtue of being in the same organization; rather, they can be considered teams only if (and when) their performances sustain each other and the social situation as a whole – in other words, if they are mutually dependant (p. 82). As discussed in the previous chapter, in the parallel structures of the strip club, third parties and strippers are interdependent but, in many ways, also operate independently of each other. In addition to collaborating in performing in the front region, being on the same team further requires that members are privy to the requirements of each other's performances and share in preparations in the back region (Goffman, 1959). This chapter explores the various situations and extent to which third parties and dancers are on the same performance team.

Parallel Structures, Shifting Back Regions

The front and back regions together make up what Goffman (1959) calls the "setting." As the scenery and props for the interactions it stages, the setting comprises both the physical facilities and their allocation for particular activities, including shared and role-specific front regions where performances "play out" for customers, and back regions where performers ready their illusions. Like the disparate goals of the parallel structures, the setting can be seen as serving a dual purpose: to stage the performances of third parties and staff, which are geared toward making money for the club through alcohol sales, and to facilitate dancers' performances and provision of services to customers.

The different regions of the club are designed to accommodate various and changing performances and interactions by dancers and third parties. Both perform in the front region of the strip club, which is visible to customers. This region comprises the stage, the club's central visual focus; and the "floor," the public area where customers and dancers interact. The VIP section, a separate area divided into unenclosed private lap dance booths (participants used the terms VIP and champagne room interchangeably to describe both the area and individual booths), is a front region used more heavily by dancers than third parties, although the latter periodically circulate through it to monitor dancers' interactions with customers. There are also multiple back regions in the strip club. Strippers' back region is, of course, their change room. To guard the secrets of the illusion dancers are crafting – and, more practically speaking, to protect their privacy and safety – change rooms are often located on a different floor than the customers, or secured behind a locked door. Some clubs are also furnished with a private smoking room or patio for dancers. Third parties prepare, or take respite from, their performances elsewhere – managers in their office; bouncers, bartenders, and waitresses in their own change room(s) (at some clubs).

Both dancers' and third parties' designated preparation areas are off limits to customers. To some extent, third parties and dancers have access to each other's preparation areas, but, because third parties (along with other staff) maintain the setting for dancers, they generally have more access to dancers' spaces than vice versa. For example, although dancers may go to the manager's office to make schedule-related requests, or be summoned there to get disciplined or receive their shift pay – interactions in which a back region to the customers momentarily becomes a front region in which the manager performs his authoritative role for dancers who respond as strip club workers – it is otherwise a back region inaccessible to (or not frequented by) dancers. By contrast, while the DJ booth is a back region to customers, it is a space open to strippers, who frequent it in order to register for, enquire about, and renegotiate their stage times, interactions in which both actors perform their respective roles, with sometimes competing interests.

Just as third parties' roles circumscribe them to particular regions of the club, their access to a back region imbues them with certain responsibilities, with implications for dancers. For example, at Donna's (dancer) club, "they had the DJ booth right next to the dressing room, and so the DJ monitored the dressing room at all times ... It impacted my privacy because we didn't have a place where us girls could just go and do our makeup and fix our hair and bitch about customers." From a booth adjacent to the dancers' change room, DJs may also "nag us about stuff like, you know, 'Get out onto the floor. Stop taking so long to do your hair'" (Sasha, dancer). Other club employees, including managers, bouncers, and wait staff, may also access the dancers' change room to deliver messages or food, monitor their behaviour, or help ensure their safety (e.g., by breaking up a fight). In this respect, third parties' and dancers' performances are directed toward different audiences at different times and spaces in the club (see Goffman, 1961; Hacking, 2004). Just as Bolton and Houlihan (2010) argue that service managers' role involves attending in distinct ways to workers and customers, strip club managers and DJs may be performing as authority figures in front of dancers in the change room, temporarily transforming the space into a front region for dancers as well. Rather than relaxing out of view of customers, in these moments dancers must instead contend with third parties' (gendered, as chapter 4 will show) expectations of them as strippers.

The Training Gap and Dancer Self-Governance

Even though third parties may occasionally pass through the dancers' change room, this does not mean that they entirely appreciate the work strippers put into, and the artifice of, their occupational performances. Moreover, because third parties work for the club and are concerned primarily with its profits, they are only very peripherally involved in how much money dancers make. In this context, it appears third parties are ill equipped (or unmotivated) to provide them with guidance. Indeed, dancers consistently noted that third parties provide very little training or support to new "hires" (see also Murphy, 2003). As Marie (dancer) explained,

> You walk in and nobody tells you how to dance, nobody tells you how to talk to customers, nobody tells you what to do other than you have to go on stage. You kind of look at what the other girls are doing and then, little by little, you learn. As far as training on how to talk to customers or how to behave with other dancers or anything, that's all stuff that you learn [yourself], I guess ... Because they [third parties] don't really care how you do, right, as long as you bring the DJ [i.e., house] fee – and you look pretty, they don't care how much money you make. That's all up to you.

Given the variety of responsibilities managers' role involves, Tony (manager/DJ) framed his hands-off approach vis-à-vis the dancers as a matter of priorities: "To literally, um, start somebody, you know, in front of an audience that has no dancing experience is not really what I want to do. Cause it takes away from the stuff that I have to be doing anyway, and I really don't have time for that, ya know?"

To compensate for this dearth of training, Monica and Marie (dancers) looked to online stripper communities for advice, whereas Jill and Jen (dancers) accompanied a friend with more experience dancing on their first night. Scott (bouncer and manager) spoke of just such a woman – an informal dancer third party – in the first strip club where he had worked:

> We had, like, a stripper mum. She was the one who's been in there the longest. She kind of earned, uh, respect amongst the other dancers. So, when some dancers came in, she would actually show them ... I remember one of my early shifts, I think the first month or two, I was patrolling ... the champagne room and, uh, she was teaching a new, uh, woman, girl how to dance, how to work the client. So, I was walking by. She said, "Could you sit down for a second?" So, I sat down and I know it's like inappropriate now, but, at the time, you know, you're like, "Eh, why not?" You know, sit down. So, I had the, like, the strip club mum perform on me, dance, you know, tease me and everything. And then, she got up and then she got this eighteen-year-old blonde bimbo kind of girl to do the same thing. And then, they did it a few more times, correcting, you know, her correcting the other one. It was an interesting experience. And then, after that, I had to go back to work with like the hardest hard-on I had in a while.

While this was an important moment of training for a new dancer, it also, as Scott notes, constituted less than professional conduct on his part. Yet, as chapter 4 will discuss, the necessity for dancers to perform in a continually sexy and appealing manner in the regions of the club visible to customers can impact the perceptions of and their relationships with third parties.

Speaking to the separateness of the parallel structures, and managers' role as director of the staff (but not the dancers') team, third parties felt they were not capable of training the dancers, or that it was not necessary. As Gilles (manager) put it, "I could train more, like, waiter, bartender, doorman, DJ than the dancer." Although Adam had not trained strippers per se – he jokingly noted, "I've never taught anybody to swing around the pole" – as a DJ, he had offered advice if someone had never danced before, albeit "not from experience": "My advice is always simple: 'Go up there and pretend you're having fun and smile ... Always stare out over top of their heads and focus on something on the other side of the room and smile. And then, the only time you want to look anywhere else is to make sure you're not walking off the end of the stage.'" Dalton (DJ and manager) similarly offered advice to new strippers, suggesting they should watch the stage shows of their more experienced counterparts; he would also insist that they dance to songs they already knew and liked. However, this kind of advice appears to be rare and, perhaps, not necessarily helpful, as Reverend's (manager/bouncer) observation suggests: "Most girls have some experience coming in, but you do have the odd few that are completely green with no experience, and most of them learn by the seat of their pants as they go, which is quite amusing to watch sometimes."

This lack of guidance can also have implications for strippers' interactions with customers. As noted in the previous chapter, rules are neither clearly communicated nor consistent across clubs. In this regard, few dancer participants had received clear directions from third parties about how they should follow municipal bylaws – namely, those prohibiting sexual touching. This was a source of frustration for Jill (dancer), who felt that unclear physical contact rules complicated communication with customers:

> Whenever there's ambiguity or it seems like, contrary, it creates like, this feeling of conflict ... They'll be like, "What are the rules?" and I'm like, "Well technically speaking, the rules are you're not actually supposed to touch me. You're not supposed to be sexually touching me – don't touch my tits, don't touch my ass, don't touch nothing." But like, the reality is that when you're looking around, that shit is going on all over the place, you know? So it just seems like bullshit to say one thing and then to completely disregard that, which then in turn can make you feel like there's no fuckin' rules.

Jill's exasperation suggests that dancers do not feel they are on the same performance team as third parties in their service interactions with customers; indeed, third parties are neither involved in the preparation (e.g., by not communicating the rules) or delivery of service (e.g., often not physically present in the VIP area), and, as chapter 5 elaborates, strip club security is generally more reactive than proactive. In this context, dancers emphasized the importance of deciding on and, in turn, taking responsibility to maintain, their own sexual/service boundaries. As Ashley put it matter of factly, "you better start making some guidelines and rules for yourself so that you know what the fuck you are doing. Regardless of what the club is telling you to do, you better make sure you know what you want to do and what you are going to do and what you're not gonna do." In concert with the tension between municipal regulation and lap dancing, the limited reach of third-party surveillance makes these boundary decisions all the more important.

Surveillance and Performing Rule Enforcement and Adherence

The extent to which third parties, usually bouncers or managers, monitor the VIP (lap dancing) areas depends on the numbers and responsibilities of third parties, as well as their interpretations of the club rules and/or municipal bylaws. Additionally, dancers may elect to take customers to more or less easily accessible areas of the VIP section. The latter decreases their risk of being caught providing services that are not sanctioned by the club ("extras") – as Sasha (dancer) noted, "they monitored some champagne rooms, but there were definitely some that were sort of tucked away in certain corners that girls who did extras, like, would go there with their regulars" – but also means that third-party help may be relatively inaccessible. Yet, even if they are vigilant, bouncers and managers cannot monitor the VIP area at all times. Moreover, the VIP area is supposed to be a place for dancers and customers to interact relatively privately, making it a region where dancers are often engaging in performances in which third parties play little to no role. Donna (dancer), for example, contrasted times when "I'm on the floor; there are people everywhere, so I don't really feel unsafe," to "sometimes when I was in the champagne room, especially when it was a day shift or a Sunday night, I was, you know, I'd be all alone," at which time "it was nice to have the bouncer walking around and making his rounds." The latter remark underscores the importance of third parties – their presence, reliability, and practices – to dancers' sense of safety, a matter that is further explored in chapter 5.

The extent to which dancers' conduct is monitored also varies from club to club – "some clubs are dirty and some clubs are clean, and it's good to know what the expectations are, and what you can get away with" (Jenna, dancer). The range of condoned services also (albeit not always) aligns with the image the club is attempting to project, with "classier" clubs projecting an image of "clean" dancing, while, "at the lower-end clubs, it's cheaper," not only for house fees charged to dancers but also often champagne-room rates charged to customers; consequently, "they kind of turn their head away, and it's a lot harder to make money without doing extras" (Kristen, dancer) (see DeMichele & Tewksbury, 2004; Deshotels et al., 2012; Lilleston et al., 2012). Given the previously discussed aesthetic restrictions that inform hiring, dancers who do not conform to Eurocentric beauty norms may find themselves at a low-end club, where there is greater pressure to provide additional sexual services.

At some clubs, third parties use signage to support the impression of rule enforcement. In contrast to what Lavin characterized as "proactive social control through signs" (2013, p. 370), however, dancers in this study agreed that signs are not an effective mode of social control or communication. Rather, dancers suggested that management did nothing more than "just put up signs" (Jill) about rules or bylaws that were not followed, enforced, or relevant – for example, "a notice from the ministry saying what kind of contact would constitute a public health risk" (Kristen). This suggests that the intended audience may not be customers or dancers but rather bylaw officers.

Similarly, although they are responsible for ensuring that dancers follow the bylaws, third parties, occasionally or routinely, wilfully ignore touching during lap dances and, sometimes, other activities as well. Third-party participants suggested that doing so is in the interest of protecting the club from legal ramifications and maintaining customer satisfaction.[1] As Adam (DJ and manager) explained, "if you've got a bouncer wandering around and poking his head in the booths every five seconds … you've ruined it for the client, who's paying good money to enjoy, you know, a dance." When he was a manager, Dalton attempted to navigate the tension between customer satisfaction and municipal regulation by "put[ting] a front on that you were following all the rules." Limited oversight of lap dances, then, is an instance in which third parties' and dancers' financial interests overlap.

Third parties and dancers also collaborate in performing compliance – in effect, forming momentary performance teams – in the face of municipal or police surveillance. For example, Marcus (bouncer) was instructed to collaborate with dancers in fostering an impression of rule adherence for municipal inspectors, despite a laissez-faire approach to "extras": "We'd do a special little knock on the booth just to warn them that there was police around … We were just basically told, you know, if it's going on, just make sure that the dancer's not getting hurt and that everybody is being safe, but also warn them if police came in." Dancers also momentarily feign compliance in the presence of municipal inspectors: "I remember being three girls to one guy, and we were all just standing around him … in a semi-circle, like talking to him" (Jill, dancer). Jill's perception that such a performance "does not look like a [VIP] booth – this doesn't look real" illustrates the extent to which a different audience can impact an interaction: although standing around talking may not meet the customer's or the strippers' expectations of a service interaction, it does meet municipal officials' expectations of no sexual contact (or, at least, fails to meet official definitions of unacceptable behaviour).

Finally, dancers perform rule adherence for third parties in order to sustain an overall impression of bylaw compliance. For example at

Monica's (dancer) club, "when the bouncer walks by, you stand up, and that's all you have to do." Comparatively strict rule enforcement at other clubs, however, can be frustrating; in Ottawa, for example, managerial interpretations of the municipal bylaw against touching manifested in a "rather ridiculous" rule requiring dancers to keep one foot on the ground at all times while performing lap dances, "even if I was sitting next to my customer [in the champagne room] and just wanted to have a drink and put my feet up because they hurt" (dancer).

Lateral Surveillance: Dancer Price- and Service-Fixing

Illustrating the pretence of the bylaw- and rule-compliance measures described above, the range of services and individual boundaries at any one club can vary considerably. Indeed, there has long been disagreement among dancers as to what level of physicality is appropriate in service interactions (Bouclin, 2006, 2009; Bruckert & Parent, 2007; J. Lewis, 2000). Although strippers' attitudes toward "extras" and their colleagues who provide them appear considerably more understanding, compared to the anger and stigma evident among dancers in the late 1990s and early 2000s, when lap dancing was still relatively new (Bouclin, 2004, 2006; DERA, 2002), extras remain a contentious issue. In spite of contemporary dancers' accepting (or resigned) attitudes toward physical contact, even what constitutes an extra is a matter of debate; as Ashley (dancer) noted, "a lot of different people have a different idea of what is an extra. What's extra, you know?"[2] Ashley herself sometimes kissed customers she liked, at no additional charge, and did not consider this to be an extra, even while acknowledging it was against the rules. Although they reported that some of their colleagues considered it acceptable for customers to suck on their nipples but did not frame this as an extra, Kristen and Monica (dancers) considered this activity to exceed the boundaries of a lap dance as well as their personal comfort level. In spite of contrasting opinions and different personal boundaries, none of the dancers who participated in one-on-one interviews identified themselves as providing extras (focus group participants did not offer such information).

Many of the dancers who participated in the study were against the provision of sexual services such as fellatio and manual stimulation in the club. As Kristen (dancer) explained, extras can undermine dancers who adhere more closely to the rules: "It affects the income of all the other girls. Because if one girl's giving blowjobs for twenty bucks a song, no other girl who doesn't do that is gonna make any money, because she can't compete with that, because they're [customers are] not going to choose you if they can get more." Similarly Jenna (dancer) was concerned with the price of extras: "I don't care if you're a ho, just try not to be a cheap one! That undercuts me." Strippers further emphasized of the role of visibility in managing client expectations: for example, Sasha reasoned, "if I can't see it, then that means my customers can't see it, so it doesn't affect me." Similarly, with the exception of Monica, the dancers in this study did not object to their colleagues escorting outside of the club as long as they left with clients discreetly.[3]

These comments suggest that dancers' primary concern in regard to additional sexual services is financial rather than moral. While their concern for fair competition may not judge, neither does it alleviate the additional barriers to making money faced by strippers who do not conform to Eurocentric beauty norms – most especially Black women – who may consequently have to work harder and/or offer extras or lower prices to earn a liveable income (Brooks, 2010; Law & Raguparan, 2019).

In this context, to encourage fair competition among themselves as independent contractors sharing a work space, and to minimize the impact of extras on their finances as well as pressure from clients for services they are not comfortable providing, dancers informally and collectively engage in peer or "lateral" surveillance (Andrejevic, 2005).[4] This practice does not involve, but may coincide with the interests of, third parties, insofar as it minimizes legal risks for the club and its employees. Indeed, it appears that some third parties rely on lateral surveillance as an effective regulator of dancers' behaviour: "A girl who's not clean [i.e., who provides sexual services] either has to clean her act up – or usually, you know, the girls assume or deter it to make the girl go away ... The girls sort of police themselves that way" (Adam, DJ and manager). In this respect, peer surveillance supplements the dearth of consistent rule enforcement and surveillance by third parties. Moreover, as a collective effort operating through an informal social network between dancers, lateral surveillance dovetails with the image of the club: dancers at an "upscale" club may strongly discourage extras (or at least the overt provision or underpricing thereof), whereas dancers at a working-class club – like Shane who contended, "it's none of my business ... I just would want her to be safe that's all, not get caught by management" – are less likely to interfere if their colleagues offer additional services.

Sasha (dancer) illustrated how lateral surveillance operates: "We had this new girl one time, and she didn't really have any boundaries, and she was just doing whatever customers wanted, so the girls – the schedule[d] girls – kind of got together and shamed her out of doing that ... Her behaviour is [now] more in line with the rest of the girls." Lateral surveillance can even commandeer the organizational authority of third parties, as Scott (bouncer and manager) explained: "When you had a club and one girl was known for giving extras, we would get rid of her, not just because of the legal reason, [but] because the girls who didn't want to do the extras, they got upset because they were losing money." Thus, as a preventive and punitive mechanism that regulates prices and services in the agglomeration of entrepreneur-like workers that makes up the dancer structure, lateral surveillance can be understood as a means to foster fair competition among peers – and not an internalization of managerial authority and training (see Foucault, 1995), as some scholars have described dancers' self-regulation (see Egan, 2004; Murphy, 2003).

Informal strategies arising from peer surveillance, including "gossip campaigns" (Sasha), can be an effective way for dancers to protect their health and business interests by limiting customers' expectations of extras. Yet, as Kristen (dancer) pointed out, such campaigns, meant to limit unfair competition, can themselves be unfair:

> The girls will gang up and attack girls for things like that [i.e., providing extras] sometimes, even though it's hypocritical, because half the girls attacking the other girl will be doing that themselves. But it's about whether you get caught, and whether other people are aware of it, so it's about how discreet you can be, and that's what's really valued, is being discreet.

Highlighting the tension among competing independent contractors in the dancer structure, sometimes gossip is not true: "Sometimes girls would get jealous if you were doing a lot of dances, and they would just say that you were doing something [inappropriate]" (Monica, dancer). Thus, in a manner comparable to Hafen's (2004) observations about gossip in mainstream workplaces, gossip among strippers can function simultaneously as social control (peer regulation) that reinforces performances supporting the broadly agreed-upon impression of the club as a classed environment of sexually charged fun but not prostitution; resistance to managerial authority, insofar as it pre-empts and supersedes third party surveillance (Bruckert, 2002; Prasad & Prasad, 2000); and social comparison and boundary maintenance – for example, to exclude new or unpopular dancers from the "in" crowd (Law & Bruckert, 2016).

Although the lateral surveillance network may often coincide with managerial interests, sometimes dancer price-fixing manifests as defiance. For example, Sasha (dancer) recounted an instance in which dancers subverted management's sudden imposition of a 10 per cent cut of their cash earnings, which they felt to be an unreasonable portion of their income. In contrast to Egan's (2004) study, in which dancers resisted paying the cut on an ongoing individual basis, this was a collective act of passive noncompliance: "[Dancers] just kind of complained about it to each other, and then ... everyone just stopped cooperating, and then the managers never talked about it again" (Sasha). Jill (dancer) recounted another income-protection strategy that had spread through the dancer network at her club, one that counters the principles of customer service: "There are many girls, and I do this too, if it's busy, I'll just, if a customer comes along, I'll be like, 'There's a five song minimum.' I don't – I'm not gonna take off my clothes for a song, sorry." It is interesting to note that dancers in this study seldom conceptualized these and other strategies as resistance, even though they certainly contested the claims of management, in much the same way as Scott's (1985) peasants engaged in "everyday resistance" that contested relations of power through small acts that supported their self-interest. Perhaps the informality of such acts prevents third parties from recognizing them as resistance as well, which works to dancers' advantage.

Bridging Competing Interests and Parallel Structures: The Economy of Favours

As shown in chapter 2, third parties below the ownership level are workers who can be more concerned with their own careers and interests than those of their employer, and may, in turn, resist organizational rules. Analogous to behaviours of mainstream lower-tier managers who occasionally subvert organizational hierarchy by colluding with employees in working around surveillance measures to produce seemingly desirable results, third parties sometimes collaborate with strippers to resist without actively challenging, breaking, or sabotaging the rules and practices of the organization (Ball, 2010). In strip clubs, this practice has been characterized as an "informal economy of favours" (Bruckert, 2002, p. 108) made up of negotiated, instrumental relationships forged between dancers and third parties through which each endeavours to maximize their own income and/or well-being. The economy of favours manifests in covert business negotiations, quid pro quo exchanges, cooperative and mutually beneficial team performances, manipulation, or blatant opportunism.

Tipping practices are illustrative of the range of opportunism or mutual benefit in the economy of favours. Tipping is particularly important for DJs, who inhabit a contradictory position insofar as they exercise a modicum of authority at the same time as relying on dancers for tips to supplement their income (Bruckert, 2002). Participants indicated that there was some variation in DJ pay structures, making tips more or less important. For example, at some clubs, DJs receive a portion of each dancer's house fee in addition to salary and tips. In spite of DJ claims that tipping "is voluntary, not mandatory" (Adam, DJ and manager), most dancers agreed that it is customary to tip the DJ at least $5 per shift: "I really can't remember not – other than a handful of times – not tipping ... It's not like you tip for good service, you just tip for service [laughs]" (Marie, dancer). According to DJs, tips average between $5 and $25 per dancer. Kristen (dancer) underscored the importance of a good relationship with the DJ, in which tipping and politeness are essential:

> [The DJ] can make the difference, like in how – you know, he can just be like, "Oh, well, this girl's next on stage," or he could be like, "The amazing, beautiful, So-and-so is about to rock your world!" You know, they can get the crowd worked up, they can make your lights better or worse, they can make your music quieter or louder, they can put you after, you know, the most athletically gifted girl in the club, or they can put you after somebody who's brand new – they can make you look better or worse. They do have that power. And tipping them has a big reflection on how you're treated.

Likewise, the amount a dancer tips a DJ will depend on his attitude toward her. As Fuzzy (DJ) explained, "I tend to leave there with more money than the other DJs on any given night, and I think it's because I try to connect a little bit with the girls." DJs' tips can also vary according to how many different dancers perform a stage show. In this regard, Jimmy (DJ) endeavoured to make stage shows more appealing to maximize his tips. His strategy was

> under-promise and over-deliver. So you would say to a girl, if she wants to go on stage, ... "Uh, I don't know. I might not need you. Maybe?" But in your head, you definitely do ... That's how you make tips or whatever. People will be like, "Ok, what if I give you money?" And immediately, it's, "Yes, sure" ... You had to make it look like these stage shows were really hot tickets, and like, "Oh you want to be on stage, girl. Everybody's gonna watch you."

A good relationship between dancers and DJs is essential to the smooth operation of the stage; indeed, DJs are the third parties who interact most often and most closely with dancers – as Jill (dancer) put it, "I probably talk to them [DJs] more than ... anyone else who, like, officially works in any capacity for the club." For his part, Dalton insisted that part of his job as a DJ was "to be positive for the girls, and be positive about the work that they're doing." Nonetheless, there is also an element of exchange, or fees for additional service, between DJs and dancers that pivots on the centrality of lap dancing in Ontario. Unlike in the United States (Bradley-Engen & Ulmer, 2009) and western Canada (Althorp, 2013), where, respectively, dancers earn money from customers' tips or from the club for their stage shows, dancers in Ontario are compensated/tipped very little for this aspect of their labour. As a result, many dancers in this study framed stage shows as taking away from valuable time in which they could be earning more money doing lap dances. In this context, a dancer may make a request to the DJ to be moved down or off the stage roster in order to spend an extended period of time dancing for a customer, whose attention she may not be able to keep in the time it takes to do a stage show – as Ashley (dancer) pragmatically observed, "he either goes and finds another girl or he leaves." The DJ may expect an additional tip for this accommodation. One dancer found that there was a standard rate in Ottawa clubs for moving one's stage show: "You'll tip him $20 and he'll not put you on stage, but ... usually the flat rate is $20 – they won't do it for less than that." In this respect, the economy of favours can be a way for third parties to exercise power over dancers' otherwise autonomous entrepreneurial activities – a levelling of dancers' superior income and third parties' organizational authority (see also J. Lewis, 2006; Reed, 1997).

Not all DJs are interested in this particular exchange, however. Studley (DJ/supervisor), for example, found that allowing dancers to reschedule merely made his job more difficult:

> I'm not flexible at all. I expect the same work from everybody. I don't care how much money they offer me. I've had girls offer me $100 before to skip their stage, and it's, "No, I'm sorry." I just – it's not worth the hassle for me because the other girls catch on, and essentially, what you're doing is you're making somebody else have to work harder so she has to work less by doing that. And it's not worth the headaches I get from the other girls for it, and it's not fair to them.

Of course, this decision has implications for Studley's income from tips, which he must earn through other means: "The only way I can really affect my profits whatsoever is through my attitude ... I try to, you know, keep them at ease. If a girl wants, you know, some music downloaded or something like that."

The matter of tips is more controversial with regard to bouncers. Although some bouncers claimed that most dancers do not tip them, some clubs have a small mandatory fee that dancers must pay daily (e.g., $2 each) to supplement bouncers' wages. Some dancers found that additional tips were required for bouncers' cooperation – "the only time a bouncer would really do anything for me was if I tipped him" (Donna). Leigh (dancer) found this to be problematic: "I don't want to have to tip for my well-being and safety ... I think that should be a non-tipping item. That's what they're being paid to do." Yet, as George (bouncer) explained, the economy of favours works both ways: "You try your hardest to get the girl the money, and then with some of the girls, even then, the girls treat us like assholes ... So it's hard to go out of your way the next time." Thus, friendliness (or, in this case, a lack thereof) also plays an important role in the economy of favours (Bruckert, 2002).

Bouncers also provide services to dancers that are not part of their job description. For example, they may arrange dancers for customers, or vice versa. Scott (bouncer and manager) remarked that customers "would say, 'I'm looking for this, I'm looking for this kind of girl' ... I hook the girls up with the client. The girl might give me a tip if they make a lot of money." For Sasha (dancer), this understanding can lead to a beneficial "cycle":

> So if you tipped the bouncers ... when they got you a champagne room ... they would get you more champagne rooms, so yeah, that could be good. You know, you could just be standing around looking at your cell phone, and then the bouncer would be like, "Come over here. Go in there with those guys," and then suddenly, you'd be making, like, $600. So you'd want to give them 50 bucks out of that or something ... because you would have missed the boat otherwise.

By contrast, Jill (dancer) found this practice to be unfair and manipulative:

> Basically if patrons come in and they're like, "Yeah, we're good to go now," they will get immediately shuffled into a [champagne] room ... It's a coordinated effort – one bouncer will stand in front of the door to the room and start calling to people on his like little microphone thingy, and then other bouncers in other areas of the club will start rounding up certain girls ... that they like and that will tip them well if they put them in this room. So, if they're standing in front of that door and you try to get in that room,

they will be like, "No," and they'll lie to your face, and they'll tell you that they want these specific girls, but literally, they don't ... I remember, one of the guys that was in that room was staring at me, and I didn't even bother with him, cause I'm like, dude, you've been in there for fuckin' hours ... and then he came over, and I made money off of him in the last half hour of the night ... And he's like, "I didn't even like the girl that I was with," and ... he spent $1500 on his girl. That could have been my money.

At times, such arrangements between bouncers and dancers can facilitate extras or exploitation. Sometimes dancers instigate these arrangements: according to Sasha (dancer) "girls who did extras ... tipped out the bouncers" to turn a blind eye (see also Blowdryer, 2009). Other times, they manifest as brazen opportunism by bouncers, as in the following example described by Reverend (manager/bouncer):

We've even had doormen ... who would try to extort from girls, whether it be financial or sexual ... Basically, you catch a girl in a position where she's already breaking the rules to the point where she'd probably just get fired on the spot, but instead, it's like, "Oh, I'll let this go if" – I don't know – "You sleep with me or you pay me or both."

Managers' involvement in the economy of favours appears to be less monetary than that of other third parties, perhaps because, as the highest position in the organizational hierarchy below the owner, they are paid more than other third parties, who earn relatively modest service industry wages as employees. Jenna (dancer) explained that, instead of tipping, dancers at her club foster good relationships with managers by bringing them cookies or coffee. That said, Donna (dancer) had worked at a club where it was customary for dancers to tip the managers, and at Jill's (dancer) club, dancers occasionally tipped the manager for favours (e.g., wilful ignorance of rule breaking). While the possibility of receiving a tip made recommending dancers to customers more appealing to Sal (manager), for Dalton (manager), arranging a customer "when one of your best girls is not making any money and she's bitching and she wants to leave" was not a matter of favours but, rather, an important strategy for retaining top-earning dancers, whose popularity among customers made them valuable assets to his club.

The final alliance in the economy of favours is between dancers and bar staff. At the club where Jill dances,

The waitresses ... will do things to help us hustle customers and also rip off customers a little bit, time-wise, like they'll knock off like fifteen minutes from an hour [in the VIP room], and they'll be like, "Ok, your hour's done." They will encourage customers to be generous. We, in turn, do the same, at least I do. Like when the customer is paying his bill, I'll be like, "She was awesome! She left us alone; let's give her lots of money!" And she'll also usually do the same for me.

Similarly, as a bartender, Kelly has alliances with dancers based on mutual respect: "Customers kind of ask for recommendations, I guess. So obviously I choose my friends." Jill tipped waitresses for not collecting her club's fee on dances paid by credit card – an arrangement in which both Jill and the waitresses benefited at the expense of the club: "If I'm going to make $300 even and clear, then I'm going to give you $20 cause you know, otherwise I would have to give like fuckin' $45 to the club."

Finally, like their counterparts in other studies (Barton, 2006; J. Lewis, 2006), dancers sometimes make arrangements with bar staff to give them false drinks so they can avoid alcohol without refusing customers' offers to buy them drinks – an agreement that is beneficial to the dancer's health without being detrimental to the financial interests of the waitress, bartender, or the club. Although Kristen (dancer) had "heard of girls, you know, splitting that money with the person they have that set up with," the dancers in this study were generally more interested in not drinking than in profiting from this arrangement.

Broadly speaking, then, whether the arrangements it fosters are mutually beneficial or favour one side and are exploitative, the economy of favours is a bridge between the otherwise divergent interests of the parallel structures. Since it unfolds covertly, out of view of superiors and customers, it can also be seen as a momentary back region shared by third parties and dancers.

Concluding Remarks: Parallel but Interdependent

As this chapter has highlighted, the parallel organizational structures that make up the strip club inform third parties' and dancers' interactions, priorities, and use of space – in particular, their use of different back regions to prepare for their occupational performances. Although few back regions are completely fixed as such, given the occasional need for third parties to enter strippers' back region or vice versa, their often discrepant back regions and job-related concerns generally align with the parallel structures. As independent contractors, dancers defend their collective and individual financial interests and bodily autonomy through lateral surveillance, peer knowledge-sharing, and personal rules. As employees of the club, third parties strategically relax or neglect to enforce rules and bylaws that would hinder clients' enjoyment of lap dances – and, in turn, the club's and dancers' profits – or temporarily collaborate with dancers in performing compliance for municipal authorities, thereby defending the overlapping interests of the parallel structures. Perhaps the most robust bridge between the parallel structures is also the most informal: the economy of favours, in which individual dancers and third parties negotiate more or less mutually beneficial arrangements beyond their ordinary occupational tasks and responsibilities, resulting in momentary team performances whose preparations and goals remain invisible to customers and, often, to superiors. Beyond this, as evinced in the lack of formal training for new strippers, and third parties' general lack of concern in regard to dancers' activities and income, the parallel structures operate for the most part as separate teams.

Considered together, these interactions, negotiations, and practices illustrate how the parallel structures inform how strip club actors ready their performances and collaborate or operate as distinct teams (albeit sometimes with overlapping interests). In this regard, this chapter has elaborated on the metaphor of parallel structures: while the dancers' status as independent contractors means that they are not included in the organizational structure that comprises third parties and other employees, these two bodies of workers are also parallel insofar as they are similar or interdependent in tendency, depending on the audience, challenge, or performance task at hand.

Chapter Four

Frontstage: Impression Management in a "Party" Environment

Turning the focus frontstage, this chapter explores third parties' and dancers' performances, and how they together contrive a gendered, racialized, classed, and sexualized "party" – that is, a commercial performance that appears effortless, relaxing, uninhibited, and fun.[1] As chapter 3 has shown, although they may collaborate in creating an impression for customers in the front regions of the club, third parties and dancers are not necessarily, consistently, or equally privy to each other's preparations in their respective back regions. This means that, in addition to performing for customers in the publicly visible areas of the club, they are, to a certain extent, simultaneously maintaining the definition of the situation for one another – in other words, third parties and dancers both produce and consume the ambiance of the strip club. At the same time, these workers are also aware that they are performing for various audiences, including peers and superiors, which may mean enacting multiple, strategic, and possibly conflicting roles. Thus, in addition to being a "party," complete with alcohol and (unofficially tolerated) drugs, the ambiance of the strip club also functions as an organizational culture. As critical management studies scholars argue, organizational culture is more than shared interactional norms and understandings that underlie workers' interactions with customers and each other; it is also shaped by workplace power relations that both inform and exist in tension with workers' deployment of gender and sexuality (Brewis & Linstead, 2000; Knights & Willmott, 1987).

Whereas the previous chapter focused on the goings on in the back regions closed off to customers, the present chapter considers the public-facing performances that emerge from these preparations. In so doing, it examines how third parties and strippers mobilize gender, class, and race in their occupational performances and, in turn, how the "party" environment shapes professional interactions between third parties and dancers, which can manifest as flirtation or sexual harassment by third parties, or opportunistic adaptation of the stripper role to intentionally manipulate third parties. Ironically, then, even as third parties and dancers routinely work alongside each other, their performances in the club's front regions undermine professionalism and their appreciation of each other's work. The chapter closes by situating these dynamics in relation to sexual harassment and racist micro-aggressions in other labour sectors to reflect on common issues, contributing factors, and existing standards and response mechanisms.

Putting on the Suit: Third-Party Personal Fronts and Masculine Scripts

Scholars have extensively examined how dancers contribute to and perform in the strip club environment, including how they embody and manipulate gender, sexuality, class, and race (see Bruckert & Frigon, 2003; Frank, 2002b; Liepe-Levinson, 2002; Ross, 2009; Ross & Greenwell, 2005; Sanders, 2005; Trautner, 2005), and how this informs interactions with, and the experiences and perceptions of, customers (see Egan, 2006a; Frank, 2002a; Murphy, 2003; Wood, 2000). Even though the subject has attracted considerably less scholarly attention, third parties also perform to affect customers' behaviour and experiences: they must exude a relaxed but firm authority (in the case of bouncers and managers) or animate, structure, and punctuate customers' leisure consumption (DJs, bartenders). As with strippers, third parties do this by tailoring their "personal front" – made up of expressive equipment, which includes clothing (e.g., a uniform); gender, size, race, age, or other physical attributes; and inflections of speech, gestures, or facial expressions (Goffman, 1959, p. 24) – to their particular occupation.

Since an occupational performance serves to define a situation and structure the social interaction in which it occurs, its success relies on the communication of shared meanings. Thus, performances also encompass and are evaluated according to social scripts, which Longmore defines as "normative clusters that specify the parameters for lines of action in given social contexts" (1998, p. 51; see also Simon & Gagnon, 1986). Although performance suggests that an individual can follow or refuse to follow a script (McInlay, 2010, p. 234), scholars who have studied women's engagement with normative gendered, sexual, racialized, and classed scripts in sex work – for example, the whore, the sexually aggressive woman, or the exotic racialized other – disagree about whether such performances are resistant ("a heroic overcoming of gender norms, a high-water mark of autonomy and agency"

(Showden, 2011, p. xvii)), reproduce entrenched social hierarchies and male privilege, or constitute a complex and contradictory mix of both.[2] Academics espousing a labour perspective agree, however, that engaging with normative scripts is as effective as it is necessary in sex work.

So, too, with men who work in the sex industry – who, of course, contend with a considerably different set of scripts. Studies focusing on male erotic dance, as well as those that compare women's and men's stripping,[3] highlight a number of ways in which men and women engage with and benefit and suffer from (hetero)normative gender expectations in very distinct ways. For example, male sex workers are expected to be well groomed but, more importantly, muscular (Mercer, 2003; M.D. Smith et al., 2015; M.D. Smith & Seal, 2008), with scholars and third parties assuming that their physical strength is a protective factor against client violence (Dennis, 2008), in turn minimizing the occurrence and importance of violence – especially if the clients are women (e.g., Montemurro, 2001; Scull, 2013).

Men who are third parties are subject to a slightly different set of norms, scripts, and expectations. Some of these norms are comparable to those for male sex workers, as well as for other traditionally masculine jobs. For example, bouncers in strip clubs are expected to be muscular and strong, qualities sought after not only in male sex workers but also bouncers in other kinds of nightclubs (DeMichele & Tewksbury, 2004; Hobbs et al., 2005; Rigakos, 2008). However, managers employ expressive equipment and scripts used by management in white-collar workplaces – including impression-management tactics that are assertive and dominant (Guadagno & Cialdini, 2007), and professional-looking clothing, namely suits. Indeed, looking the part was of paramount importance to Dalton, who as a manager "dressed in slacks, a button-down shirt and a tie, always. Always, always. Always had a tie on. And that's just to get respect … And that was the only costume that I would wear." As Adam (DJ and manager) explained, this presentation of self is designed to impress a particular image of the business on customers: "As a manager, you're the face of the bar towards the clientele." Similarly, because they are prominent in the front regions of the club, bouncers "have to look a certain way … We have to wear dress shoes, dress pants, dress shirt" (George, bouncer).

Although there appear to be fewer clothing-related expectations for DJs, who are not generally visible to customers, Jimmy (DJ) observed that wearing a suit also shaped his interactions with dancers: "If you dress like somebody who doesn't have control or power, people will step on you … If you have a suit on, they'll be like, ok, this person clearly has some sort of self-respect and I shouldn't disregard what he says; like, I should take him seriously." Having dressed more casually during his first month as a DJ, Jimmy followed advice from a manager he admired, who "told me if you dress the part, people will respect you for it." He, in turn, noticed a significant difference in how he was treated by dancers once he began wearing a suit at work: "It was night and day." Thus, even in a strip club, donning a suit conveys archetypically male organizational authority (see Whitehead, 2002). Interestingly, the only racialized men to be employed by strip clubs in this study, Jimmy (DJ) and Dalton (DJ and manager), were also the only third parties to explicitly say that wearing a suit to work contributed to their being respected by strip club workers as well as customers. This suggests that, in keeping with the archetype of the organizational leader (see Acker, 2009), donning the occupational "costume" of the suit allows third parties of colour to strategically tailor their "personal fronts" to the professional masculine respectability with which they are not normatively associated.

For Sal (manager), along with the suit came a work persona:

> When I go into work, like, the same way the girls become a character, right, and they use like a stage name and stuff, and the makeup and the high heels and all that stuff, and you know I'm the same way, right. I gotta go into work and you know, I put on my best-looking Sopranos suit and play the role, you know? ... I have to be, like, sometimes, like, aggressive, like, physically aggressive, and that's not me at all. Like, I haven't been in a fight, outside of work, since I was in grade school probably. Yeah, so it's just a persona.

Sal's reflection demonstrates that managers' occupational roles, which include security as well as hierarchical authority, also draw on masculine scripts of toughness.

As with dancers, bodily attributes can be an important part of third parties' "personal front." This is especially the case for bouncers, visible in Marcus's experience of being judged to be more suitable for security than tending bar: "I was going around looking for bartending jobs and ended up going to some adult entertainment ones, and they're like, 'Well, we don't need a bartender but we need a doorman.' Cause I'm like a pretty big guy – I'm 6'3", 300 pounds – so they're like, 'Yeah, do you want to be a doorman?'" This finding echoes the literature on nightclub bouncers, which emphasizes the immense importance of bouncers' physicality (Hobbs et al., 2005; Rigakos, 2008). Thus, like sex workers, bouncers – and, to the extent that they are involved in security, managers – engage in body work, that is, "gendered as well as material" labour comprising aesthetic (e.g., masculine posturing), physical (e.g., manual labour), and bodily (e.g., handling customers) dimensions (Brents & Jackson, 2013, pp. 77, 81).

All of these dimensions of body work converge in bouncers' performance of aggressive masculinity to control customers, as the following chapter will examine in greater detail. These performances in the front region also make an impression on dancers – Sal (manager) maintained that the presence of physically intimidating bouncers can increase dancers' sense of security. Aware of this impression, bouncers may also feel pressured by what they perceive to be their co-workers' expectations:

> A lot of them [co-workers] felt that I had a non-violent approach, like I was a sissy at one point, because I went like a month without fighting or something like that. And then, it takes one fight, you know, you take on four guys by yourself kind of deal and you, you walk away, then, you know, it's almost like you need to re-establish yourself every once in a while. Uh, that's within the staff. Because of the fact that they all knew I was going to university, they expected me to be, you know, walking with spectacle glasses, the educated. It was a weird balance between the two, being a strip club bouncer and a university student. (Scott, bouncer and manager)

In this passage, class, gender, and racial scripts – of the "soft" scholar versus the working-class "man's man" (see Kimmel, 2013; Whitehead, 2002; Willis, 1977), whose significant contrast with stereotypes characterizing Black men as rapists (Crenshaw, 1991) or pimps (Benson, 2012) highlights the role of racialization in the construction of toughness as risk or security – intersect in Scott's perception of his colleagues' expectations of him (see also Pinel, 1999). Scott's narrative further suggests that, in order to fulfil organizational expectations, bouncers must bolster their masculine performance with occasional displays of physical aggression. This finding echoes Hobbs et al.'s framing of "bouncing as class work," in which violence is drawn upon as a resource (2005, p. 10; see also Rigakos, 2008; DeMichele & Tewksbury, 2004) – in this instance, to convince co-workers as well as customers of their masculinity and effectiveness.

The "Party" Environment as Front Region: Balancing Perceptions, Expectations, and Conduct

These masculine performances regulate, support, and aim to protect strippers, who are performing femininity in the party environment. Echoing Frank's (2003, p. 65) characterization of the strip club as an atmosphere that allows male patrons to engage in stereotypically masculine behaviours, including vulgarity and aggressiveness, DJ Jimmy described an ambiance "like a clubhouse ... where whatever they say is safe." In this context, strippers are faced with various forms of harassment from customers, which are exacerbated by third parties' financially motivated and selective wilful ignorance of overconsumption of alcohol and illicit drugs. As Jill (dancer) explains,

> When you're in the club, gentlemanly behaviour is sort of like tossed out the window, and guys get really basic. And because people are so drunk most of the time, or inebriated on whatever they're on, like um, there's no room or place for, like, political correctness ... When you think about a strip club, it's supposed to be like, wild, happy, fun, party! You know, not "Let's be on our best behaviour kids!"

This appears to be the case regardless of a club's purported "classiness." For example, as a manager who helped open a new venue, Dalton branded his club as "upscale," but at the same time recalled that it was also "pretty rowdy." Indeed, as long as it is not seriously disruptive, third parties tolerate boisterous behaviour among desirable strip club clientele, almost invariably identified by third parties as white, middle-class, middle-aged men – a demographic perceived, and in turn prized, as affluent and low risk (Brooks, 2010; Frank, 2003; Ross & Greenwell, 2005). Considered alongside the hiring and scheduling limitations on Black dancers – informed by a Eurocentric interpretation of feminine beauty (see chapter 2) and perceptions of Black men as risky (see chapter 5) – this selective tolerance of rowdiness suggests that "classiness" is an effect of constructing the club as a white environment.

In this context, especially for racialized dancers like Jill, discrimination is ever present: "I don't feel like I'm a person or girl at my work, I feel like I'm an Asian girl at my work." Jill experienced discrimination from third parties as well as customers, who perceived her as an exotic other:

> I'm stereotyped a lot ... People call me, you know, kind of like, offensive names, but I find that, like [sighs], being offensive in a strip club is totally acceptable, basically ... There used to be a manager who worked there who creeped me out because he would tell me that he thought that Asian women were so beautiful, and he would just like randomly tell me that ... And yeah I get it from customers all the time, like, all the time, like [mocking a customer's voice], "Oh, I think, you know, Asian women are really beautiful," or, they just have all kinds of opinions ... I have been called China girl by multiple bouncers.

Jill's narrative speaks to how women of colour experience sexism and racism as profoundly intersectional (Crenshaw, 1989).

The brand of boisterous masculinity tolerated from customers in the party environment also informs strip club organizational culture insofar as it permeates workplace norms and understandings shared by third parties and strippers. Dancers recounted micro-aggressions by third parties as well as customers – "brief and commonplace daily verbal, behavioral, or environmental indignities, whether intentional or unintentional, that communicate hostile, derogatory, or negative racial slights and insults toward people of color" (Sue et al., 2007, p. 271) or "express hostility or indifference toward women" (Basford et al., 2014, p. 341). Inasmuch as third parties' behaviour routinely exhibited gendered, racial, and sexual under- or overtones, dancers expected such behaviour, with some tolerating it and others being offended by it.

Interacting in the Front Region: Losing Sight of Professionalism in the "Party"

More than infusing third party–dancer interactions with sexuality, the party environment conceals their professional qualities or requires them to minimize these qualities, which, after all, are not conducive to an impression of effortless fun. As a result, in the public spaces or front regions of the club, their interactions are informed by their necessarily ongoing performances: the dancers as beguiling seductresses (as opposed to reliable or rights-deserving workers); the managers and bouncers as tough guys (as opposed to organizational superiors or service providers with whom workers can reason and negotiate). Thus, although third parties may be aware that, at work, "everybody in there is wearing a mask, you know. Nobody is who they really are" (Studley, DJ/supervisor), there may be little chance for them to become acquainted with who dancers "really are," and vice versa. Third parties' and dancers' perceptions of each other are also informed by the parallel structures: as discussed in the preceding chapter, dancers are not privy to all of third parties' back region activities, and third parties do not see all of dancers' performances (e.g., in champagne rooms), often making them into separate performance teams (Goffman, 1959) and fostering an incomplete understanding of what the other does. In this context, to make sense of each other's performances, third parties and dancers rely on organizational and popular discourses and stigmatic assumptions (see Hacking, 2004; Hannem, 2012), in turn reproducing them and undermining professional relationships and emotional well-being in the workplace.

Taking Care of the "Girls": Third-Party Condescension

Tellingly, as in the findings of Bruckert (2002) and Price (2008; Price-Glynn, 2010), third parties predominantly used the word *girls* – not *workers* or *women* – to refer to dancers. While strippers also refer to their colleagues as *girls*, sex worker rights organization Stella (2013) notes that sex workers use the term not only "as shorthand for working girls" (2) but also as an empowering reclamation of a word commonly used to invisibilize sex workers' agency and the distinct experiences of girls, as well as to infantilize women. Among strip club third parties, then, the habit of referring to strippers as girls reflects both the dominant association between youth, desirability, and sexiness that informs stereotypical tropes of feminine foolishness and vanity, and as an infantilizing term that frames dancers as unreliable, unskilled, and unprofessional. Both associations are visible in a comment by Adam (DJ and manager) about the importance of screening dancers before hiring them because "not all good-looking women are smart or sane [but] the best-looking women tend not to have any brains, and they require a lot of babysitting." This sentiment was also evident in the way some third parties talked about, or compared themselves to, dancers. For example, in a discussion about the skills required for his job and how he learned them, Scott (bouncer and manager) said, "I learned some negotiation skills ... I mean, I can't believe I'm saying this; I learned a few things from the dancers." Thus, whether through a dichotomous view of women as either beautiful or smart, or simply by positioning them as inferior (to men), these comments suggest perceptions of women in general, or dancers as a particular *type* of woman, as unintelligent.

However strategic, dancers' performances can also perpetuate this perception, as Marie (dancer) pointed out:

> Talking to customers and stuff, they don't want to hear about, like, your career goals and – well some of them do, but, generally speaking, no ... To make more money you act, like, dumber ... and you don't talk about serious things or about goals and about school, cause when you do, some guys would get turned off by that, cause some guys [clients] want to feel like they're in power, or they're, you know, superior to you ... So yeah, I guess by your actions you kind of perpetuate that stigma ... or stereotypes against dancers, I guess.

While Marie consciously used it to her advantage, choosing to limit her conversation about other life goals with customers, this stereotype of strippers may inform third parties' impressions as well. Indeed, dancers reported that managers did not expect them to be in school. For example, when Marie came to work from class,

> I'd be dressed in, like, student clothes and with my bag to go to work, and then I got in to work and the strip club manager, he's like, "Oh you know every time I see you I always think that I would never guess that you're a dancer" … And then you think, well, what is it supposed to look like, you know?

Donna (dancer) had similarly received a mix of condescension and praise: she "had some managers be happy for me that I was in school and say, 'Good girl. Good girl. Spend your money on school.'"

What Monica (dancer) described as "a very, very, sometimes condescending attitude towards dancers" can inform managerial approaches. According to Shane (dancer), DJs, bouncers, and managers "would treat the dancers in very dehumanizing ways, like, I guess, a different class of women, and then, like, just more like children I guess, but in a weird sexual way." Not wanting to threaten their professional relationships, dancers tolerated comments made by third parties that were indicative of such paternalism and condescension. For example, Sasha (dancer) reported that, "one DJ that I worked with … spent a lot of time complaining about how stupid the girls were, which I didn't really like, but I wanted him to be on my side, so I kind of just listened to that."

Third parties also described dancers as irresponsible, unreliable, and in need of counselling and close supervision. In this regard, seven out of fifteen third-party participants used the word "babysit" when describing their responsibilities in regard to strippers. Although his job was security, George also described himself as "a glorified babysitter … I'm either babysitting drunk, immature men or I'm babysitting women that are drunk and can't defend themselves or … that do extras." Also notable in George's comment is his judgment of customers' behaviour, which he tolerates but does not condone, highlighting that even though third parties may also consume dancers' performances, the party environment is nevertheless work. Kelly (bartender) similarly used the word "babysit" to describe the way she feels attempting to ensure that dancers do not drink and drive, as well as monitoring their drug consumption.

Framing the dancers as "girls" who require "babysitting" also speaks to perceptions of dancers as unprofessional. Chico (DJ) said he would "like to see girls treat it more as a 9-to-5 job, like if you come in for five hours, kick some butt for five hours, you know. Do your job; don't bitch; don't complain … [have a] take it seriously kind of attitude."

Such perceptions may impact third parties' responses to dancers' work-related grievances. For example, after a client refused to pay, Jenna (dancer) recalled:

> Basically for three hours it was supposed to be $1200, and he [the manager] got me $700 and said: "Well I think you've made enough money today" ... It's not like the guy didn't have the money or whatever, it's that after $700, he stopped pressing for the matter, like he just thought that was arbitrarily enough. And it's, like, that's half of the – you know, a little more than half.

In deciding how much money was enough for Jenna, her manager failed to recognize her as a worker and a victim of theft of service. Thus, third parties' perceptions of strippers as immature "girls" they have to "babysit" invisibilizes dancers' grievances, as well as their skills and judgment, as workers.

Performing and Manipulating Appropriate Femininity: Dancers' Class and Attitude

Third parties' perception of dancers as non-workers is fostered by the continuity of strippers' performance for customers in the public areas of the club. As Kristen (dancer) explained, dancers are expected to act as outgoing salespeople who are simultaneously ultra-feminine:

> You kind of have the perception of being a diva by the people that are familiar with the industry, so the managers, the bouncers ... I was told I was not high-maintenance enough, that I would be more successful, more likeable and all this, if I was more high-maintenance ... You know, "Buy me a drink," instead of waiting 'til you're offered. You know, instead of talking to somebody for a bit, kind of feeling them out, and then maybe asking if they are interested in a private dance, you kind of would go, "Hey honey, let's go for a dance" ... [like] a high-maintenance shark – you're like a pageant girl and a shark at the same time.

While being a "high-maintenance shark" may be an effective way to interact with customers, third parties also criticized dancers who had too much or the wrong kind of "attitude" or caused "drama." According to Kelly (bartender), such behaviour can emanate from inebriation: "They're rude, and they yell, and they want what they want right now, and they don't care if they're fifth in line or tenth in line, they're gonna get it." For Jimmy (DJ), "attitude" from dancers was insufferable: "I don't want to be treated like I'm lesser than you. And often they'll [dancers] do that. They'll be – they're on this horse where it's just so high, and they're like, 'Nobody can touch me. I make this much money a week. Blah blah blah. I drive a leased Lexus.' ... I just didn't have any time for people like that." Jimmy's comment suggests that third parties' adherence to discourses of gender superiority and organizational authority (see Whitehead, 2002) may be informed by feelings of being undervalued by, and having little control in, the organization (see Willmott, 1997).

According to dancers, "drama" – for example, fights between co-workers or scenes resulting from extreme intoxication – elicits heavier discipline from third parties than do drug use or "extras." Sal (manager) confirmed this perception: "I let them [dancers] bend some of the rules a little bit and stuff, and so that makes me, like, cool in their eyes. So they know that as long as they just go in and do their thing, there's no drama and they're not, like, starting shit with other girls and stuff like that, then everything's gonna be cool." Jimmy's (DJ) description of this "drama" drew on tropes of female hysteria and underclass toughness: "You get to see these crazy sides of these girls. They get into fights sometimes, and one girl the other day was, like, fighting another girl with scissors."

Although condemned for creating "drama," dancers can augment their perceived value to third parties by presenting as "high maintenance," as suggested by Kristen above – and it is here that class becomes important. Having come from an economically disadvantaged background, Shane (dancer) reflected on how her working-class "personal front" (Goffman, 1959) had impacted her success as a dancer:

> I definitely was like, tacky looking. I wasn't, like, fancy; I didn't have, like, expensive outfits or anything ... and my outfits, a lot of them were handmade, so, um, I didn't notice that that was affecting me at the time. But now in my life [as an escort], I definitely, like, go the extra mile to, like, at least pretend I look a little classier so I can make more money ... Looking rich in the sex industry is important if you want respect.

For Shane, the last statement was also true of her relationships with third parties in the strip club; she had "just felt so disrespected by [bouncers]" at one club, who severely disciplined and humiliated her. This treatment affected her security insofar as she did not feel comfortable asking for their help. In sharp contrast, Monica, a middle-class, blonde woman who had been financially successful as a dancer in her late teens and early twenties, recalled seldom being disciplined by third parties even when she disregarded her club's scheduling policy: "It didn't matter when I came in; I never seemed to get in trouble ... I just, like, wouldn't show up or I would come in when I wanted, and just drift in and out." Monica's recollection echoes DeMichele and Tewksbury's finding that the most conventionally attractive dancers, who are also often "big money makers," are virtually exempt from disciplinary repercussions for rule breaking (2004, pp. 548–9).

Some dancers used "attitude" strategically in negotiating with third parties – Monica referred to her approach as "kind of demanding ... aggressive," while Sasha approached the manager at her club with a "nagging" tone when negotiating her schedule. These approaches can be seen to conform to the familiar trope of female "bossiness." Notably, however, whereas aggressiveness and self-promotion are interpreted unfavourably in women in mainstream organizational leadership roles (Guadagno & Cialdini, 2007; Rudman, 1998), they appear to be both expected and effective qualities in female erotic dancers. Thus, while scholars have characterized such applications of heteronormative gender scripts as subversion of organizational hierarchy (see Bruckert, 2002; Colosi, 2010a; Frank, 2002a, 2002b, 2003; Lavin, 2013; Murphy, 2003), if third parties expect this behaviour, it is also – somewhat paradoxically – acceptable and normalized in strip club organizational culture.

Racialization can additionally inform the way third parties distinguish between "high maintenance" and "attitude," as evinced in the following comment by Tony (manager/DJ):

> A couple weeks ago I got a call from the bartender at [club A] saying there's two Black girls that gave him terrible attitude, so they were almost physically removed from [club A], and they called us to give us a heads up, cause they heard, they were overheard saying, "Well let's go to [club B]" ... so we, you know, watch each other's back.

Tony's specification that the two dancers with "terrible attitude" were "Black girls" suggests heightened surveillance and suspicion of racialized (and, given Jill's relatively conflict-free relationship with managers, specifically Black) women – not only by individual third parties but among them and across clubs. These views can be seen as yet another dimension of the employment and equity barriers that Black women face in the erotic dance sector (see also chapter 2).

Alternatively, strippers may manipulate gender and sexual scripts in order to avoid being read as having too much "attitude." Finding that the bouncers and managers were not always willing to intervene when she needed them, Jenna (dancer) sometimes elected to "just look really, really sad until they just fix it so that you'll stop pouting and bothering them [laughs]." At the same time as it confirms third parties' impression of dancers as childish, this strategy also draws on stereotypical assumptions about third parties – namely, that as men (and not professionals, for example) they are susceptible to dancers' feminine wiles. Yet, as Studley (DJ/supervisor) suggested, such strategies may not be consistently effective:

> The stereotypes are only temporary until they get to realize that I'm not who they've stereotyped me to be, and then they're more surprised, I think, than anything, you know, or – not always pleasantly, either. [Laughs] You know, like I say, once they realize that they can't sweet-talk me to get their way or flash me a bit of boob or something, that – you know, then the attitudes change drastically.

Other dancers adopted more casual approaches that sidestepped the gendered assumptions tied to their stripper "personal front." Marie (dancer) attempted to use her "positive relationship" with third parties as a platform for straightforward negotiation:

> I find just being the most honest is what helped me, like just saying, "Listen, I've had this really crazy day; I'm exhausted; my contact lenses are going to fall out of my eyes [laughs], like can I just go home?" And, yeah I guess sometimes it would work, they'd say yes, but sometimes if the manager was in a bad mood or the bouncer, he would just say no, or if there was not enough girls – it depends on a lot.

Ashley (dancer) similarly fostered good working relationships with third parties by being earnest and friendly without feeling she had to perform like she did with customers. In return, like Marie, she found that, for the most part, third parties acted professionally. It is important to note that Ashley and Marie both conform to the Eurocentric beauty ideal as white, blonde women, which may have contributed to the success of their casual approaches. At the same time, considering that Marie's honesty yielded inconsistent results, "bossiness" may be more effective. Thus, although not all dancers espoused it, "high-maintenance" aggressive femininity, when performed in a manner consistent with intersecting expectations of "classiness" and whiteness, appears to be a relatively acceptable and efficient strategy for dancers to win favour with or contest the authority of third parties. Because such performances do not disrupt third parties' normative expectations, however, they more closely resemble "ambiguous accommodations to authority" (Prasad & Prasad, 2000, p. 388) than resistance.

Acting the Part: Friendliness versus Professionalism

Dancers' "personal fronts," in concert with the party environment, inform third parties' perceptions of and approaches to interpersonal workplace relations in problematic ways. In the sexually charged atmosphere of the "party," it is difficult for some third parties to separate friendliness from flirtatiousness. In turn, their interpretations of friendliness, or flirtatious responses to dancers' performances, risk being defined by dancers as unprofessional or as sexual harassment.

Some third parties framed flirtatiousness and professionalism as mutually exclusive, associating the former with sexual harassment or assault. Underscoring his professionalism, Jimmy (DJ) proudly stated:

> I never ever done anything to [dancers], never made any advances, never made any moves, because I knew that if I was gonna do this job, the only way to fly straight and to be, I guess, safe, was to not be that creepy DJ … like, just when they're picking their music, they're putting their hands all over the girls and stuff, and like, getting them to sit on their lap. I'm not about that. I was raised a very respectful person. I know that, if I come to work, it's really all I'm there for. I'm not – you know, you don't mess around. And I was respected for that.

Similarly, when he first began his career as a DJ, Sal recalled dancers advising him not to make sexual (and especially physical) advances. With time and a promotion to manager, Sal grew increasingly uncomfortable with dancers flirting with him:

> I'm thirty-six now, and I've got girls who are, you know, like I guess I'm almost old enough to be their father and they're like, you know, flirting with me and stuff like that, and it's kind of weird … When I was in my twenties and even when I was, like, thirty or something, like, if a twenty-year-old girl came up and flirted with me, I didn't feel strange about it. I was like, hey, cool, yeah. But now … I'm not the one hitting on them, but I feel like a creep [laughs].

Sal's and Jimmy's experiences suggest that organizational authority does not necessarily foster sexual harassment (see Brewis & Linstead, 2000), and, moreover, that, in the party environment, dancers' behaviour can also make third parties uncomfortable.

Other third parties use flirting as a strategy to relate to dancers. Describing his approach as "professional, up-front," Studley (DJ/supervisor) said "I flirt a lot when I'm working … It helps me break the ice with the girls a bit and kind of keep it on an unserious level." Similarly, Fuzzy (DJ) endeavoured to maintain a fun atmosphere by "harmlessly flirt[ing] with [dancers]. They will harmlessly flirt back, but at the end of the day ... they all know that I'm just talk." Although it is not possible to know if Fuzzy's last remark accurately reflects his colleagues' perceptions of him, his comment illustrates that the party environment shapes organizational culture and interactional norms.

While some dancers described third parties with whom they worked as both (or interchangeably) flirtatious and professional, others felt that sexual comments negated professionalism. Nonetheless, aware that many third parties engage with them and/or their colleagues flirtatiously, dancers instrumentally (and sometimes begrudgingly) accommodate third parties' invitations to participate in sexual banter or flirtation. For Brigitte (dancer), these invitations felt like expectations she had to accommodate: "I would feel like if I didn't flirt back with them that, like, it would cause problems." That said, Carrie (dancer) was of the opinion that "flirting ... will just get you so far." Not all dancers elected to respond to this behaviour in kind, however. Charlene (dancer) insisted "I don't flirt"; instead, resisting the seemingly common expectation among third parties of a sexualized interaction, she kept her conversations personal but professional in order to ensure that "they're always willing to help me out because I'm always interested in what they're doing as people." At the same time, Leigh and Jen (dancers) recounted instances in which approaching third parties professionally was less effective than flirting. Others simply preferred to avoid interacting with third parties altogether.

Because some dancers interacted with him in the same way that they performed for customers in the front region, Scott (bouncer and manager) felt entitled to take certain liberties, which some other dancers did not welcome:

> You know, with some girls, you know, they're in character, they're being the ... seducing kind of girl or happy boppy go happy, I'm fun kind of girl, whatever. It's a second persona they develop on stage. And, sometimes, they do it with us as well, doormen, whatever. You know, they come in; they tease us. You know, they might come in and just grab our cock, you know, playing at one second and walk away, that sort of thing. You know, I might walk up and slap another one's ass. Now, with some girls, that was okay ... Some other girls ... they don't appreciate [that] and they give me shit.

Scott's comment illustrates how some dancers' conforming to what they perceive as an expectation of flirtatiousness may be advantageous for them but may encourage behaviour that other dancers experience as sexual harassment. At the same time, it is important to note that third parties who interpret flirtatiousness on the part of some dancers as a unilateral invitation to make sexual advances on any others are effectively disregarding the issue of consent, or individual dancers' right to refuse them.

Only one dancer, Marie, expressly indicated she had not experienced inappropriate behaviour from third parties. With the exception of two focus group participants whose experience was not clear, the remainder of the fifteen dancers interviewed for this study reported inappropriate (e.g., sexual or sexist) comments, and nearly half (six) had been subject to unwelcome touching or aggressive advances from third parties. Some dancers recounted behaviour by third parties that exceeded what Jenna (dancer) described as "touchy feely" workplace culture, including termination for resisting third parties' advances, and sexual assault. Generally speaking, many participants (third parties included) suggested that the way some third parties interact with dancers is at best unprofessional, and at worst sexual assault and grounds for dismissal in a "mainstream" work environment. While the frequency of this problematic behaviour suggests that it is normalized in the party environment, there appear to be at least some limits: Jimmy (DJ) and Reverend (manager/bouncer) explicitly condemned such behaviour, and Sal (manager) was fired from his previous club after what he described as a dancer seducing him at work.

It is nevertheless important to note that not all dancers felt that the sexual attention they got from third parties was problematic, unmanageable, or particularly troubling. Participants enumerated consensual sexual interactions between workers: in spite of rules and advice by (other) third parties against it, six third parties in the study had dated dancers, and two dancers reported having had romantic or sexual relationships with third parties. Other dancers were simply unperturbed by sexual comments. Ashley (dancer), who described third parties as being "overly friendly" yet also "pretty professional," suggested that what Erickson (2010) characterizes as a "sexually overt work culture" is not unique to the erotic dance sector:

> I don't think that that's exclusive to a strip club. I've worked in other places before where men have made comments about me, so I didn't take offence, or even really – it didn't even really, like, throw me off, because, you know, as a woman, in many places ... men make comments about you being an attractive person.

Somewhat similarly, Shane (dancer) recounted working with a DJ whom she felt "was very sexually inappropriate with me." He "would, like, come up behind me and grab me and just stuff like that. But he was like, he was nice and friendly, he wasn't like, scary." Sasha (dancer) also found such behaviour to be manageable but ultimately chose to manage it in a different way:

> I had this creepy manager at this one club that especially liked me, and he would always, like, try to touch me while he was giving me the shift pay, so I just told him to stop that one day, and he was very surprised. I guess not a lot of people do that ... I was like, "This is not a lap dance." And he was like, "Okay." And that was that.

As a sexually overt work culture, the party environment normalizes sexualized talk and touch, and complicates labelling such behaviour as sexual harassment or assault (see Erickson, 2010). But, as Ashley (dancer) pointed out, "a lot of where your money comes from is how you act towards other people," and, in a workplace in which tipping plays an important role, unprofessional behaviour and unwelcome advances may negatively impact third parties' income.

"They Just Stand around and Jingle Their Change": Third Parties as Not Working

While dancers' performances in the front region may cloud third parties' perceptions of them as workers, it seems that dancers may not recognize some third parties as working either; instead, some participants had the impression that bouncers and managers were "just stand[ing] around" (Leigh, dancer) the strip club, much like the men in the audience. From dancers' vantage points, and recalling that they are not privy to third parties' back regions, this makes sense: if bouncers and managers regulate customer behaviour by being aggressive masculine presences ready to react but not wanting to disrupt the party environment unnecessarily, it is understandable that dancers may fail to recognize this performance as a conscientious effort.

Dancers' perception of third parties as not working also draws on their own classist perceptions of blue-collar workers as unskilled, unintelligent, or dubious:

> I guess [pauses] it's not always kind of the people with the best judgment who are hired to work in strip clubs or who choose to work in strip clubs ... like males, adults, who've been working in the entertainment industry

for a long time, like, people who are, like, doormen or bartenders and they kind of make a life out of it, you know, like people with not much education or who don't necessarily have a lot of other career options, you know, so it's kind of, some people it's like a last resort … When you're fifty and been a bouncer all your life, where are you gonna go? (Marie, dancer)

This comment is comparable to stigmatic assumptions about dancers, whom some third parties perceive as choosing stripping as a desperate solution in the face of few options. In this respect, normative judgments by both dancers and third parties can be seen to diminish solidarity, empathy, and respect between them.

Such perceptions embolden some dancers to resist third parties, and can underlie the "attitude" they convey. Monica (dancer) shared Marie's opinion of third parties as underclass men, and additionally thought of them as undeserving of her respect. Reflecting her middle-class perspective, Monica described "just seeing through them [third parties] and seeing them as ineffectual monkeys … and so I treated them like they didn't have any power." Thus, like third parties who perceived themselves as superior to dancers by virtue of their gender and/or occupation – the "status shield" (Ashforth et al., 2007) garnered from not participating in sexual labour directly – dancers who felt superior in class saw third parties as non-workers and/or as people not deserving of respect.

Just as dancers did not appreciate third parties' surveillance duties, it appears that even some club owners, who are seldom in the club and therefore less likely to appreciate the nuances or utility of third parties' performances, interpret bouncers' presence as non-work. As Scott (bouncer and manager) explained: "[The owner] felt that the doormen were getting paid to stand around … So, he started dropping more and more work for us. That includes going in the back and restocking the beer bottles, removing the empty beer boxes, clearing tables at the end, things like that." Of course, as Reverend (manager/bouncer) admitted, when things are running smoothly in the club, "you have the easiest job most of the time. You get to sit around; you get to chill out; you almost get to just chat with people and relax." When trouble does arise, however, security work is "very physically demanding … You literally put your life on the line at times. You go from having – I'm relaxing – having a cigarette to literally running straight into a brawl sometimes to break it up." This dramatic change of pace is a reminder of the potential volatility of the party environment. In this context, diverting bouncers' attention away from monitoring customers – especially around closing time, when customers may be most inebriated and thus more likely to cause trouble – may have negative ramifications for workplace safety and dancers' safety in particular.

Comparing the Strip Club to Mainstream Workplaces

So far, this chapter has shown how the party environment can shape strippers' and third parties' perceptions of and interactions with each other, with ramifications for professional relationships, dancers' safety, and the incidence of sexual harassment and sexualized interactions. In order to avoid the hasty conclusion that only the strip club (and, by extension, the sex industry) is an environment where unprofessional, inappropriate behaviours and gendered/sexual aggressions flourish, a comparison to other workplaces is warranted.

While some aspects of strip club work are particular to sex work – for example nudity, and (negotiated) physical touching between customers and dancers – as Erickson (2010) has argued, a "sexually overt" work culture is not unique to the sex industry and can be found in service industry workplaces such as restaurants and bars (see also Spradley & Mann, 1975). Sexual harassment is also prevalent in highly gendered mainstream workplaces like the military, whose members were characterized in a government-commissioned investigation as unable (or unwilling) to differentiate between fraternization and sexual harassment (Deschamps, 2015). Looking across the labour market additionally reveals that workplace sexual harassment is far from unique to labour sectors in which sexuality and gender feature prominently in organizational makeup or culture. In fact, rates of sexual harassment in the workplace appear to have remained steady since the 1980s, leading scholars to argue that it is the most prevalent form of sexual victimization of women in Canada (Crocker & Kalemba, 1999; McDonald, 2012). In a nationwide survey, 30 per cent of workers, of whom 94 per cent were women, reported experiencing sexual harassment in the workplace during the preceding two years (Canada, 2017).

Unlike strippers who are classified as independent contractors, some employees in more conventional occupational sectors – such as the military, the public service, health care, and even the House of Commons – are able to draw on labour protections, including provincial employment standards or (for federal government agencies) the *Canada Labour Code*. Yet, in spite of regulatory mechanisms prohibiting, and mandating responses to, sexual harassment and discrimination, women often do not report sexual harassment out of fear of personal or professional adverse consequences (Bruckert & Law, 2018b). Thus, women facing even considerable workplace sexual harassment – for example, in Canada's armed forces – are discouraged from reporting, not only by the potential costs for their careers (e.g., being "diagnosed as unfit for work"), but also by the rarity and/or inconsequentiality of sanctions (e.g., online sensitization training) (Deschamps 2015, iii). The latter appears to be common across mainstream labour sectors, where human resources departments – including those of large entertainment media companies highlighted in the #MeToo movement – have been critiqued as woefully inadequate in preventing and responding to sexual harassment (Flanagan, 2019; see also Basford et al., 2014; Brewis & Linstead, 2000).

Racial and gender discrimination and micro-aggressions, similarly, persist across the labour market in spite of organizational and state frameworks endeavouring to mitigate them (Acker, 2009; Basford et al., 2014; Brewis & Linstead, 2000; Green, 2005). As Basford et al. (2014) note, although blatant discrimination may have declined in the mainstream workforce, it is not disappearing but is increasingly manifesting subtly and ambiguously through interpersonal interaction (micro-aggressions), including in hiring processes that, for example, assess people based on "fit" to sidestep anti-discrimination measures and privilege already-privileged candidates (Acker, 2009; Green, 2005). This issue is perhaps most evident in tech start-ups, which Lyons (2017) has described as steeped in "bro culture," in which workers are hired based on "culture fit" – an expectation of shared patriarchal values akin to the recruitment practices of "high risk" fraternities (Boyle, 2015; see also Sanday, 1992) – and women, racialized, and older workers are marginalized, excluded, and harassed. As with strippers and other sex workers (see Raguparan, 2017), racialized workers in office-type settings also feel pressured to perform professionalism in a way that compensates for their racialization and upholds organizational norms and hierarchies through "additional, invisible labor" that Wingfield and Skeete refer to as "racial tasks" (2016, 48).

In response to both the continuing pervasiveness of sexual and racist harassment, and the inadequacy of policy and human resources responses, critical research on mainstream workplaces has pivoted toward highlighting the potential of progressive organizational leadership. Reviews of best practices suggest that management can set the tone for a respectful workplace by recognizing discrimination and harassment as organizational issues and fostering diversity and inclusiveness (Campbell & Chinnery, 2018; H. LeBlanc, 2014). However, translating such lofty rhetoric into action has proven challenging, particularly in occupations in which gender roles and inequalities feature significantly, such as the military and the police (Bastarache, 2020; H.

LeBlanc, 2014), but also in relatively progressive institutions such as universities, which have struggled to effectively implement anti-racist policies (Dua, 2009).

Nevertheless, that large mainstream employers such as these have implemented programs endeavouring to train management and staff to better prevent and respond to racism and sexism is at least an acknowledgment of these issues. In this regard, and in recognition of the fact that strip clubs are smaller organizations that likely do not have the capacity to implement such training themselves, another way to reduce workplace harassment at strip clubs might be through municipal licensing processes. Currently, like several strippers in the study, as well as key informants and sex worker organizations, Sal (manager) found adult entertainment licensing to be stigmatizing and without value, noting that, "with my [adult entertainment operator] licence came absolutely no education whatsoever." Similar to training that is provincially mandated to equip mainstream workers such as security guards and bartenders to promote people's well-being and respect applicable regulations at their places of work, the education Sal suggested is lacking could map on to an existing licensing infrastructure – municipal adult entertainment licensing – helping to impel strip club managers and owners to prevent and respond to workplace sexual harassment and assault, and, through the inclusion of provincial human rights information, welcome a more diverse roster of dancers.

Concluding Remarks: Considering Responses to Sexual Harassment

Comparing stripping to other kinds of jobs reveals that sexual harassment is a common problem – albeit one that is more readily apparent in a context in which the performance of gender and sexuality is overt. As this chapter has shown, dominant expectations surrounding professionalism – and discouraging sexual impropriety – are not met (or are flouted) at strip clubs and mainstream workplaces alike. At strip clubs, these expectations conflict with the performances that are necessary to the ongoing production and maintenance of the party environment; in turn, third parties' impression of dancers as unreliable and untrustworthy "girls" may foster inappropriate behaviours, including sexual harassment. Across workplace contexts, however, intersectional gendered harassment betrays attitudes framing women and racialized people as inferior, unprofessional, and undeserving of respect.

At the same time, there is evidence of some change in mainstream gendered workplaces like the Royal Canadian Mounted Police, which issued an apology to its female members after two class action suits concluded in 2016, admitting that the national police force was replete with systemic gender and sexual harassment and discrimination that undermined women's health and well-being, success, and professional contributions. That said, a report following the resulting settlement asserted that creating "a more inclusive and respectful workplace" could be achieved only through collective, sustained effort requiring "vision, leadership and determination over a decade or more" (Bastarache, 2020, p. vii). Strippers and other sex workers have argued that recognizing their work as legitimate labour – for example, through granting them employee status, union membership or support, or access to labour protections – would allow them to more effectively fight back against (at least the more egregious instances of) inappropriate conduct by third parties (Gall, 2016; Gillies et al., 2019). Analogously to efforts to reform mainstream workplaces, peer-led groups advocating for better working conditions for strippers and the decriminalization of sex work have achieved some success in the courts (e.g., *Canada v Bedford*, 2013; *Work Safe Twerk Safe v Ontario*, 2021a) and sympathy in the media, but have so far been unable to secure commitment from policymakers to mandating meaningful change (Beer, 2018).

However, even in the absence of labour protections and political support, problems like sexual harassment and lack of professionalism at strip clubs are not insurmountable. As Roscigno and Hodson (2004) have argued, "workers' sense of dignity and satisfaction are formulated on an ongoing basis, and relative to what occurs in their particular workplaces" (p. 15). As this chapter has demonstrated, many strippers are able to manage, avoid, or subvert sexual harassment and sexist and racist micro-aggressions through the use and manipulation of their "personal fronts." While performing sexualized, classed, and racialized iterations of gender is in some ways counterproductive to collegial relations, as it can perpetuate stereotypes, it is also a means to relational or practical (e.g., scheduling) outcomes that works in the party environment and with the organizational norms fostered and circulating therein. At the same time, that some dancers opted to approach third parties professionally speaks to the availability of alternative, non-gendered means to confront harassment and relate to third parties. In turn, the fact that some third-party participants in this study conscientiously approached dancers professionally rather than flirtatiously suggests that third parties are able to relate to dancers differently.

Chapter Five

Safety and Security: Unpacking Danger, Mitigating Risks

As discussed in the previous chapter, the gendered, sexualized work culture of strip clubs informs the risk of sexual harassment by third parties in ways that are both distinct from and comparable to mainstream workplaces. The presumed risk of *client*-initiated violence is another matter altogether, and tends to be met with a different response than the lack of regulatory scrutiny of worker-on-worker harassment and violence. Political and community objections to strip clubs as bad for neighbourhoods and women reveal considerable cultural anxiety about the risk posed by clients, framing them as the fuelling demand that leads to sexual exploitation – *the men who buy women and girls* (Hubbard, 2009; Weitzer, 2012).[1] In response to such reductive and sensationalistic framings, critical scholars have argued that criminalizing clients – the solution put forth by those attempting to end the demand for commercialized sexual activities and reflected in Canada's prostitution laws (see *Protection of Communities and Exploited Persons Act*, 2014) – does not alleviate important labour, occupational health and safety, socio-economic, and gender-related issues, which have been highlighted in the previous chapters (Bruckert & Hannem, 2013a; Fuckförbundet, 2019; Sex Workers United Against Violence et al., 2014). Moreover, the risks that sex workers face are conditioned by the particular sector and context in which they work (Bruckert & Parent, 2018; Law & Raguparan, 2019; Weitzer, 2012). A significant body of scholarly research has found that street-based sex workers face the highest rates of violence, while indoor sex work venues are relatively safe – in part because indoor workers are not exposed to predatory violence from passers-by, and in part because the security provided by third parties in indoor venues can prevent and minimize client-initiated violence (Brents & Hausbeck, 2005; *Canada v Bedford*, 2013; Lowman, 2000; O'Doherty, 2007). Brents and Hausbeck (2005) further argue that non-criminalized sex work venues are less stressful as well as less risky for workers. This is not to say that strip clubs are risk-free, or to deny that gender informs how strip club workers perceive and respond to risk. Although situational or client-initiated violence is a risk with which a variety of direct service workers – including nurses, taxi drivers, and teachers – contend (M. Leblanc & Barling, 2004), at strip clubs the risk of client violence is informed by the "party" environment discussed in the preceding chapter.

This chapter unpacks the question of risks in strip clubs. In so doing, it examines how third parties manage (or fail to manage) security, legal, and financial risks to dancers, themselves, and the club through policies as well as perceptions and performances that mobilize gender, race, and class. All of this takes place in the party environment, which contributes to the risks workers face at the same time as it constitutes the context in which security issues must be resolved with minimal disruption. Drawing on research participants' interpretations of and responses to risks, the chapter demonstrates how dancers and third parties confront risks particular to their unique roles (sexual and physical assault, respectively) as well as shared risks (e.g., financial, legal) that they manage together as well as separately.

How Risky Are Strip Clubs? Insider Wisdom on the Question of Risk

Turning to dancers' and third parties' perspectives on the risks in and related to strip clubs reveals a considerably different picture than the dominant framing of stripping as inherently risky. This dominant framing is, in large part, based on stigmatic assumptions about customers, who are erroneously assumed to be a distinct, immoral, and dangerous sub-population (Hubbard, 2009). In contrast, strippers' and third parties' perceptions of clients are informed by their positions as people who are, in Goffman's (1963) terminology, "wise": familiar with and sympathetic to the stigmatized – in this case, the customers with whom they interact on a daily basis.

Third-party participants agreed that clients are just ordinary people – "your average working white-collar guy, or a lawyer, or a doctor, or a judge. I've seen them all" (Tony, manager/DJ) – some of whom are nice and some of whom are "annoying" (Dalton, DJ and manager), "party animals" (Jimmy, DJ), or "total fuckin' creeps" (Sal, manager). As George (bouncer) put it, "I don't really have an opinion of a client unless they do something bad – like, I don't judge people for what they do." At the same time, third parties acknowledged that, practically speaking, customers are the people whose behaviour is most likely to violate the rules of the club (no matter how lax), whether through inappropriate sexual touching, aggressive or violent behaviour, or irresponsible alcohol or drug consumption. In Sal's words, "they're a lot of time the biggest wild card." In turn, Sal felt he was at risk of getting involved in physical altercations, "and it makes my stomach turn." As third parties' encounters with violence discussed later in the chapter demonstrate, the risk of client violence can manifest in significant injuries – particularly for bouncers and managers, who are charged with managing the security of the club.

Third parties' perceptions of clients as simultaneously ordinary and "wild cards" can be seen as a recognition that average men whose behaviour is ever informed by gendered socialization and who are imbibing in the permissive context of the party environment may behave more aggressively or irresponsibly than they would in other contexts. Fuzzy (DJ) surmised that these factors are mutually reinforcing:

> You've got to remember that each of these guys have had a few drinks, and you know – they were picked on in school and, you know, that's the reason they're here. They're – you know, women have probably abused these guys all their lives, and they're here in the club, and finally, they're top dog, so yeah, they're going to act like jerks because they feel like that's what the popular guy is supposed to do.

Fuzzy's analysis is analogous to those of academics who have argued men's violence, ranging from sexual harassment, to intimate partner violence, to school shootings, is informed by the immense pressure to "measure up to the norms of hegemonic masculinity" (Kimmel & Mahler, 2003, p. 1440; see also Boyle, 2015; Godenzi et al., 2001), the "most culturally exalted form of masculinity," which works to sustain the "institutionalization of men's dominance over women" through homophobia, sexism, and sexual violence (Carrigan et al., 1985, p. 592; see also Connell & Messerschmidt, 2005).

Scholars have also reflected on additional factors influencing men's violence against women, including the role of alcohol. While they have found that alcohol can exacerbate aggressive behaviour because it impedes cognitive functioning and communication, they argue that the relationship between alcohol and men's risk of sexual offences or transgressions is correlative rather than causal (Lorenz & Ullman, 2016; Boyle, 2015). In other words, alcohol is not an excuse for sexually assaulting or for blaming victims; rather, academics argue that alcohol merely lowers men's inhibitions against acting on, or encouraging peers to act on, misogynist beliefs to which they already adhere (Boyle,

2015; Godenzi et al., 2001). Analogously, Boyle (2015) argues that men who do not subscribe to sexist beliefs and attitudes, and whose peer group shares similarly non-sexist values, are considerably less likely to engage in behaviour that is disrespectful to women. Although Boyle's study focused on fraternities, her findings accord with third parties' and dancers' perception of a considerable portion of clients as relatively well-behaved, and suggest that strip clubs where sexual hostility is more tolerated may be more likely to attract patrons whose beliefs about gender may pose greater risk to dancers. Of course, the presence of third parties at strip clubs is an additional level of oversight not present at fraternity parties – in this respect, Boyle's research can be read as applying more generically to male peer groups (see also Godenzi et al., 2001) than to sexually charged workplace environments. Taken together, these insights suggest that some men, and some male peer groups, are more likely to act aggressively in various contexts. In short, there is nothing especially risky about men who patronize strip clubs – but this does not make risk management any less important to the maintenance of a business and leisure space that is enjoyable for all.

Fuzzy's above assessment of clients further illustrates how, at the same time as they are "wise," strip club workers nonetheless subscribe to some normative judgments about customers. Some of these assessments are informed by scripts of inadequate masculinity intersecting with stigmatic assumptions about sex industry clients. For example, Sal (manager), Chico (DJ), and Kelly (bartender) perceived at least some customers as lonely; similarly Studley (DJ/supervisor) admitted, "you know, I see a lot of them that come in the doors, and I think, 'Jesus, what a loser.'" Other gendered assessments of risk mobilize intersecting racialized and classed tropes of dangerousness, culminating in screening practices (elaborated in the coming section) that disproportionately target Black men as presumed "pimps" or trouble-makers.

For their part, dancers, who also insisted that clients are, for the most part, ordinary men, were careful to specify that only some behave inappropriately, even as many endeavour to negotiate or test their boundaries. Monica's description of the types of customers she had met over the course of her stripping career is illustrative:

> Like, there's good and bad customers, and, ultimately, the bad ones made me quit, but it was – I think the bad ones are a much smaller percentage. And I think, eventually, I was able to weed them out, and vet for them and stuff too. Most customers fall in the neutral range, I guess, like, you say no and you tell them a couple times, and then they'll wait a couple songs

to see if you changed your mind, and then they give up. But I was always fine with that.

Generally speaking, dancers reported feeling safe at work. As Sasha (dancer) put it, "I've always been more concerned about my financial security rather than my physical safety." Thus, similar to the workplace sexual harassment discussed in the previous chapter, dancers usually felt safe in a context in which customers "try and get away with whatever they can get away with" (Ashley).

Comparing dancers' and third parties' perceptions of clients and the risks they pose demonstrates that their respective roles – both in terms of gender and occupation – inform the risks they face: while dancers are primarily concerned with theft of services (refusal to pay for dances) and sexual assault, third parties are more likely to be faced with physical violence in altercations. How third parties approach these risks is conditioned by the context of the party environment and clubs' reliance on alcohol sales; in this sexually charged "party," where alcohol and drug (ab)use by customers as well as dancers is overlooked as long as it does not disrupt the ambiance of the club, third parties' strategies are more often reactive than preventive.

Assessing and Preventing Risks through Normative Assumptions and Practical Considerations

There are two important exceptions to this relatively tolerant approach to potential risks. First, as in other sectors of the sex industry (see Brents & Hausbeck, 2005; Bruckert & Law, 2013), the mere presence of third parties is a deterrent to client-initiated violence. Second, as with other kinds of nightclubs and bars serving alcohol, strip clubs are in the habit of screening – indeed, are legally required to screen – patrons entering the establishment, in order to exclude those who are already overtly intoxicated, not of legal age to enter, or otherwise deemed imminently or inherently risky.

In one respect, screening is practical: managers affirmed that the club's first line of defence is at the door, making screening an important tool to prevent trouble by refusing entry to potentially disruptive customers (see Hobbs et al., 2005). To this end, Sal's (manager) club employs an intentionally vague dress code as a tool third parties can use to prevent men they perceive as overly intoxicated or otherwise unsuitable from entering the establishment: "We have a sign at the door, sort of like a disclaimer, saying 'Dress code is in effect' ... We'll just say, like, to guys, 'Sorry, you don't meet our dress code.'" As a preventive strategy aiming to exclude undesirable others, screening is often directed toward Black and/or underclass men, reflecting Hunt's (2003) assertion that risk assessment frequently derives from stereotypes through which particular ethnic and/or sexual attributes are read as morally dubious (see also Lilleston et al., 2012). Bruckert and Hannem (2013b) similarly argue that fixating on a particular attribute like race or class and associating it with negative characteristics (e.g., sexual predation, violent tendency) forms "a social profile, indicating the type of person who fits into this stigmatized category" (p. 298). In this regard, bouncers often subtly or explicitly direct their attention to Black men whom they perceive as fitting the profile of pimps or gang members. This social profiling is additionally informed by an interest in protecting the comfort of middle-class clientele, visible in Dalton's rationale for not allowing gang colours (e.g., motorcycle club logos) in the club he managed: "The colours scare the rest of the customers away." Even at Sal's working-class, "biker friendly" club, the presence of gangs must be mitigated, both for the comfort of middle-class clientele and to prevent conflict: "You kind of almost have to choose a side … You can't have both of them coming to your club or there's gonna be a shit storm, so, um, you gotta kinda be friendlier to one [gang] or the other."

If men matching any such risky profiles do gain entry into the club, third parties are likely to pay particular attention to them. Describing a policy that overtly relied on racial profiling, Marcus (bouncer) recalled being "instructed by management to keep an eye mostly on Black males." At the club where Studley (DJ/supervisor) worked, management was particularly attentive to certain attributes ("Black guys") and behaviours that they associated with "pimps": "None of them want a drink, none of them want to pay cover, 'Oh, I'm just waiting to talk to so-and-so,' or whatever, then every girl that walks by, they're calling them over." Other policies tangentially related to security are informed by the same normative assumptions. Participants reported that, almost universally, music guidelines at strip clubs strongly favour classic rock, which is perceived to appeal to white, middle-class, middle-aged men, the demographic that third parties characterized as the most desirable and most lucrative, while rap and sometimes also hip-hop is not allowed because it is imagined to attract "G bangers" (Scott, bouncer and manager) – that is, risky, racialized men. Fuzzy (DJ) suspected that racial tropes also informed his club's limit of "five Black girls" per shift: "They're trying to limit the amount of pimps they let into the club, and, I guess, the thought is that Black girls will bring in the Black guys" who are presumed to be pimps.

Although screening directly and indirectly facilitates racial and social profiling, it is an example of a legal requirement that works *with* the business and security interests of the club, which would be hindered by admitting unruly, drunk men. Attesting to the legal riskiness and vulnerability of underage dancers, Studley's club additionally made a point of over-conforming to provincial liquor regulations: "You only have to be eighteen to be in there, but by our personal rule, we don't allow anybody [i.e., dancers] under nineteen." Another regulatory requirement that attends to dancers' concerns and facilitates third parties' security practices is a stipulation about private lap dancing areas. Dancers in both Ottawa and Toronto appreciated that the champagne rooms at their clubs had been redesigned to facilitate surveillance when municipal edicts were revised.[2] At Monica's club, "when they cut the [champagne room] walls down and things became more open ... the DJ himself could probably see a lot of what was happening." Similarly, at the club where Jill (dancer) works, "they used to have like semi-opaque partitions separating the booths ... and now, they're clear partitions, so that if the bouncer is walking by, he can totally, clearly see into the booth, rather than like, having to like peek around the corner to look in." However, it appears that these regulations have not been consistently heeded, as Ashley (dancer) worked at a club where "the VIP rooms are super secluded and like, really private and really small ... I didn't like it."

Neither mobilizing stereotypical scripts of riskiness nor employing tactics particular to strip clubs, preventive security policies attending to financial considerations are comparatively banal and practical. For example, along with other bouncers at his club, George endeavoured to minimize financial disputes by noting each dancer's time of entry into a champagne room with a customer, in order to keep track of how many $20 songs have passed, and therefore how much money is owed. Similarly, dancers described bartenders, managers, or waitresses explaining the hourly rates to the client at the beginning of a champagne room session in order to make sure he is well aware of how much money he is committing to spending. Dancers also noted that clubs post "signs that ... [say] '$20 per dance'" (Monica), and that some oblige dancers to collect the money they are owed from customers after one, two, or five songs. According to Scott (bouncer and manager), the latter policy is designed to prevent customers from spending more money than they can afford or be forced to pay. However, dancers complained that the latter policy challenges dancers' ability to maintain customers' impression of the situation, interrupting the "flow" with business-like demands that undermine the feeling of intimacy that they are attempting to sustain

(Goffman, 1959). Shane (dancer) identified an additional challenge in regard to collecting payment: "You don't ask for your money up front because you don't know how many songs you're gonna do up front." Accordingly, many of the strategies used by third parties (and, in the absence of sufficient or, sometimes, any responses from third parties, dancers as well) must work seamlessly with their gendered performances.

Managing Risk in the "Party" Environment through Gendered Performances and Perceptions

Security is, in many ways, a gendered endeavour at strip clubs. As noted in chapter 1, performing aggressive masculinity is an important part of bouncers' job: it informs the tasks they are assigned and spaces of the club they occupy and monitor. For example, as a manager, Adam had made a point of stationing an imposingly large bouncer at the door of his club to deter customers from misbehaving. This strategy echoes Bruckert's (2002) finding that clubs use bouncers' conspicuous presence as a preventive security strategy.

As with the screening practices noted above, security tactics at strip clubs are informed by how third parties read customers' behaviour, which shapes the approach and timing of their responses. Such decisions are key to a successful intervention, in order not to disrupt the individual customer's impression of the situation, or the party environment as a whole, as Sal (manager) explains:

> Let's say we really have a really loud, boisterous customer who's being obnoxious ... If he hasn't done anything that actually warrants him being kicked out, and you ask him to leave, he's probably gonna freak out. So I'll sit back and wait, because I know that, like, within the next hour, this guy is gonna do something stupid enough that we can be like, "Ok man, it's time to call it a night." So, you know, you go over and give them some warnings and that, and just sort of sit back and wait, and then eventually it'll happen ... It's a fine line you gotta watch pretty close – make sure that he doesn't, like, go too far over the line too quickly without you actually being there to prevent it.

As Sal's narrative evinces, intervening to prevent customers from further misbehaviour, whether by giving them a warning or ejecting them from the premises, can be a delicate interpersonal interaction. Aware of this, Marcus (bouncer) taught dancers hand signals to subtly communicate their issues to bouncers in the VIP area without alerting their customer or disturbing neighbouring lap dances.

Third parties endeavour to manage customers' behaviour by mirroring their class and disposition (which may be interpreted through racialization), in an effort to approach them in a way they will understand. Thus, Marcus attempted to appeal rationally to customers he perceived as rational, while Sal adopted a gendered and classed aggressive "street-level" persona to interact with men he perceived to be pimps attempting to recruit dancers at his club:

> I've had some pretty harsh words with some of them just because I knew that they're like, they're street-level guys ... I've literally gone over and said to guys, like, "These are *our* girls, so don't come in here and think you're fuckin' recruiting any of these chicks, cause they're ours," and that's totally possessive of me to say, and they're not ours at all, but I just say that cause it sounds tough [laughs] and hopefully they'll get the message, right, is to just leave these [dancers], leave them alone. (Participant's emphasis)

Another strategy to manage customers is invoking the spectre of the law. This might involve denying further service to intoxicated patrons by referencing the liquor inspector, or threatening to call the police to resolve a dispute. Marcus had a fixed order of tactics for dealing with payment disputes between dancers and clients, in which violence was a last resort: he would first try to reason with the customer; next he would call two or three colleagues over to appear more intimidating; he would then threaten to call the police, evoking possible ramifications on other aspects of the customer's life, such as his wife and workplace finding out about the situation – at which point the customer usually capitulated. In making reference to criminalization (the police), his position as head of a nuclear family (his wife), and his socio-economic status (his job), this strategy effectively calls the customer's attention to the moral threshold of his normative gender and class affiliations to regulate his behaviour. It also highlights how bouncers' performance of authoritative masculinity, through the use of manipulation, pressure, intimidation, and threats of violence, can allow them to avoid actually using physical violence (see also DeMichele & Tewksbury, 2004).

While some third-party participants insisted that violence is necessary in certain situations, especially when physical and/or sexual assault are involved, it is not the preferred conflict-resolution method. As violence enacted for security purposes may pose a legal risk to the club and the third party or parties involved in the altercation, bouncers are usually instructed to use violence judiciously and, as George (bouncer) phrased it, to "mak[e] sure I get hit first ... because once that happens, my butt is covered [legally]." As he elaborated, "the physical portion of it, in restraining people, it's a very grey area for security guards, even when we've been assaulted. It's – you can only hold someone for so long before it's forceful confinement, even if you're waiting for police to show up." However, "hands-on" approaches may not necessarily be violent; for example, bouncers may (though, as dancers noted, sometimes do not) run after customers who leave the club without paying, and managers or bouncers may hold a piece of a customer's property, such as a cellphone or driver's licence, as collateral until he pays the money he owes a dancer.

Reflecting the complexities of an environment produced as both gentlemanly and rowdy, legal and risqué, managers and bouncers framed social skills as a first resort and a valuable security tool. This perspective stands in contrast to Scott's mention of feeling pressured to prove himself to colleagues through displays of physical aggression (see p. 76), but research on nightclub bouncers by Hobbs et al. (2005) and Rigakos (2008) demonstrates that the preference for verbal over physical approaches to conflict resolution is common in night-time entertainment venues. Supporting this finding is Adam's (DJ and manager) suggestion that third parties' verbal and negotiation skills can reduce the risks of violence from customers: "Your reaction to people is what determines how much risk you're in. I think if you're, you know, nice and polite and civilized, I think you lower your risk significantly. I think, if you're a dick, I think you raise your risks significantly."

The sole woman third party to be interviewed in this research, Kelly (bartender) relied exclusively on verbal strategies. Furthermore, she argued that her approach to negotiating with customers to resolve payment disputes was gentler and, as a result, more effective than those of her male colleagues. Jill (dancer) offered a similar assessment of a female manager with whom she had worked. Thus, while evidently relatively marginal, considering the paucity of women who work as third parties, performing (hetero)normative femininity can also be an effective and non-violent risk-management strategy.

Sometimes, however, the risk of violence is impossible to mitigate. Reverend (manager/bouncer) recounted "running straight into a brawl sometimes to break it up where I've had my head cracked open; I've had my jaw broken; I've broken ribs; I've taken layers of skin out of my head, broken a collarbone, my hand, my nose." This litany of workplace injuries draws attention to the physical risks faced by third parties, contrasting starkly with stereotypical tropes reproduced by scholars who, in equating stripping and prostitution with violence, frame third parties themselves as risks (e.g., Farley, 2003; Holsopple, 1998). In contrast to this stigmatic and gendered assumption, bouncers and (to a lesser extent) managers face considerable (albeit, as DeMichele and Tewksbury (2004) note, not necessarily frequent) risks of physical assault. Having witnessed physical assaults on bouncers but not dancers, Marcus (bouncer) wryly noted, "the risk is probably higher for security than it is for dancers because the security people are usually the ones who are stopping you from doing what you want to do." He further surmised that, if weapons are pulled, bouncers are the most likely targets.

Legal Risks and Wilful Ignorance in the "Party" Environment

At the same time as they are tasked with mitigating security risks, third parties must also mitigate legal risks to the club and its employees and dancers. As noted in chapter 3, third parties monitor lap dances more strictly than usual when police or bylaw officers are present, thereby interrupting the "party": "It was just basically like a buzz kill until they were gone, like no one would really be able to sell dances" (Monica, dancer). In the absence of uniformed officers, third parties often endeavour to balance the club's business and legal interests – that is, customers' enjoyment and the risks of administrative or criminal sanctions – by purposely limiting their attention to, overlooking, or ignoring intoxication and prohibited sexual activities.

Strip clubs, like other nightclubs, earn most of their profits through alcohol sales (Rigakos, 2008), and Kelly (bartender) commented that overserving customers is quite common (in spite of its contravening provincial liquor regulations): "We're supposed to always encourage bottle service, but, like, if they're drunk, you can't, but we're supposed to … Sales are, like, the most important. So we're also not supposed to serve anybody when they're intoxicated, by the rulebook, but it happens." Similarly, dancers are allowed, and even encouraged (see also Chapkis, 2000; Maticka-Tyndale, 2004), to drink at work – as Ashley (dancer) put it, "you could get fuckin' hammered and … they wouldn't care." Indeed, it appears that most third parties employ what Lavin (2013) refers to as a "path of least resistance" approach (p. 362; see also DeMichele & Tewksbury, 2004) to alcohol and (albeit to a lesser extent) drug (ab)use by dancers: "Girls can't be, you know, falling-down drunk or, you know, under the influence of some drug that they can't do their show. Aside from that, most of it's overlooked if they don't – if the girl doesn't look too bad" (Chico, DJ). Sal (manager) explained his rationale for overlooking a modicum of drug consumption among dancers: "I don't know very many girls who don't drink or smoke or do other things … A stoned dancer is a happy dancer so let them do their thing

... In the long run they're probably gonna do their job better, and that will only benefit the club." Although their occupational roles do not permit them the leeway granted to dancers, it appears this approach sometimes applies to other club workers as well. Recalling being allowed to drink as a DJ, Jimmy had also "seen doormen drink on the job; I've seen management drink on the job; I've definitely seen dancers drink on the job; servers, yes. And I mean, that's like that party atmosphere – you can't control everything. And the owner's barely there."

As in other night-time entertainment venues with sexually charged atmospheres replete with intoxication (see Purcell & Graham, 2005), for some clients the availability of illicit drugs is part of the appeal of strip clubs. Frank (2002a) has argued that drugs like cocaine reinforce customers' socio-economic standing at the same time as they engender rowdiness – both key elements of the upper-/middle-class masculinity of the "party." Indeed, participants spoke of (suspected) drug dealers in clubs where they had worked; some accepted them as part of the environment, whereas others were troubled by their presence. As a manager, Adam adopted a practical approach informed by his understanding of the fabled "house dealer":

> It's just a business that caters to that sort of thing. Better to know the person who's in there selling stuff. You don't necessarily have to be friendly with them. But, you know, you know who they are. And, you know, and it's generally better to have a good relationship with them because you don't know who's behind them. And, on the other side of things, in that way, you can protect your ... club by not allowing ... anybody else in there other than the person you know. The worst occasion is having two people doing the same thing, and them having a conflict in the middle of your bar. So, that's my philosophy: it's better the devil you know than the one you don't.

Other participants suggested that drug dealers may not necessarily be outsiders. While Marcus (bouncer) and Sasha (dancer) reported working at clubs where bouncers sold drugs, Kelly (bartender) had been instructed by management to report dancers whom she suspected were dealing drugs to customers. Thus, at the same time that third parties and dancers are generally aware of drug and alcohol abuse in the party environment, third-party responses, while varied, share the goal of attempting to minimize the *visibility* of overt intoxication and illicit drug use.

In an environment lenient about substance use, third parties nevertheless endeavour to minimize the risks of physical injury or victimization to strippers who over-consume. Some participants recounted trying to make sure dancers do not drive home inebriated, or helping them into a taxi. At the same time, some third parties were frustrated by irresponsible substance use: "I saw her falling down the stairs, and you know, I grabbed her and made sure she wasn't injured ... Someone told me, 'She took some ketamine.' I'm like, aw come on, you do ketamine after work, not during work" (Marcus, bouncer).

A laissez-faire attitude also applies to contact between dancers and customers that normally occurs in a lap dance, although the legal risks engendered by "extras" render third parties somewhat more trepidatious, since manual stimulation, fellatio, and penetrative sex are more likely to fall under the scope of Canada's federal prostitution laws. Third parties' moral opinions of prostitution (which chapter 6 examines in greater detail) also inform their approach to managing risks engendered by its (apparent) provision. Managers tend to endeavour to balance business and legal concerns by tolerating a modicum of touching during lap dances, and selectively, occasionally, or routinely wilfully ignoring the provision of extras. Jenna's (dancer) recollection of a manager with whom she had once worked is illustrative of overt wilful ignorance that is perhaps more tolerant of sexual services:

> When I got hired at [the club] ... he was giving me a tour of the VIP booths, and they had these fake palm tree plants, and ... he goes, "Well, my dear, ok, around here, you know, I'm not saying you have to, but I'm saying if you choose to do something other than dancing, around here what we do is we move this decorative plant ... and you put it in front of the entrance to your booth, and I just know not to look in there!" And he was like, "However, if you're in there and you're doing something other than dancing but you feel like you're in danger, don't feel shy to ask for my help." And I was like, oh, I kind of like you.

As noted with regard to rule enforcement in chapter 3, wilfully ignorant approaches can be frustrating for lower-tier third parties who are merely attempting to perform their occupational duties. For example, George (bouncer) became frustrated by discrepancies between the rules and managerial expectations regarding their enforcement: "They tell me they don't want the extras going on. They say to report it. I have reported it. I've gotten in more trouble than the dancers. So, to me, it's, what's the point of the reporting?" By contrast, Reverend (manager/bouncer) took a more measured approach to rule enforcement that nevertheless speaks to the imperative not to disrupt the party environment: "You'll find a girl jerking a guy off ... I'm not going to go in there, grab everybody, you know, throw them down and throw them out, but you know, it ends pretty quickly when you go in and you just have a chat with a girl saying, 'Come see me in a minute.'"

Although some third parties, like Marcus (bouncer) and the manager described by Jenna above, were willing to intervene if dancers offering sexual services encountered client violence, scholars have argued that wilful ignorance in effect downloads the responsibility to manage clients onto dancers and thus exacerbates the risk they face (Chapkis, 2000; Egan, 2004; J. Lewis, 2000). Deciding not to consistently monitor dancers' activities in VIP sections (or not to do so at all) increases third parties' response time to incidents of physical or sexual assault. The sometimes fine line between a lap dance and an extra also determines when third parties can legally intervene in payment disputes (or perceive they can without contravening procurement or other prostitution laws). For Kelly (bartender), this meant that, "when there's a payment dispute ... we can't charge the customer for extras, so ... I'm not allowed to collect that money."

Third parties' wilful ignorance of municipally prohibited touching and extras can also belie the above-noted threats to call the police. Indeed, it appears that third parties seldom actually call the police. Participants enumerated several reasons for this reluctance, including the possibility of drawing unwanted attention to illicit activities that may be going on in the club (e.g., recreational drugs, extras), as well as the time spent waiting for the police to arrive (see also Rigakos, 2008). This unwillingness to involve the police stands in considerable contrast to nightclubs, where police can be an informal extension of security practices: according to Rigakos (2008), nightclubs commonly invite police officers to monitor their entrances or inspect their premises. That said, there are some situations in which strip club third parties do call the police – for example, if a "payment problem" with a client (Jimmy, DJ) becomes "an impasse" (Scott, bouncer and manager). However, Reverend (manager/bouncer) was of the opinion that, "due to the circumstances of the situation, it's hard to prove everything." Scott noted that the police can do little to resolve a financial dispute except record the parties' information to begin a civil process. As a result, some clubs have policies that appear to be informed by the recognition that it can be very difficult to settle financial disputes. For example, Sasha (dancer) had worked at a club that compensated dancers up to five songs, or $100, for theft of services, and another where "they banned clients that didn't pay."

Like third parties in the incall/outcall sector (see Bruckert & Law, 2013) – and in spite of the above-mentioned drawbacks and shortcomings of police involvement – third parties were clear that calling the police is an appropriate response to sudden or escalating violence, such as significant physical conflicts with or between clients, (although relatively rare) gun violence or threats thereof, or "gangster whatever" (Jimmy, DJ) in or about the club. Speaking to DJs' occasional involvement in security as the only male staff member present besides the club's elderly owner during daytime shifts, Studley (DJ/supervisor) sometimes had to decide whether to call the police: "If there's a couple of drunks that are fighting or something, there's nothing he [the club owner] can do about it ... I can certainly call the police and let them handle it, but it needs to be handled expeditiously, so it's usually me that does that."

Even in these more serious instances, some participants remained unsure as to whether calling the police was indeed helpful. Scott (bouncer and manager) further noted that his colleagues would call the police if a dancer wanted to press sexual assault charges against a customer, but explained that this became problematic when he tried to make a client wait for the police to arrive:

> So, the male was stuck in the champagne room and he panicked, got on the cellphone, called 911, and said I was holding him hostage. Yes, imagine the look on the cop's face when they came here, confused about why I'm holding a man hostage against his will. So, then, we explained. And they took it ... I don't know what happened [in the end].

Tony (manager/DJ) related an approach that interfaced more smoothly with the criminal justice system: with "a lot of cameras" stationed throughout his club, "we can burn them a CD of the incident within a couple minutes and they have the evidence right there to take to court, which is great."

Responsibilization and Dancer Self-Management of Risks

Although challenging amid the relaxed attitude to drugs, intoxication, and extras in the party environment, the scenario Scott described above illustrates something that many participants agreed upon: the preferability of prevention. Contributing to the importance of dancers undertaking prevention – and the onus on them to do so – is a curiously contradictory perception among third parties of lap dancing as inherently risky. As Sal (manager) put it, "as sad as it is to say, a girl getting, like grabbed somewhere that she doesn't want to be – it's kind of an occupational hazard. And like, I'm more than happy to kick the guy out, like 100%, but that's sort of the risk that they take, right?" While, on the surface, this framing may appear to contravene third parties' insistence that most clients are ordinary, or harmless, it is informed by and justifies gendered responsibilization. Just as (non–sex working) women are exhorted to modify their behaviour to minimize their risk of sexual assault more often than men are discouraged from perpetrating sexual assault (Ikeda & Rosser, 2010), the security-related advice third parties give to strippers reiterates the naturalization of male sexual aggression. For example, Dalton (DJ and manager) drew on gendered and classed notions of respectability, in tandem with discourses around risk and responsibilization, to dissuade dancers from behaving in a manner that may increase their risk of sexual assault:

> If you see a girl who's, you know, getting too drunk, you know, let her know what's going on … "Listen, you know, you're better than that. You can't make any money [drunk], you know. This is not the kind of image you want to present of yourself. Think about it" … Only the bad guys want the, you know, the heavy drunk girls. They got bad intentions.

The concurrent expectation is that dancers should mitigate these safety risks themselves. When dancers' attempts to do so are unsuccessful, third parties – and, in Jill's experience, even other strippers – sometimes read their experiences of sexual assault as "extras": "rather than people being like, 'Hey, what happened the other night?' girls were like, 'Fucking girl's a whore'… So I really take great responsibility for my own personal safety, cause I know that nobody else has my back" (Jill). Indeed, in one focus group, dancers Bobby and Brigitte both told of being reprimanded for complaining about a customer's inappropriate behaviour, while Jen asserted that third parties interpreted conflicts as "always your fault."

Dancers noted additional reasons why they felt they could not necessarily rely on third parties to manage issues with customers. Jenna (dancer) found that the importance third parties ascribe to a situation may only sometimes accord with dancers' interpretation: "It depends on the discretion of the staff member involved, and like, their mood that day … Sometimes it's a bit of a crapshoot because sometimes you're like, fuck it, you know, so-and-so looks annoyed today and I just don't want to bother him over $20 or $40." Here, third parties' responsibilization of dancers may dovetail with weak morale or apathy emanating from frustration about strippers earning more than them (see pp. 15–16), their expectations for tips fostered through the economy of favours (see chapter 3), and perceptions that some security issues are more important than others. Although some dancers felt that they were more likely to be helped by third parties if they tipped (as in Bruckert, 2002; J. Lewis, 2006), Carrie (dancer) found that sometimes even then, third parties were reluctant, and Monica (dancer) was of the opinion that bouncers and managers did "nothing. I had a guy, like, whip it out basically, and masturbate onto himself while I wasn't looking, like really fast, and it was really gross and upsetting to me ... and the bouncers did nothing about it." Jill (dancer) highlighted another compelling reason behind dancers' preventive self-management of risks: by the time a bouncer or manager intervenes in an incident in the VIP section, "that shit has already happened to me, you know?"

Because strippers feel they often have to act as their own enforcers, they develop their own screening practices and interactional guidelines. In the process of selecting their customers, dancers preventatively minimize risks by screening based on intuition and sometimes social profiling to determine who is an agreeable or acceptable customer, and who is "iffy" or a "red flag" (Donna, dancer). This allows them to avoid or abandon customers they deem to be potentially risky, unmanageable, or a poor financial return on their investment of time.

Dancers also emphasized the importance of vigilantly policing their personal boundaries (e.g., the level of touch with which they are comfortable). Although former stripper Monica had found this to be emotionally straining, others talked about it matter-of-factly. Reflecting on her eleven years in the industry, Carrie (dancer) flatly stated, "You have to be tough ... You have to be diplomatic and know how to handle yourself when you're being sexually molested – literally." Thus, while some scholars characterize dancers setting and policing their own boundaries as resistance to institutional control regimes (Bruckert, 2002; Bruckert, Parent, & Robitaille, 2003; Colosi, 2010a; Egan, 2004, 2006b; Lavin, 2013; J. Lewis, 2006; Murphy, 2003), such practices are also a pragmatic and necessary security strategy. Dancers often integrate physical boundary maintenance tactics into lap dances to maintain customers' impression of the situation, which, as noted by Frank (2002a, 2003, 2005), Pasko (2002), Pilcher (2009), and Wood (2000), is essential to the continued success of the business interaction. Dancers' strategies in this regard include remaining aware of their bodies and proximity to customers and keeping a watchful eye on clients' movements.

Strippers also integrate verbal strategies, such as assertions about boundaries or services, into their occupational performances. So as not to interrupt their soft, feminine presentation, dancers invoke the authority of third parties through what Egan (2006b) calls "playing helpless," which they insist is more effective than simply telling customers no:

> I'll tell them that, for personal reasons, I can't work at other clubs anymore, and I don't want to get kicked out, and it's kind of like, this is my only place I can work right now. So I kind of use that to my advantage ... You kinda have to make it look like: "It's not that I don't *want* to, it's that I *can't*. My hands are tied." You know, because you never want to imply that, you know, "It's just not in my personal code of behaviour and you repulse me." [laughs] You can't say that. (Kristen, dancer, participant's emphasis)

As other scholars have argued, such tactics simultaneously subvert and perpetuate stereotypical gendered scripts (Bruckert, 2002; Frank, 2002a, 2003; Liepe-Levinson, 2002; Murphy, 2003; Ross & Greenwell, 2005; Wolkowitz, 2006). Sometimes, as in Kristen's example above, they also opportunistically mobilize popular assumptions about strip club third parties as unscrupulous bosses.

As with Marcus's aforementioned strategy of threatening to call the police, dancers also evoke the law, albeit in a way that reflects their own situated concerns:

> Sometimes if someone's giving me a hard time about come to my hotel or give me a blowjob or this or that, you can very innocently be like, "You know, that's illegal, and I'm just not allowed to do that, and like, you're soliciting prostitution and that, I believe, in itself is a crime." And so sometimes you can, like, totally shame them into shutting up. (Jenna, dancer)

Yet, as Marie (dancer) pointed out, this strategy may not always be effective because "some guys don't really care about the laws or they've had extras with another girl before so they think all the girls will do it." Such clientele can inspire dancers to enact other approaches. Faced with a customer "try[ing] to wear you down to buy sex," Monica (dancer) sometimes elected to "just keep saying no to that, and then they keep trying to get you to say yes, but in the meantime they're still buying dances. So ... you're still making money while arguing."

Other verbal strategies, including boundary communication and (if needed) insistence, are comparatively more overt. Marie (dancer) made a point of clearly communicating her boundaries to customers, but in a way that fit with her performance of femininity: "I would always tell them, like at the beginning of every dance, like in a jokingly, like, cute way that, like, where they're allowed to touch, just so you set the expectations right away so you don't have to interrupt them to tell them, 'No you can't do that.'" In former dancer Shane's experience, asserting herself to clients was considerably easier than interacting with third parties. Negotiation and communication are also useful tools for dancers to protect their financial security. For example, Monica (dancer) found maintaining customers' ongoing consent to be an effective measure to ensure payment: "Usually as one song ends, I'd ask, 'Do you want to keep going?' but I pretty well never just let another song happen without alerting the customer."

When clients do become unmanageable, either by overstepping boundaries or refusing to pay, dancers may act more assertively. Leigh (dancer) described an instance of the former:

> I once, actually, scared the shit out of a customer because the guy … touch[ed] me how I didn't want, and, basically, I got so angry that I grabbed him by the finger … and I told him, "Listen. What you have done is a sexual crime. You have sexually assaulted me." I said, "I did not give you permission to do that. I specifically told you ahead of time not to do that." I said, "You should give me an extra $100 for that." And then the guy didn't want to do it, and I said, … "I could take you to court and sue you for sexual harassment, like, sexual assault."

Strippers refer to the practice Leigh alludes to as "the asshole tax … I explain to them, 'You've been an asshole, give me more money or you'll get in trouble'" (Jenna) – in other words, they use extortion as revenge for boundary transgression. Dancers can also just "stop it … If I'm doing one song with you and I find that you're acting inappropriately or you're not taking my direction in terms of what you can and can't touch, then I stop the song and I say, 'You owe me $20, and this is as far as we're going'" (Jill, dancer). Alternatively they may have to manage the situation with physical force: "Some customers, you have to hold their hands down … and [be] strong with them" (Carrie, dancer; see also Spivey, 2005). Recognizing this possibility, some dancers at George's (bouncer) workplace had requested that he "teach them little self-defence moves" he had learned in the military.

Rather than emphasizing dancers' femininity, these reactive strategies instead draw on scripts of working-class toughness or drop the performance altogether. As visible in the variety of preventive, reactive, feminine, assertive, verbal, and physical approaches, dancers are immensely creative in their strategies to manage risks emanating from customers. While this kind of problem solving exemplifies strippers' agency (Law & Raguparan, 2019), its necessity highlights the shortcomings of third parties' ability and/or willingness to protect their security, a situation that is conditioned by the classification of dancers as independent contractors, sanctions on lap dancing, and the excitability fostered in the party environment.

Concluding Remarks: Conflicting Accounts and Complementary Strategies

Looking at dancers' perceptions that third parties do not do enough, as well as the variety of strategies they undertake themselves, it is easy to assume third parties care little about strippers' safety. However, dancers described some bouncers and managers as helpful, supporting the credibility of third-party participants' descriptions of the ways they helped dancers and maintained the security of the club. At the same time, the inevitable variability in individual third parties' abilities, competing responsibilities, and perceptions of the situation means that the measures third parties describe taking are not always enough. Here it is important to recall what is going on in a strip club on any given night: not only are dancers and third parties attempting to balance their own safety with their respective financial concerns in the party environment, but there are more dancers, customers, and spaces than bouncers, managers, DJs, and bartenders can reasonably continually surveil. Thus, dancers' self-protection strategies should not be read simply as evidence of third parties' inaction but also as proactive and complementary.

Reflecting on the permissiveness of the party environment sheds additional light on a possible reason underlying the paucity of preventive actions by third parties beyond not allowing already disruptive or apparently risky patrons from entering the club: telling customers not to assault women or continually scrutinizing their interactions may foster an unappealing environment that is not fun, relaxed, or lucrative for the club and workers. This suggests that security practices at strip clubs in some ways mirror and in other ways reject broader societal attitudes toward, and gendered, raced, and classed framings of, risk. Just as women are normatively expected to govern their social and sexual activities in such a way as to minimize their risks of sexual assault, third parties responsibilize dancers to mitigate this risk. At the same time, both third parties and dancers reject normative discourses constructing alcohol, recreational drugs, commercialized sexual services, and (at least middle-class, white) customers as inherently risky.

In this context, third parties and dancers engage in a number of similar strategies, including screening, performing gender and class for security purposes, talking or negotiation, threatening to bring the situation to the attention of a higher authority (the law or, in the case of dancers, third parties), restraining customers, holding a client's property until he returns with payment, physically separating customers (by ejecting or leaving them), and clearly communicating service rates.

These strategies are, of course, deployed differently – that is, in keeping with third parties' and dancers' respective occupational roles and their attendant gendered scripts. Third parties employ additional strategies to mitigate the risks faced by the club and workers, such as rotating surveillance of the floor and VIP areas; threats or use of violence; selectively following or ignoring regulations (e.g., not hiring underage dancers; ignoring bylaws prohibiting touching or provincial liquor laws against serving inebriated customers); and calling the police for issues they deem serious (e.g., significant physical or sexual violence, theft, or property damage). That dancers for the most part feel safe at work suggests that all of the aforementioned strategies are largely, but not always, adequate – if not necessarily ideal – for managing risk and minimizing harm in strip clubs. Thus, as discussed in this and the previous chapters, the risks of client-initiated and worker-on-worker violence are not necessarily greater at strip clubs than at other workplaces; what is particular about strip clubs is that these risks – and the professional relationships through which they are managed – are conditioned by site-specific and intersecting gendered, raced, and classed scripts, and, as the next chapter will show, by stigma.

Chapter Six

Stigma, Stereotypes, and Solidarity

In his history of labour, social vulnerability, and exclusion in the West, Castel (2003) argues that paid work has long been performed under inequitable conditions – a truism that, as argued in chapter 2, applies no more to sex work than it does to other kinds of labour – but also that work is essential to social citizenship and inclusion. Westcott, Baird, and Cooper similarly assert that "paid work is one of the most important social activities that individuals undertake" (2006, p. 6). However, the social and personal worth and inclusion garnered through work are limited to jobs perceived to be socially valuable: "What establishes the social dignity of the individual is not necessarily the wage-earning job, nor even the labor itself, but its social utility, that is to say, the place it holds in the production of society" (Castel, 2003, p. 420). For people labouring in the sex industry, normative judgment and stereotypes undermine their status as workers by negating the value of their work. These common perceptions are informed by stigmatic assumptions (Bruckert, 2012) – that is, tendencies to "believe the person with a stigma is not quite human" and "construct a stigma-theory, an ideology to explain his inferiority and account for the danger he represents" (Goffman, 1963, p. 5).

As a label applied indirectly – for example, through media representations – and directly through interpersonal interactions, stigma is powerful and deeply affecting to the "marked": it can culminate in shunning, othering, violence, and/or internalization leading to a tainted self-image (Bruckert, 2012; Goffman, 1963; Hallgrimsdottir et al., 2008; Hannem & Bruckert, 2012; Link & Phelan, 2001). Stigma has both interpersonal and social determinants and effects. With respect to the latter, Link and Phelan (2001) operationalize stigmas as cultural objects that are constructed in and disseminated through discourse, that transcend or supersede the experience and voices of the individuals they label, and that are informed by and produced through social structures and hierarchies. Interpersonally, "the occupational stigma [of sex industry work] is constructed as a personal attribute so that the implications extend beyond the sphere of work and the label becomes a master status that has permanence across social space" (Bruckert, 2012, p. 58). For strippers, stigma pivots on their failure to embody normative expectations of feminine reserve and private sexuality. In contrast, as the examples across this chapter will demonstrate, third parties are stigmatized as suspicious or dangerous men – for some, with considerable effects on their life and well-being. Yet, even as third-party participants noted that they suffer from stigma, they also perpetuate it: along with dancers, third parties participants denigrated their counterparts and superiors by comparing them to that most deplorable stereotype, the pimp. Like some strip club third parties' moral objections to prostitution, these judgments demonstrate the pervasiveness of stigma and the normative values underpinning it, illustrating Goffman's assertion that "the general identity-values of a society may be fully entrenched nowhere, and yet they can cast some kind of shadow on the encounters encountered everywhere in daily living" (1963, pp. 128–9). Aware of its pervasiveness, some third parties endeavour to counter stigma against themselves and dancers. This chapter reflects on such moments of solidarity as well as on the implications of its absence. It also shows how stigma nevertheless informs interpersonal and work relationships between strippers and third parties.

Third-Party Perceptions, Experiences, and Management of Stigma

As was shown in chapter 5, third parties occasionally and opportunistically work normative tropes (e.g., tough masculinity) into their security strategies. Speaking to how their performances can additionally be informed by stigmatic assumptions, Scott (bouncer) recounted an incident in which a customer's fear made the situation more difficult to manage:

> After holding and fighting the guy in a choke hold for twenty minutes, um, one time, I – and you have to also understand that it went completely to chaos. The guy was so scared, he thought, uh, he had smashed one of our windows. So, we dragged him back [into the club]. Now, in his mind, because of Hollywood and what not, he thinks I'm taking him to the, some mysterious back room to beat him with a baseball bat or kill him. So, he's fighting for his life. I'm dragging him back, because, when the cops come, we're charging him with damage to the property. So, he's really fighting it.

So, I, I had him in the hold and everything. And he defecated himself and urinated himself while he was sitting on my lap. It was not an enjoyable experience.

While this situation illustrates the risks of getting physically involved with customers – Scott stopped using choke holds after that night – it also highlights the importance of perception in interpersonal interactions and the consequences when social actors' expectations about how a particular social interaction should unfold do not align. As Scott's narrative suggests, the customer may have perceived him and his fellow bouncers as nefarious and dangerous mob-like characters rather than as security professionals.

It is not only customers who adhere to these stereotypical tropes. Third parties enumerated a range of stigmatic assumptions to which they had been subjected, and that affected not only their interactions with customers but also with acquaintances, family, and friends. Jimmy (DJ) listed some assumptions commonly identified by third-party participants: "They think I'm a pervert. They think I do coke ... They think I've got a lot of money – I don't. And you know, I'm supposed to be some sort of crazy party animal ... And people call me a womanizer." Similar to assumptions by strip club customers about bouncers having some degree of ownership over dancers, noted by DeMichele and Tewksbury (2004), Scott (bouncer and manager) suggested that most women "look down on me when they find out about [my work], because they see me as ... some sort of oppressor or even abuser ... the evil thug that, you know, abused women to make money in whatever capacity ... a violent sexualized animal." Scott also felt that bouncers were subject to particular assumptions: as a "bouncer at strip club, I'm obviously not smart, apparently." As Chico (DJ) noticed, "I would get two different reactions. One was like, 'Oh, yeah? Oh, yeah?' [excited intonation] and the other one was more 'Oh, yeah' [disappointed intonation], you know. There was never any in-betweens."

Like strippers and other sex workers (see Bruckert, 2012; Trautner & Collett, 2010), third parties engage in a number of stigma-management and information-control strategies. Three were quite private about their work – including Eric, the driver and protection provider, perhaps speaking to the more nefarious characterizations to which he may have been subject as an unaffiliated third party. Another four disclosed their work somewhat selectively (e.g., to their friends and select family members, but not their children or casual acquaintances). However, more than half (eight) of third-party participants were public about their work. Their decisions about disclosing were informed in part by what Pinel (2004) calls "stigma consciousness," a form of self-consciousness about, or a focus on, their stereotyped status, that reflects "the extent to which targets believe that their stereotyped status pervades their interactions with members of the outgroup" (p. 39; see also Pinel, 1999). Decisions about disclosure also depended on participants' social circles – for example, whether they spent their time with people who are "wise" (Goffman, 1963), that is, industry insiders, or with outsiders. Thus, Fuzzy has told "very, very few people" about being a strip club DJ because "I don't want to be objectified, and I don't want to give myself that stereotype. I want people to know me for me before they find out what I do." Like Adam (DJ and manager), Fuzzy can elect to pass as "normal" – that is, not part of the discreditable group (Goffman, 1963) – by sharing information only about his other job. By contrast George (bouncer), who is very open about his work, found that outsiders could be sympathetic. He noted, "I have a really, really good family when it comes to talking and being open," and, moreover, that, "I'm not ashamed."

In addition to managing stigma by carefully considering whether and to whom to disclose their work, third parties resist dominant stereotypical perceptions by reframing their work, by "infusing the work with positive value and/or by neutralizing the negative value" (Ashforth et al., 2007, p. 157). Third parties emphasized the positive aspects of their work, voicing pride in their responsibilities, and noting that it allowed them to build their social skills and have fun. Like dancers and other sex workers (see Bruckert, 2002; Law, 2013), third parties also counter the lack of recognition for their work by refocusing attention to how their jobs resemble other occupations as well as the specific skills they require (see Ashforth et al., 2007). For example, managers agreed that balancing all of their tasks and responsibilities required not only excellent interpersonal skills but also organizational, creative problem-solving, and mathematical or money-management skills.

As with managers in other "tainted" occupations ranging from janitor, to social worker, to collections agent (Ashforth et al., 2007), participants also managed stigma by confronting public perceptions. Subtly challenging the stereotype of bouncers, Marcus (bouncer) "did my best to break the stereotypes of what a security person in a strip club is ... [by] talking to them [customers] in a respectful way." Chico (DJ), who was quite open about his job, expressed frustrations about his family not taking it seriously:

> In the beginning, my mom used to say, "When are you going to get a real job?" and I – you know, because she was used to me being in, you know,

a career thing, like radio. And I said, "You know, Mom?" I said, "I get up every morning; I take the bus; I go to work; I do eight hours, and at the end of the week, I get paid. Where's the part where it's not a real job?" ... So I think the family had a bit of a problem with it in the beginning. It took a while. It wasn't like I was ostracized or anything, but I mean little by little, she came around.

Kelly (bartender) brought her mother to her workplace "on like a Sunday afternoon, just to check it out," to dispel her worries and misconceptions. Thus, some third parties engage in normification, making an effort to present themselves as normal – in this case, without hiding their discreditable attribute (Goffman, 1963) – by framing their work as ordinary labour.

These tactics did not always prove effective in preventing ramifications for participants' lives, in their relationships with friends and/or family members, or in their interactions with acquaintances. As with strippers (see Bradley-Engen & Hobbs, 2010), working in the erotic dance sector can have deleterious effects on third parties' romantic prospects. While Chico (DJ), Studley (DJ/supervisor), and Fuzzy (DJ) maintained that stigma had not affected their romantic partnerships with women who were industry outsiders, other third parties had not been so lucky. Adam (DJ and manager) recounted a particularly unsuccessful date:

> I went out on a blind date with a normal girl ... We went out for dinner and we were talking over a glass of wine and we ordered food and the, you know, the big question ... "What do you do for a living?" comes up and I can't not be honest with her. So, I say, during the day, I do, I tech support for, you know, for the company I worked for, and, on the weekends, part-time, I DJ at a strip club. She got up from the chair and left the restaurant.

Analogously, Reverend's job as a bouncer had played a role in his divorce, while Scott's (bouncer and manager) girlfriend simply did not want to hear about his work – something that strippers struggle with as well (Bradley-Engen & Hobbs, 2010; Bradley, 2007). To mitigate these consequences, some third parties – like some of the dancers in Bradley-Engen and Hobbs' (2010) study – simply avoided dating outsiders (whether intentionally or as a result of their social circle comprising primarily work colleagues). As Sal (manager) put it, "in my time working in strip clubs, I don't think I've dated any, what we call civilian girls." Ashforth et al. (2007) refer to this practice of restricting one's social circle to the "in-group" as "social buffering." In this respect, stigma consciousness can influence how third parties organize their social and romantic lives. The impact was quite different for Kelly (bartender), who, as a heterosexual woman, was instead attuned to how stigmatic assumptions about risk impacted her boyfriend: "He thinks it's risky, so I think he worries a bit."

Stereotypes and Stratification

Consistent with third parties working in other sectors of the sex industry who were interviewed for the Rethinking Management in the Adult and Sex Industry Project, which provided some of the data for this book, strip club third parties were asked what they thought of the stereotypical image of the "pimp" and whether it affected them or applied to their work – and, if so, how. These questions were included in order to examine third parties' experiences, but also their internalization and/or perpetuation, of stigma. Their responses to these and other unrelated questions suggest that, in spite of their awareness and experiences of stigma, third parties also sometimes perpetuate stigma and, furthermore, that being employed at a strip club positions them to do so in particular ways.

Some club-affiliated third parties discredited the labour and/or character of their counterparts by attributing to them morally impugning qualities, such as sexual impropriety and exploitation. For example, although Sal (manager) was familiar with some driving services, he confessed that, "I'd rather get, like, a cool cabby that I trust," framing drivers who focus solely on dancers as "kind of creepy." Illustrating how such an assumption can be exaggerated through racialization, several third parties presumed that any Black man driving a dancer was a pimp (see also Law, 2020). As a bartender who had worked in several strip clubs, Kelly reported that "every manager I've ever known was *not* a good person ... Except for the one ... If you want to do a job like that, you're probably a dirtbag." Although he himself had worked as a manager, Adam had also worked with managers as a DJ; reflecting on the latter experience, he described a manager with whom he had worked as "see[ing] dancers especially as a means to an end. I don't think he sees them as people at all ... just meat that allows him to have a job and make money." Additionally, like many of the dancer participants (and workers across the labour market [see Hodson, 1999]), third parties often described their superiors or peers as corrupt, apathetic, or lacking in business acumen. Such perceptions reflect Willmott's (1997) suggestion that managers derive a sense of importance and accomplishment from the perceived failings of other employees. That these ascribed failings often dovetail with the pimp trope demonstrates that third parties reinforce stereotypes and stigma while endeavouring to dissociate from them. This tendency is illustrative of "stratification," which Goffman (1963) describes as dis-identification by stigmatized persons with individuals in their group whom they perceive to be exhibiting offensive or overt behaviour embodying negative stereotypes.

Insofar as stratification pivots on the internalization of the normative beliefs underlying and justifying stigma (Goffman, 1963), third parties often distanced themselves from prostitution by specifying that erotic dance is less sexually involved and therefore less immoral. As Gilles (manager) put it, "I provide fantasy; I don't provide sex. I provide, like, an environment where you have a good time – one that's fair, that's legal. We respect all the law and regulation, and we operate a good business. We can't compare us to pimp or massage parlour; that's not what we provide at all." Here Gilles bolsters the state-sanctioned (albeit tenuous) legitimacy of erotic dance in order to shield his workplace from the stigma of prostitution and distinguish himself from the discreditable, stereotypical pimp. Echoing Tony's (manager/DJ) insistence that "it's an honest living. I'm not pimping," the majority of third-party participants actively endeavoured to distance themselves from the stereotypical pimp, a distinction that was important to their construction of their job as work. This differentiation was additionally supported by the notion of choice versus taking or controlling a woman's money: "I'm not forcing anybody to do this job. They're coming to me looking for the work" (Studley, DJ/supervisor). Just as Hannem and Bruckert (2012) argue that although stratification may protect stigmatized individuals' self-worth, it ultimately reproduces existing stereotypes and the marginalization of the group as a whole (p. 178; see also Bruckert, 2002), these assertions situate strip club third parties as superior to "pimps," even as they reiterate simplistic and spurious assumptions conflating sex work, coercion, and exploitation (see Weitzer, 2012).

Stigmatization and Normalization

Just as some third-party participants characterized their affiliated and unaffiliated counterparts as creepy, exploitative, manipulative, and pimp-like, they also occasionally made negative judgments of strippers by comparing their conduct to prostitution. Both comparisons suggest that even strip club workers reproduce – albeit minimally and likely often unconsciously – mutually reinforcing gender and (hetero)sexual norms and popular framings of prostitution as immoral. In the following account Sal (manager) voices a common observation made by third parties who had enjoyed long careers in Ontario's erotic dance sector – that touching and the proliferation of erotic massage parlours have irrevocably changed the industry:

> I can remember the second club that I ever worked at, when I was a DJ, and girls were coming up to me and they were complaining about this one girl that worked on the day shift with us: "Oh yeah, she's dirty ... She's back there in VIP and this guy is touching her boobs" ... And then fast forward, like fifteen years later or whatever and that, I think, is pretty much a standard now, and, I mean, that's sort of like the base and it just kinda [laughs] goes from there ... The only way that the strip club industry could survive, I guess, was to move in that direction, because of the rub and tugs ... I don't even know how much they are, but it's like a fraction of what you would pay for lap dances ... And you go, and you're guaranteed to get your whatever, right? Whereas strip clubs, it was $20 a song, and depending on what girl you had, you could touch her boobs maybe, or maybe not, you know? So yeah, it just kind of manifested into what it is today. And I really, really, really hated it at first ... I was trying to keep the faith in the back of my head. I'm like, you know, they're not all bad, it's just, like, a handful of these girls who are doing this stuff. You know, the rest of them are still good, good girls. And now, I just feel like it's almost gone the other way. Now there's like handful of good girls and then the rest of them are up to something.

Sal's comments refer to the initial years of lap dancing, during which time touching muddied the previously clear boundary between erotic dance and prostitution (J. Lewis, 2000), and a distinction between "good girls" and "bad girls" emerged, even among dancers (Bouclin, 2006; DERA, 2002).[1] As Sal illustrates, even though the norm has shifted from a strictly visual display (table dancing) to a visual and tactile experience (lap dancing), the good girl/bad girl dichotomy remains. Many other third-party participants similarly insisted that stripping and prostitution "should be different" (Scott, bouncer and manager) for moral and pragmatic (business) reasons. As Sal's comments above imply, the latter concern speaks to unfair competition, about which strippers are considerably preoccupied and manage through lateral surveillance (see chapter 3). As the following excerpt from Adam (DJ and manager) suggests, however, morality often featured prominently in third parties' discomfort with prostitution-like sexual activity:

Sexual contact is, for the club, is wrong. It's not supposed to be that way. Suggestive contact is exactly what it's supposed to be about. A guy comes in and gets his, gets a dance from, you know, he's married, unmarried, every guy has got a girl who's a fantasy girl. To get a dance from a girl who's the guy's fantasy girl and have suggestive contact is harmless ... Because he's fulfilled a fantasy and now he's, you know, he goes home happy. And I think that's okay.

Adam's moral justification of erotic dance as "harmless," as compared to full sexual service, recalls Castel's (2003) assertion about the importance of the social utility of waged labour. Through this lens, Adam's reasoning can be read as an argument that stripping does not pose a threat to the reproduction of society because it does not interfere with men's position as head of the nuclear family. The inference is that prostitution would have a relatively deleterious effect on committed, monogamous, legitimate romantic relationships.

At the same time, and illustrating the mutually reinforcing relationship between stratification and stigma, third parties' discomfort with prostitution was not separate from, but rather informed, their moral opinions of erotic dance, visible in the information-management strategies of those who selectively disclose their jobs. Reverend (manager/bouncer), for example, had not disclosed his job to his children. Rationalizing a similar choice, Sal (manager) noted that he "always tried to keep it away from ... the young females in my family ... cause I have a pretty good, like, relationships with all of them and stuff, and they think I'm cool, so I don't want *that* to seem cool" (participant's emphasis).

Ironically, the desire that dominated among third-party participants in this study to differentiate stripping from prostitution contrasts with the actions of Ontario strip club owners' groups, which advocated in favour of lap dancing in the 1990s (Bouclin, 2004; *Ontario Adult Entertainment Bar Association v Metropolitan Toronto*, 1995, 1997), for the softening of Toronto's touching bylaws in the 2010s, and for the integration of brothels and strip clubs shortly thereafter. This discrepancy between owners, who are apparently in favour of having additional sexual services in strip clubs, and many of the third parties who participated in this study may be related to the amount of time they spend in the clubs: whereas owners are seldom in the club, the third parties they employ to operate it confront and attempt to manage "extras" on a routine basis. Analogously, only a few third-party employees were knowledgeable about the most recent (now defunct) strip club owners' group, the Adult Entertainment Association of Canada, but those who were aware of the association held it in low esteem. Marcus's (bouncer) impression was that "they're a bit slimy," while Jimmy (DJ) argued that "they're just like, pigs in suits, trying to be all, 'Oh, we're your defence and your rights and blah blah blah.' No, you just want a little more money."

Third parties' discomfort with prostitution also informs their interactions with strippers. It appears that this is especially the case with bouncers, perhaps because they are the third parties most often tasked with monitoring dancers' behaviour in the VIP section. Unfortunately, it can be in these instances that bouncers' stigmatic perceptions of dancers affect their reactions to rule breaking, even when it is instigated by customers against dancers' will. For example, Shane (dancer) described scenarios wherein "the client was trying to finger me or something, and I flipped out ... and then I got in trouble for accusing the client of doing that ... Basically got screamed at [by a bouncer] and called a whore and all sorts of different names." This reaction by the bouncer illustrates the mutual reinforcement of the "whore stigma" and assumptions of unchastity (Pheterson, 1998),[2] as well as how, once defined as unchaste, women are understood as implicitly and generally consenting to any sexual act (Comack & Balfour, 2004; Smart, 1989). These stigmatic assumptions are especially visible in the way Kristen (dancer) came to be discredited in the eyes of a bouncer at her club, and its impact on their future interactions:

> A client made a move to touch me inappropriately, I smacked his hand away, bouncer's walking by and said I didn't smack his hand away fast enough and he became really upset with me and started accusing me of doing a lot of things that I didn't do, and he said that I was going to be kicked out ... And I had to argue my point and my case, and in the end he let me stay ... and he became very sexually grabby with me after that point, almost as if, "I let you stay here, so you're – you know, I can grab your ass when you walk in, I can tell you where I want to stick it in you," even though he was married and very open about that.

Stigma, intersecting with classism and sexism, also manifests more subtly in third parties' assumptions about dancers' lives outside the club. Discomfort with prostitution can intertwine with these perceptions, such that some third parties associated strippers with exploitative or abusive romantic relationships (sometimes assumed to be pimping relationships); "bad relationships with their parents" (Adam, DJ and manager); "bad backgrounds, abusive backgrounds" (Studley, DJ/supervisor); lack of marketable skills; financial desperation; and addiction. These impressions echo stereotypical characterizations of strippers (and sex workers in general) as damaged, underclass women, and stripping as a last resort rather than an informed, contextualized, and/or constrained occupational choice (see also Jeffrey & MacDonald, 2006a, 2006b; Hallgrimsdottir et al., 2006). At the same time as it relates to their perception of dancers as not really workers, this framing can coincide with, or be informed by, sympathy for dancers experiencing difficult circumstances – something that featured prominently in participants' narratives as an emotional toll of working in the erotic dance sector. For example, George (bouncer) described his personal struggles with the effects (as he perceived them) of the party environment on dancers, including harassment and stigma:

> Having to watch some of these girls go through what they have to go through ... it's tough, and I see it takes a toll on them ... And even myself – I know, like, two weeks ago, I had to go home for a week because I just – I caught myself getting more and more – I guess – agitated, not only with the dancers but also with the customers where I would, I guess, try to provoke fights ... I just needed a break.

Some third parties did not subscribe to these stereotypical tropes. Unlike Jimmy (DJ), who was so disturbed by the party environment that it led him to quit the business, Dalton (manager and DJ) was sympathetic to the challenges faced by some dancers but refrained from generalizing their experiences, instead making sense of them in relation to stigma:

> Mainly, I didn't like seeing the hurt looks on the girls, girls who were hurt, girls who were broken. I met girls who were in the business for the wrong reasons. Or girls who had gotten into it for one reason and found out that it just wasn't what, uh, what they wanted. And, um, you know, it was bad. It was bad to see someone who, um, example, young girl, probably eighteen ... And she was a little crazy. She made, I think, $1400 the first night she worked. Which is incredible for a first night. I'm like, "Whoa!" But then, you know, you find out what she was doing for it ... you have to reprimand her ... Then, she comes back and she does it again ... Three days later, [her] boyfriend beats the [inaudible] shit out of her ... [But] I can't go beat him up. Right? And, you know, other girls who ... at one time, they were beautiful. You know, and [now] they're old. And, uh, they, they don't want people touching their breasts. You know, because they're not from that generation. They're from a burlesquey kind of generation. You know and, so, their time is over. And watch, you know, and looking at them and going, "What's going to happen? You have no education, you have no

> other job skills. What are you going to do?" Watching girls come back after they had said, "I'm out. I'm finished" ... And then ... three months later, saying, you know, "I need to come back to work." Right? You know, and that, the dejection on their faces when they say that ... You know, stories that you just don't want to have to deal with, right? ... "The Children's Protective Agency [Children's Aid Society] is taking my kids." You know, that's – you just get ill.

As Dalton intimates, the various issues faced by dancers he had encountered are not inherent to stripping but rather emanate from stigma intersecting with labour market discrimination (in barriers to mainstream jobs), gendered violence (in jealous or abusive intimate partners), and normative constructions of motherhood (in perceptions of sex work as morally corrupting to children). Together, these discursive and concrete implications speak to how being a sex worker marks women as "lower class" and limits their class mobility (Brown, 2005). Echoing Pheterson's (1998) assertion that the "whore stigma" is the most significant and deleterious label a woman can face, Dalton had observed across his career that, "[people] really do look at the dancer as a whore and as just a nobody."

Although the above quotes certainly suggest that he was sympathetic to their struggles, Dalton did not perceive strippers as exclusively victims of circumstance – indeed, he maintained:

> I always saw it as, as an emancipating kind of a job. Because I saw so many, so many women come into that work and stay in it and stay happy, or stay in it, leave happy. Right? They were in it for whatever reason they needed to be there for. They did it. They fulfilled their needs. And they moved on. Right? They had fun and they had a great time. You know? And it didn't affect them at all.

Analogously, not all the dancers who participated in this study reported feeling stigmatized by third parties, nor did most (save for Shane) think that third parties were universally unprofessional. Marie (dancer) "never felt judged by them for [being a dancer]. Like, I think to them, it's normal." Jenna (dancer) argued that a non-judgmental attitude is appropriate and, moreover, expected in strip club third parties:

> Well they work there too, so I don't think they should have much of a high horse to be on ... There have been a few crazies that, you know, maybe have mentioned that like, we're slutty or something, but I don't think they generally last long or are well liked, and, you know, I don't think you can do well with that attitude.

It is interesting to note that Dalton (DJ and manager), Marcus (bouncer), Gilles (manager), Sal (manager), and Tony (manager/DJ), the third parties who most appeared to see dancers as ordinary workers, also reported high levels of satisfaction with their job. Dalton and Marcus, who had both been in committed romantic relationships with sex workers (a dancer and an escort, respectively), shared the sentiment that the erotic dance sector comprises "a huge spectrum of women and their ideas" (Dalton). Gilles also thought of dancers as "like any worker I work with and for since – just a worker." Similarly reflecting a rejection of normative judgment, Kelly (bartender) provided information about a local sex worker organization to dancers who offer sexual services outside of her club.

Consistent with research about managers of other kinds of stigmatized or "dirty" jobs, third parties felt they were, in some respects, "in the same boat as" their stigmatized employees (Ashforth et al., 2007, p. 157). Rather than distancing themselves from or blaming workers, they managed stigma alongside them and on their behalf, including defending dancers when they encountered stigmatizing opinions. Marcus was particularly passionate in this regard and recounted how he would try to educate acquaintances about erotic dance:

> I would challenge them. I'm like, "Why is it disgusting? They're just working like anyone else would. Who cares if they're taking their clothes off?" Yeah, like, you know, "Nude artists' models do the same thing and no one says they're disgusting, like what's the difference? They just happen to be dancing." Like [in a boorish voice], "Ughh, I just couldn't do that." Like, "Well don't do it! [Laughs] Don't bug the people who are doing it. Like sure, it might not be the choice that you make, but it's still a valid choice for someone who wants to do that."

Marcus reacted in a similar manner to stigma from customers: "A number of people that I kicked out of the club – they're like [imitating a client], 'What's the big deal? She's just a dancer!' I'm like, 'Well no, she's a human being, and you don't treat people like that.'" For Dalton, the stereotype of dancers as public health risks (Bruckert & Dufresne, 2002; Jackson, 2011) was particularly egregious:

> I would doubt that there's a dancer out there, even if your club said yes, or turn the blind eye to whatever hand jobs, blow jobs, sex ... that would do it without a condom ... So, it blows my mind when people say, you know, "Yes, you're going to get all kinds of dirty diseases from a dancer." You're just not.

Dalton's assertion echoes sex workers' insistence that their body is the most important and valuable tool of the trade, which means that they are incentivized by both their short-term financial and long-term health interests to protect themselves by engaging in safer sex practices (Brents & Hausbeck, 2005).

Other third parties incorporated sympathy for the stigma faced by dancers into their managerial approach. Although his attitude was informed, in part, by stigmatic assumptions about dancers having "some scars from their past," Sal (manager) noted that "showing that you care … goes a long way in this business … It's, like, 'I'm gonna go be a dancer – it's probably gonna be like, I'm gonna get treated like shit.' And then if they come to work for us and we treat them differently then, you know, it makes them loyal." For Sal, demonstrating that he cared included charging a reasonable house fee and treating the dancers in a professional manner. Some dancers in one of the focus groups noted that another way in which third parties had shown them that they cared was to provide "reference letters … to say that I was a good, reliable employee. Sometimes they were kind enough to disguise it [the job] so I wouldn't be prejudiced [discriminated against]" (Leigh, dancer).

For some third parties, concern about the consequences of stigma on dancers manifested in a feeling that clubs should be more proactive in regard to worker well-being and labour rights. Acknowledging that the parallel structures foster problematic labour conditions for dancers, Chico (DJ) admitted, "We don't treat our employees right, or you know, we don't treat everybody as equal employees … I mean, racism is a big part of [it]." Like some other third parties, Chico wanted to see "more protection for the worker … It'll be better for the entire industry." Although, as noted in chapters 2 and 3, labour protections have not been a panacea in the mainstream labour force, Chico's reflections underscore their potential to address egregious violations such as racial discrimination in hiring and scheduling practices.

Concluding Remarks: Togetherness and Stratification in the Strip Club

As this chapter has shown, third parties are subject to stigma in ways that are informed by gender, class, and racialization: they are perceived as underclass men who are either dangerous or lacking in intelligence/education, risky (particularly if they are unaffiliated), and sexual deviants. As with dancers (Thompson & Harred, 1992; Trautner & Collett, 2010), for third parties, managing stigma involves continually navigating the tension between the insider knowledge of working as and with stigmatized workers, and the dominant framings of both – in other words, they adhere to some stigmatic assumptions about dancers, themselves, and their counterparts, even though they should and, in many respects, do know better. When third parties manage this tension successfully, they are able to better enjoy their work and suffer fewer social consequences. Further, when third parties consciously reject dichotomous normative tropes such as exploiter/exploited and good girl/bad girl, the results can include better organizational practices and labour relations, and the promotion of positive perceptions of dancers. As Chico (DJ) put it, this can also be good for business: "We're all in this together; let's have a good time, you know ... If we're going to work ... and if we enjoy ourselves, I think we'll do well because the entertainment aspect is – anybody who looks like they're enjoying themselves, they're usually at their best." Conversely, third parties' perception of dancers' (presumed) conduct as immoral can lead to abuses of power, including severe discipline, humiliation, or sexual harassment – illustrating how the "whore stigma" can precipitate concrete effects that perpetuate perceptions of unchastity and defilement (Pheterson, 1998). Thus, the pervasiveness of stigma and its power to stratify and divide has particular consequences for workers in the erotic dance sector: it exerts a considerable influence on interpersonal relations and third parties' and strippers' abilities to cooperate with and help each other, even as – and because – both suffer from it in significant ways.

Conclusion

The Good, the Bad, and the Future of Strip Club Management

As this book has argued, there is more going on at strip clubs than the impressions conveyed through strippers' and third parties' performances: like other kinds of organizations, strip clubs "are communities of people, and therefore behave just like other communities. They compete amongst themselves for power and resources, there are differences of opinion and of values, conflicts of priorities and of goals [and] ... clashes of personality and bonds of alliance" (Handy, 1993, p. 291). Examining third parties' roles, and personal, organizational, and business relationships with strippers allows us to understand what third parties do (and neglect to do); see beneficial as well as problematic practices and relationships; distinguish degrees and kinds of abuse and exploitation (including workplace sexual harassment and unpaid labour); and identify pragmatic solutions that could be possible or already exist within broader legal and labour market structures. This chapter extends these arguments to a broader scale to consider their implications for strippers and other sex workers. It begins by summarizing best and bad practices in the erotic dance sector and then turns to consider how they relate to regulatory approaches and mechanisms. In closing, it offers a reflection on the continued relevance of understanding workplace issues in the erotic dance sector and their implications for the management and regulation of other sectors in the context of a changing sex industry, labour market, and society, even in the face of an uncertain future for strip clubs.

Respecting Workers and Women: Industry Best Practices

While this chapter focuses mostly on key issues facing dancers, in order to suggest changes to government policies and strip club practices that would help address these issues, it is also important not to overlook good practices. To this end, this section presents descriptions by research participants of a number of third-party practices that demonstrate care, highlight the necessity of the services that third parties offer, and could serve as industry standards against which individual workplaces and third parties could be measured. Illustrative of what it means to be a good and fair boss, service provider, support person, or security provider, these practices pertain to safety, rights, professionalism, and equitable hiring.

Across their diverse responsibilities and job titles, good third parties care about strippers' safety and well-being. This is visible in their realistic assessments of the risks posed by customers (e.g., acknowledging theft as well as violence) and also the risks not presented by dancers (e.g., rejecting the moralizing framing of strippers as vectors of disease). It is also evident in their responses to these risks, both in terms of preventive policies such as screening and informing customers of service prices, and in the consistent practice of risk-management measures, including reasonable surveillance and quick and appropriate responses to problematic customer behaviours. Other ways third parties demonstrate that they care are through their efforts to protect strippers from dangers associated with substance (ab)use by supplying alternatives to alcoholic drinks, ensuring that overly intoxicated dancers get into a cab safely, and providing a private place to smoke. In a similar vein, when absent of gendered responsibilization, advising dancers to refrain from getting (too) inebriated at work can be practical advice that, notably, would not be considered unreasonable in mainstream workplaces, and that shows that third parties care more about dancers' safety than about the club profiting from selling a few more drinks.

Professional conduct was another quality dancers appreciated in third parties. For some strippers and third parties, professionalism among managers, bouncers, and DJs simply means being approachable in a way that is mindful of the difference between friendliness and sexual harassment. Furthermore, some third parties suggested that they would like to see strippers be more professional and/or successful, and they encouraged these outcomes by helping dancers with clients (e.g., when managers or bouncers set dancers up with a customer without expecting or demanding a tip in return) or with aspects of their stage show (e.g., DJs who help with music selection or editing, or communicate stage show times well in advance). Given that the parallel organizational structures of strip clubs can, in concert with the onus to perform in the presence of customers, lead third parties to (mistakenly) share customers' impression of dancers as flirts rather than workers, such efforts may be difficult in the "party" environment. Inasmuch as the party environment informs organizational culture, however, Lerum (2004) has argued that a sexualized work environment can feel like camaraderie rather than sexual harassment if subordinate workers do not feel precarious. From this perspective, other organizational practices and policies become relevant to workers' comfort in interactions with management, which will be undermined if dancers fear unpredictable and unreasonable reprisal for rule breaking or worry they may be fired for a change in their appearance, such as weight gain. Thus, more professionalism and respect, accompanied by fairer personnel-management practices, could change strip club organizational culture for the better.

Research participants enumerated some good practices relating to staffing (an area that, as the coming section elaborates, could be improved in many ways). Some of these practices evince a recognition that stripping is not a universally or necessarily lastingly appealing occupation. For third parties charged with hiring, like managers, this recognition meant not pressuring waitresses or waitressing applicants to become strippers. Indeed, in contrast to Barton's (2006) observation about management exerting such pressure, none of the research participants indicated that they had ever seen or done this (at least intentionally, recalling the admission of Reverend (manager/bouncer) that sometimes he mistakenly initially assumed aspiring waitresses were applying to be dancers). Further, Dalton's (manager) trial process for new dancers (circling the room in their underwear) in effect prevented women uncomfortable with stripping from working even one night. Owners and managers offering waitressing jobs to dancers who want to retire from stripping or letters of reference for apartments similarly evinces a recognition of other particularities of stripping – namely, that dancers may encounter barriers to conventional employment opportunities and housing due to stigma.

Underlying the abovementioned good qualities and practices, albeit perhaps indirectly, lies concern for dancers' human and labour rights. This was evident in third parties' objections to punitive regulations such as the criminalization of prostitution and bylaws prohibiting touching, as well as to inequitable organizational practices such as racist staffing and scheduling, and arbitrary firing. Unfortunately, the third parties who espoused these critiques were usually too low in the organizational hierarchy – as DJs, bartender, bouncers, and managers rather than club owners – to change workplace policies, which also demonstrates their precarity and vulnerability to termination as low- to medium-waged, non-unionized workers in a stigmatized segment of the private sector. Other actions in support of dancers' human rights can be carried out at the individual level. For example, speaking out against stigma – as some third parties did to customers, family members, and acquaintances, as well as disrespectful or shame-filled colleagues – would contribute to both strippers' and third parties' well-being.

Examining Sectoral and Organizational Bad Practices Intersectionally

While bad third-party practices are, simply put, the absence or opposite of the above-mentioned good practices, it is important to note that they occur at and are facilitated through various intersecting and mutually reinforcing mechanisms. In other words, they are not merely individual but organizational, systemic, normative, and regulatory, overlapping with and informed by broader social inequalities. Among these are a number of issues relating to racial and gender inequality.

For dancers, limits on the number of Black women allowed on club rosters and per shift is not only a significant trend across Ontario's erotic dance sector (even though it is not practised in every club); it is also informed by broader beauty standards that continue to privilege white, feminine, and also young and slim, women. There is some evidence that suggests the beauty and fashion industries are slowly changing – for example, beauty products catering to an expanding range of skin tones, record-breaking beauty pageant wins for Black women (Zaveri, 2019), and somewhat more diversity in race, age, and size in fashion shows and shoots (Entwistle et al., 2019). Nonetheless, lookism continues to pervade mainstream labour sectors, such that those who embody a conventionally attractive aesthetic (middle-class, white, heterosexual, and fit) are rewarded with more income and employment opportunities, especially if they are women (Cawley, 2004; Hersch, 2008; Liu & Sierminska, 2014). Meanwhile, racialized people working in predominantly white organizations continue to feel pressured to manage their presentation of self to appear professional in the face of normative assumptions and micro-aggressions that undermine the recognition of their work and skills (Sue et al., 2007; Wingfield & Skeete, 2016). These apparently contradictory cultural and labour market trends suggest that transforming normative conceptions of beauty and competence will take time. Moreover, in contrast to mainstream enterprises like beauty and fashion companies, which are concerned with managing their public relations, public scrutiny that is directed largely at the presumed exploitation of women in general by strip clubs presents no motivation for strip club operators to improve specifically discriminatory practices.

The paucity of women managers, bouncers, and DJs at strip clubs can also be seen as employment inequality, although it should be noted that these positions may be relatively less appealing to women, who may not want to work surrounded by scantily clad strippers and fully dressed men, or confront the stigma and/or risks that third-party work entails. Nevertheless, the rarity of women strip club managers is somewhat analogous to broader occupational inequities, given that men occupy nearly two-thirds of management occupations in Canada (Statistics Canada, 2020). Although it is difficult to estimate the proportion of women managers in Ontario strip clubs on the basis of a qualitative study such as this, anecdotally it appears to be much lower than the overall proportion of women managers in Canada (35.9 per cent) (Statistics Canada, 2020), even though participants suggested that women are equally capable of performing managerial and security duties at strip clubs (albeit using different gendered strategies). The low proportion of women in third-party positions at strip clubs could, in turn, play a part in the more problematic elements of organizational culture – namely, the tolerance of workplace sexual harassment and apathy toward or neglect of dancers' safety concerns. On one hand, organization scholars have found that minority representation of at least 30 per cent, along with buy-in from organizational leadership and the provision of training, is required to change gendered organizational norms and power dynamics (Centola et al., 2018; Coe et al., 2019). On the other hand, research on other sectors of the sex industry where women operators are more common suggests that women may not be better or fairer bosses than men, even if they have sex work experience (Bruckert & Law, 2013) – an important reminder that alleviating gendered inequalities in the workplace does not negate the inherent inequality of employer-worker relations.

The precarity and inapplicability of labour-protection mechanisms engendered by club management's classification of strippers as independent contractors are also problematic. Moreover, the fact that Ottawa dancers are subject to mandatory unpaid scheduling obligations – and so are treated, in effect, like Toronto "housegirls" but without the (paltry) shift pay – demonstrates that strip clubs in Ottawa continue to violate the distinction between independent (freelancers) and dependent contractors (scheduled dancers) drawn in the *Canadian Labour Congress (Canadian Association of Burlesque Entertainers, Local Union No. 1689) v Algonquin Tavern* (1981) decision (*CABE v Algonquin Tavern*). That dancers, furthermore, do not appear to have the collective organizing capacity to compel clubs to enact this distinction highlights some significant limitations of provincial labour mechanisms. The enforcement of the *Occupational Health and Safety Act* requires collective action – for example, the proactive formation of a joint health and safety committee, or a worker representative who can accompany a ministry agent on a workplace inspection. At the same time, the comparatively reactive *Employment Standards Act* is an avenue through which individuals can claim unpaid wages but is available only to dependant contractors (Vosko, Tucker, et al., 2011).

As this book has highlighted, dancers' status as independent contractors also informs their relationship with club-affiliated third parties. Without the incentive (for many) of a wage, or a guarantee that third parties will protect them from customers who violate their personal boundaries but not the ambiance of the club, it is understandable that strippers may not be motivated to arrive on time for scheduled shifts, or may try to avoid or reschedule a stage show. The divide between the parallel structures of the club is, in turn, shaped and exacerbated by the onus on third parties and dancers to continually maintain their performances for customers in their shared front region. In this contrived "party," third parties can believe strippers' performances too much, such that this impression invisibilizes dancers' status as workers and delegitimizes their labour rights and occupational health and safety claims (e.g., about inadequate service or facility upkeep).

At the same time, it is important to acknowledge that, for those below the level of club ownership – like the managers, DJs, bouncers, and bartender who participated in this study – third parties' perspective on their own work and (for some) their apathy toward it is informed by their position as wage labourers who feel precarious and who are also subject to money-saving strategies by club owners, including not paying benefits and relying on formal or informal tip-out policies to supplement wages. In this context, resentment toward dancers, whom they perceive as earning comparatively more money, is understandable (but nevertheless unprofessional). In a workplace where occupational performances are gendered for both third parties and dancers, earning less than dancers may also feel like an affront to third parties' masculinity, illustrating the far-reaching effects of the stubborn norm of the male breadwinner that has produced and maintained the gendered wage gap (Vosko & Clark, 2009). Thus, bad practices of individual third parties and problematic policies at particular clubs are informed by intersecting systemic factors including labour regulation and gendered, racialized, and classed constructions of work, professionalism, and desirability.

Navigating Nebulous Laws

Other practices, norms, and policies at strip clubs are harder to classify as beneficial or harmful to dancers because they are informed by inconsistencies between municipal, provincial, and federal criminal regulations and their enforcement by state actors. In this context, third parties elect to follow the regulations least likely to interfere with the financial goals or ambiance of the club. For example, dancers reported that, at least in some clubs, third parties put up signs indicating the risks of sexual contact and that physical contact is not allowed. While dancers may not think public health signage is relevant or that posting the touching rules is effective, both practices are in keeping with public health and bylaw compliance responsibilities,[1] and a realistic outlook on the provision of "extras." Signage can also serve as a visual reminder to customers and a resource for third parties (and dancers) should they need to reference official regulations in their attempts to manage customer behaviour.

In addition to proactively observing bylaws that are low cost and easy to follow (i.e., that do not compete with lap dancing or alcohol sales), third parties also adhere to regulations that are actively enforced (and therefore high risk to ignore). According to participants, municipal surveillance for the purposes of bylaw compliance attends only to egregious violations of the sexual touching prohibition, and to compliance with recordkeeping in regard to dancers (in Ottawa) or with the validity of adult entertainer licences (in Toronto). Evincing municipal authorities' preoccupation with moralistic, rather than health and safety, concerns, third parties and dancers noted that inspections by police and other municipal agents routinely neglect to attend to the physical conditions of the establishment, in spite of bylaws stipulating that "premises and all fixtures and equipment ... shall be regularly washed and kept in a sanitary condition" (*Toronto Municipal Code*, 2019, 545, s. 377(b); see also Ottawa Bylaw No. 2002-189, ss. 23(1)(b) and (e)). In turn, dancers reported that club management largely ignores bylaws stipulating cleanliness and proper maintenance of facilities. In the context of COVID-19, third parties and municipal authorities have paid closer – though, according to strippers, not necessarily adequate – attention to workplace public health protection measures (Kassam, 2020), ushered in by stigmatizing comments about strip clubs by municipal and provincial leaders (Krishnan, 2020). These requirements (masks, social distancing, contact tracing) have, of course, been pandemic-specific, and it remains to be seen if they will lead to any lasting changes in strip club occupational health and safety practices or enforcement.

While the failure to adhere to health and safety standards operates exclusively to dancers' detriment, the flouting of municipal bylaws against drug and alcohol intoxication as well as provincial liquor regulations against over-serving can benefit them – and, of course, the club's profits – by contributing to the party environment and encouraging customers to stay and spend, even as it may increase clients' likelihood of engaging in offensive or dangerous behaviour. This conflict may explain why only one stripper participant reported calling bylaw authorities about her club's physical conditions: dancers may see calling bylaw enforcement as too risky, given that they are vulnerable to being charged for violating the provisions against sexual touching. Moreover, as contractors, they also stand to lose income if the club at which they usually work is temporarily closed as a result of failing to respect occupational health and safety standards or liquor regulations.

In the dual context of an apparent decline in touching-related bylaw infraction charges and the continued criminalization of facilitating the provision of sexual services, third parties are motivated to wilfully ignore touching and (to varying extents) the provision of extras. In one respect, wilful ignorance by third parties leaves dancers free to decide their own boundaries, but in return, third parties (to varying extents) expect dancers to manage their own issues with customers. With such responsibilization comes blame (which, in the context of a sexualized occupation, and especially the provision of sexual services, is compounded by stigma). Wilful ignorance can also limit third parties' ability to respond to dancers' security concerns in a timely manner. While it appears that at least some municipal staff and representatives in Toronto are privy to and concerned about such issues (see Law, 2015), the most recent review of Toronto's bylaws (in 2012) fell short of implementing changes that would alleviate them – for example, by removing bylaws around touching or rewording them to centre consent.

This grey area between regulation and enforcement is further complicated by the above-mentioned inapplicability of labour protections, making the absence of training all the more salient. Given that licences are required for owners and operators (i.e., third parties with managerial responsibilities) in Ottawa and Toronto, municipalities are missing an important opportunity to educate new and renewing strip club operators, not only about pertinent health and safety–related bylaws such as those relating to facility upkeep and cleanliness noted above, but also about what kind of behaviour by customers or other workers constitutes a violation of criminal law (including that the lowest threshold of sexual assault is any unwanted touch) or workplace harassment or discrimination according to provincial labour law, and to provide guidelines about how third parties should respond. Such education may address some of the problematic reactions reported by dancers, including of third parties not taking seriously their complaints about customers who refuse to pay the amount owing for services provided, or who cross their boundaries or attempt or commit violent sexual assault. Here it is important to remember dancers' assessments of customers as mostly harmless, which suggests that what they do report to third parties is indeed serious enough to merit a response, and that that strip clubs would not be empty of customers if such rules were properly enforced.

Dancers, too, would benefit from being provided with more information by municipal authorities upon application for or renewal of a licence or through printed or online materials or visits to clubs. Useful information might include an explanation of the bylaws and of dancers' rights (the services and standards to which they are entitled) and responsibilities (what kinds of touching and services are prohibited) specified therein. Greater awareness of such information among strippers could increase the use of existing municipal redress mechanisms, such as Toronto's Municipal Standards Complaints and Information Line. At the same time, given the historical lack of interest in the enforcement of occupational health and safety regulations, as well as dancers' entrepreneurial interests and vulnerabilities, peer education among dancers would remain important. On this point, participants reported a number of informal peer-training practices, including more experienced strippers mentoring new colleagues on how to give lap dances, watching each other's stage shows, and peer surveillance with the goal of ensuring consistent services and prices and fair competition. At various times, strippers have also offered information more formally through peer organizations.[2] Given that dancers ultimately decide what they are comfortable and not comfortable doing in their interactions with customers, their practice of deciding on and reinforcing their own boundaries will remain an important part of their work and self-protection strategies regardless of changes to bylaws.

The last point underscores the importance of prevention – not only of sexual assault at strip clubs but also of sexual harassment by both customers and third parties. As chapter 1 has argued about third parties and chapter 5 about clients, the men who manage and patronize strip clubs are not a separate and deviant sub-population but rather ordinary people who participate in mainstream work and social activities (see also Egan, 2006a; Lowman & Atchison, 2006). Prevention efforts should, in turn, be aimed at the general population, which would benefit not only strippers but women (and other groups marginalized for their gender expression or sexual preferences) across workplaces, entertainment venues, educational institutions, intimate partnerships, and the criminal justice system. Scholars have argued that the most promising approach to preventing gendered violence is broadly inclusive sexual education programming offered throughout children's school years, touching on topics such as gender norms and expressions, gender and sexual diversity, relationship building, sexual consent and communication, respect and boundaries, risk-reduction tools and measures, and emotion management (Schneider & Hirsch, 2018; SIECCAN, 2019). Michau et al. (2015) have similarly lauded broader approaches to preventing gendered violence, such as community education programs and coordinated efforts across institutional settings that aim to change not only behaviours but also gender and sexual norms in romantic relationships, families, and workplaces.

As feminist scholars (e.g., Pheterson, 1998; Smart, 1989; Vance, 1992) have long argued, however, as long as women's sexual activity and pleasure remain taboo, and acceptable sex remains confined to non-interactional, private relationships in which women are the gatekeepers of consent and of men's sexual pleasure, sexual and gender relations will remain unequal. Until these norms change, the responsibility will continue to fall on women to protect themselves. This is just as true for strippers responsibilized to police their sexual boundaries and blamed by third parties when these efforts fail to prevent sexual assault as it is for university students advised to not dress like "sluts" and/or to exercise vigilance to minimize their chances of being sexually assaulted (Ikeda & Rosser, 2010; Reger, 2014), and for women complainants whose "provocative" behaviour or outfit or "risky" lifestyle is scrutinized by police, defence lawyers, and judges in their responses to sexual assault, especially if the complainants are Black, Indigenous, or visibly poor (Craig, 2016; Crenshaw, 1991; DuBois, 2012). Such expectations also serve as an important reminder that engaging in the politics of sexual respectability, even in the name of women's best interests – for example, in campaigns to rid neighbourhoods of strip clubs or street-based sex work, or to educate Indigenous women and girls to help them not become victims of trafficking – only perpetuates the disposability of othered women (Chateauvert, 2013; Lowman, 2000; Maynard, 2015).

Strip Clubs Now: Reflecting on Contemporary Trends and Future Implications

Even as strippers are impacted by, and would benefit from general efforts toward addressing, issues relating to intersectional gendered and workplace inequalities, it is important to note that the erotic dance sector is already undergoing significant change informed by broader social trends. Indeed, industry change was a topic broached by a number of research participants – third parties and strippers alike – who voiced concern about the decline in the novelty, popularity, and financial success of strip clubs. The strip club landscape in Ottawa and Toronto over the past decade is telling in this regard: at the beginning of the data-collection period for this research (2011), there were seventeen strip clubs in Toronto (two having closed in the two years before the study) and nine in Ottawa; at the time of publication, there remain only seven licensed adult entertainment clubs in Toronto and three in Ottawa.

News reporters and academics have speculated and disagreed about why strip clubs are declining, citing a range of socio-cultural trends that may have contributed. These include the proliferation of other sexual services delivered through other types of venues (e.g., erotic massage parlours) and online platforms (e.g., webcam sites); the value of the land strip clubs occupy and the temptation for owners to sell to condo developers in a booming housing market; the "changing tastes of millennials" (Villeneuve, 2017, n.p.); and the shrinking appeal of a no-longer-as-taboo form of entertainment (Brents & Sanders, 2010; Deachman, 2019; Dmitrieva, 2017; Hayes, 2018; Hunter, 2017). Economic trends – including the global 2008 recession; the decline in the quality, stability, and salary of working-class occupations; and more women in formerly male-dominated (and strip club–going) occupations such as investment banking – have also informed a decrease in dancers' income (Brents & Sanders, 2010; Hardy & Sanders, 2015; Hayes, 2018; Lister, 2015). Meanwhile, in spite of inflation and increases in house fees over the past few years, lap dances remain $20 per song.

More recently, the COVID-19 pandemic and the accompanying restrictions on gatherings and non-essential businesses have had particularly significant consequences for strippers (and other in-person sex workers), including outbreaks, inadequate managerial prevention measures, and temporary closures, as well as public health guidelines (e.g., mask mandates, reduced hours and/or capacity, socially distanced dancing) that shifted numerous times during the pandemic (Kassam, 2020; Work Safe Twerk Safe, 2020, 2022). In this context, dancers – some of whom, like other economically marginalized sex workers, did not qualify for federal pandemic relief funds (Benoit & Unsworth, 2022; Lam, 2020) – had to look for other income-generation avenues. For some, this has meant migrating online – a notably different environment than in-person stripping, and one that involves different skills and privacy concerns. Online work allowed strippers who had been excluded because of conventional beauty standards to organize, most notably in a series of virtual strip events featuring Black queer performers put on by Toronto sex worker organization Maggie's with Strapped TO (Gowland, 2020; Singh, 2020). With the relaxing of provincially mandated quarantining and social-distance measures, clubs have reopened, and customers have returned, but strippers have observed that venues have shorter hours and are open fewer days of the week, and are more likely to demand stage shows (Work Safe Twerk Safe, personal communication, 6 October 2022). In addition, searches of Toronto's business licence database reveal that three clubs closed between February and October 2022.

Although the above-noted trends suggest that strip clubs are a shrinking portion of both the sex industry and Ontario's cultural and economic landscape, they nevertheless remain an important site of income generation for a considerable number of women. Scholars have suggested that stripping has become a more palatable job to a broader swath of women due to an increase in both push (e.g., rising tuition fees) and pull (e.g., more sexual open-mindedness) factors (Brents & Sanders, 2010; Hardy & Sanders, 2015). Some have argued that this apparent contradiction has increased competition among dancers and, in turn, has heightened pressure to provide extras (Bouclin, 2006; Lister, 2015; Maticka-Tyndale, 2004). Considering the broader labour market context – the COVID-19 pandemic aside – these factors do not necessarily mean stripping has become a worse option. Hardy and Sanders (2015) surmise that wage declines in conventional jobs may be increasing women's reliance on informal work such as stripping as a secondary source of income. This hypothesis is supported in general terms by data gathered by Statistics Canada linking a growth of self-employed informal labour in Canada ("gig" work) between 2005 and 2016 to a "growth in the percentage both of gig workers who earned no wages or salaries (T4 income) and of gig workers who combined gig work with wages or salaries" (Jeon et al., 2019, p. 6).

Far from meaning that the information gleaned from a study such as this is unimportant, the decline of strip clubs provides evidence that has significant implications for what we know (or, rather, assume) about the sex industry and its management and regulation. First, the fact that the erotic dance sector is legal and also declining counters a key claim of prostitution prohibitionists: that the legalization of commercialized sexual services (which they understand as not qualitatively different from decriminalization) leads directly to the expansion of the sex industry (e.g., Farley, 2004; Raymond, 2003). Anti-prostitution activists further claim that the removal of criminal sanctions incentivizes criminals to funnel trafficked women into strip clubs because they are less likely to be caught. Yet, as Weitzer (2012) argues, it is more plausible "that most club owners would be averse to hiring trafficked or coerced dancers, for fear of attracting attention from law enforcement and perhaps losing their business license" (p. 1359) – an argument that accords with the observations and experiences of participants of this study.

Second, changes in the erotic dance sector in recent years also counter sex industry prohibitionists' corollary claim: that prohibitive regulation – in this case, municipal bylaws against sexual touching – is effective in combating sexual exploitation. This assertion comprises two interrelated claims: that prohibitive regulation prevents commercialized sexual services and also (simultaneously, because prohibitionists frame them as one and the same) sexual violence. In fact it does neither. Bylaws prohibiting sexual touching have not stopped client violence, as evinced by third parties' and dancers' ongoing concerns about and strategies to manage it – a finding analogous to the slight increase in workplace violence in other sex industry sectors since Canada criminalized the purchase of sexual services (Machat et al., 2019). In spite of being overly broadly construed, bylaws prohibiting sexual touching have also failed to stop lap dancing. On the surface the decline in the number of strip clubs may appear to suggest that prohibitive regulation engenders a decline in business. Yet, the relaxing of enforcement practices over a period in which touching and extras have increased evince that commercialized sexual practices can become normalized in spite of prohibitive regulation. This further suggests that the market appeal of lap dances has not been hindered by prohibitive regulation but, instead, by other socio-economic factors such as those enumerated above.

Third, Ontario's erotic dance sector provides an important example of legalization that can be compared to other countries where sex-related businesses have been legalized rather than decriminalized. As Bruckert and Hannem (2013a) explain, legalization – that is, the creation of laws specific to sex work, an approach distinct from decriminalization, which simply removes criminal laws prohibiting sex work – often manifests as structural stigma because it seeks to manage particular risks sex work is presumed to pose in a way that is not actually beneficial to sex workers. For example, Ontario municipalities' zoning and operator licence restrictions are comparable to brothel licensing in Nevada and the Netherlands, both legalized jurisdictions where administrative responsibilities and costs prohibit small-scale entrepreneurs from opening businesses. As a result, competition is minimized, and larger operations can continue to engage in exploitative labour practices, including classifying sex workers as independent contractors and charging exorbitant fees to work (Bruckert & Hannem, 2013a; van Wijk & Mascini, 2019). Similarly, limits on the number of strip clubs, as well as the administrative hurdles and expense involved in transferring or applying for a new licence, make it too costly and onerous for Ontario strippers to open their own club in order to provide better working conditions (Hayes, 2018). Such morally informed surveillance accompanied by a dearth of labour oversight – typical of legalized approaches (Bruckert & Hannem, 2013a) – demonstrate that the current approach to strip clubs in Ontario is not beneficial to strippers, nor is it as a model for how the regulation of sex work in Canada *should* look.

In contrast, decriminalization, as evinced in New Zealand's approach to sex work, can improve sex workers' relationships with police[3] and facilitate their access to labour, human rights, and health and safety legislation, fostering "a sense of entitlement to protection [among sex workers], as opposed to a sense that nothing can be done" (Healy et al., 2017, p. 56). Notably, with regard to prohibitionists' and strippers' respective concerns, decriminalization in New Zealand has neither increased the participation of women and organized crime in the sex industry nor eroded the distinction between stripping and prostitution (Abel et al., 2009; Healy et al., 2017). Brothel licences, mandatory for establishments employing five or more sex workers, were introduced in New Zealand as a means for the state to exclude organized or otherwise unscrupulous criminals from operating sex industry businesses. The legislation also combats exploitation by allowing for smaller sex-worker collectives and independent workers (Healy et al., 2017). As Bruckert and Hannem (2013a) argue, however, while New Zealand's approach, for the most part, regulates sex work as labour, it retains some elements of stigma, visible in "provisions that are redundant in light of existing criminal laws prohibiting sexual assault, sexual exploitation, blackmail, assault, and drug trafficking," betraying a modicum of "acceptance of the prevailing discourses linking sex work with exploitation and drug use" (p. 60). These remnants of stigma notwithstanding, New Zealand's approach can be described as focusing on health, safety, and well-being – a direction that Ontario municipalities, which already have strip club–specific occupational health and safety regulations in their bylaws, could shift toward, if they cared to do so. In short, if there is anything to be learned from the regulatory mistakes made in regard to Ontario strip clubs, it is that regulating sexual labour as labour is effective, or possible, only when there is a conscious shift away from moral regulation, that is, regulatory effort emanating from and reinforcing "the wrongness of some conduct, habit or disposition" (Hunt, 1997, p. 280).

Although, in the context of the sex industry, strip clubs are relatively tame, insofar as they offer only limited sexual contact, the arguments made in this book can be extended to brothels, erotic massage parlours, and escort agencies. These are businesses run by ordinary people who can be apathetic, shrewd, or caring business operators and whose approaches haves consequences for workers: sex workers will not be able to improve their working conditions if no one cares to enforce the regulations, such as those related to occupational health and safety, that they want enforced. Descriptions provided by participants of individuals unaffiliated to strip clubs – for example, drivers offering services comparable to taxis as well as those who also offer security, and relationships that sounded more like financial intimate partner abuse than organizing, supervising, or coordinating a stripper's work (see also Law, 2020) – can similarly apply to other sex industry sectors, insofar as they demonstrate the importance of empirically examining rather than relying on normative assumptions about third parties. In this regard, qualitatively differentiating between exploitative, neutral, and beneficial third-party relationships can help gauge when and precisely what responses are appropriate – for example, criminal sanction, peer support, or workplace oversight – or alternatively, when no intervention is required.

Final Remarks: Stripping, Sex Work, and Management in Perspective

As this chapter has suggested, much of the conflict between strippers and third parties and many of the problematic aspects of strip club management are related to broader socio-economic trends. In this respect, the challenges faced by and strategies of strip club workers can be seen as analogous and related to the struggles encountered by workers in other sectors of the contemporary labour market. As highlighted in chapter 2, strip club operators were early adopters of approaches to employment relations that have since become popular in the wider world of work, visible in the expansion of precarious labour and the gig economy. The attention dancers brought to their working conditions in *CABE v Algonquin Tavern* (1981) culminated in recognition by the Ontario Labour Relations Board (OLRB) of scheduled dancers as dependent contractors subject to employment-like conditions of control over their labour. *CABE v Algonquin Tavern* became a "seminal case" that facilitated the identification of "relevant factors" to which the OLRB "has consistently returned ... when examining whether an individual or group of individuals are acting as dependent contractors or independent contractors" (*Canadian Union of Postal Workers v Foodora Inc.*, 2020, para. 81). At issue in *CABE v Algonquin Tavern* and many subsequent OLRB cases were concerns shared by strippers and other workers alike that speak to the divergent interests of workers and management with respect to wages, benefits, and the right to collectively defend their interests. Food deliverers for the app-based delivery service Foodora, who, like dancers, were classified by the company as independent contractors, recently challenged that classification. In February 2020, in its "first decision with respect to workers in ... 'the gig economy'" (*Canadian Union of Postal Workers v Foodora Inc.*, 2020, para. 171), the OLRB ruled that Foodora workers are dependent contractors, because the employer exercises control over them by setting their pay rates and controlling their shifts. Shortly thereafter, Foodora announced it was closing its Canadian operations. Because the decision had allowed them to unionize, however, former Foodora workers were able to win a $3.46-million settlement from the company (CUPW, 2020).

Although the *Algonquin Tavern* decision excluded freelance dancers, affirming that they were independent contractors because they could work for multiple establishments and control their own schedules, another important element of the case applies to all strippers: like subsequent court cases brought by dancers against management (see the discussion in chapter 2; see also Bouclin, 2004; Gall, 2016), it highlights the difference regulation makes. *CABE v Algonquin Tavern* (1981) pragmatically and non-judgmentally compared and contrasted labour relations at strip clubs to those in other types of sectors and occupations – including musicians, journalists, and photographers – and has since been used to facilitate comparisons between strippers and construction workers, taxicab drivers, and truck drivers, among others. Conversely, the winning strategy adopted by the appellants, their lawyers, and interveners in *Canada v Bedford* (2013) – a constitutional challenge brought by sex workers to Canada's prostitution laws – was effective precisely because it redirected popular assumptions about the dangers of sex work toward the dangers posed by the constraining effects of the law. They argued that the criminalization of bawdy houses and communication had facilitated the murder of street-based sex workers by serial killer Robert Pickton. Nonetheless, as Lawrence (2015) argues, the federal Conservative government subsequently mobilized the spectre of Pickton to instead "[represent] the grim reality of sex workers' lives, or rather, deaths" (p. 7) and introduce a new set of laws that effectively recriminalized many of the aspects struck down in *Canada v Bedford*.

These federal laws, introduced in 2014 via the tellingly titled *Protection of Communities and Exploited Persons Act* (*PCEPA*), criminalize the purchase but not the sale of sexual services, in order to condemn sex buyers and managers and to "encourage those who engage in prostitution to report incidents of violence and to leave prostitution" (preamble). Following an international trend often referred to as the Swedish or Nordic model, this approach conflates sex trafficking (coerced participation in the sex industry involving forcible confinement and/or debt bondage) with sex work (consensual exchange of sexual services for material reward) by framing managerial individuals as people who facilitate sexual exploitation. Sex workers have critiqued this "partial" criminalization as ideological rather than evidence-led, and as having the same effects as full criminalization, insofar as they are still harassed, ignored, charged, and even deported through the intermeshing of anti-prostitution and immigration laws that forbid migrants from working at relatively legal (i.e., licensed rather than criminalized) sex industry businesses, including strip clubs (Fuckförbundet, 2019; Lam & Lepp, 2019; Sex Workers United Against Violence et al., 2014).

A recent constitutional challenge against these new laws by the Canadian Alliance for Sex Work Law Reform (CASWLR), a coalition of sex worker rights groups, "challenges all of the sex work offences together … and includes legal arguments related to a much broader range of Charter rights" (CASWLR, 2022, p. 3) than *Bedford* or previous post-*PCEPA* cases (e.g., *R v Anwar*, 2020). The CASWLR argues that sex workers' rights to equality, bodily autonomy, and freedom of expression and association – in addition to the right to life, liberty, and security underpinning *Bedford* – are violated by the *PCEPA* (CASWLR, 2022). In its inclusion of a broader scope of rights, this challenge expands beyond the narrow purview of criminal law, which constrains the focus even of arguments contesting it to risk as a proxy for moral judgment (Bruckert & Hannem, 2013a; Hunt, 2003). The challenge was heard in the Ontario Superior Court only in October 2022, and the CASWLR expects the battle to be lengthy (CASWLR, 2022; Chu & Clamen, 2022). In the end, though, the case may open the way for workers across the sex industry in Canada to avail themselves of non-criminal legal and rights mechanisms to contest unequal power relations and problematic managerial practices.

Strippers' engagements with civil and administrative law illustrate both the potential of such avenues as well as their limitations and frustrations. Individually, some strippers have filed and won racial discrimination claims (*Varma v G.B. Allright Enterprises*, 1988; *Roberts v Club Expose*, 1993), but other civil or employment-related claims have not been successful (e.g., *Peck v Chomyc Hotels*, 1989). Moreover, the paucity of such claims by strippers in Canadian legal database records, particularly in the lap-dancing era, evinces how stigma can be a barrier to legal processes, especially those requiring and then documenting one's legal name. On this issue, a recent collective legal action has been successful, even though its main objective was derisively dismissed in court: in its judicial review contesting Ontario's stigmatizing approach and lack of consultation of dancers in its governance of strip clubs during the COVID-19 pandemic, peer-led stripper group Work Safe Twerk Safe (WSTS) first had to petition the court for anonymity for its affiants. The court granted the anonymization motion on the basis that WSTS had "demonstrated risk of harm that is more than speculative and more than embarrassment or humiliation" (*Work Safe Twerk Safe v Ontario* 2021a, para. 29). The group lauded this decision as a recognition of the risk of reprisal from management but also, and more importantly, a possibly precedent-setting recognition of stigma as a reason for anonymization in legal claims of marginalized groups (Work Safe Twerk Safe, 2021). This decision allowed them to move forward with the judicial review, which did not aim to limit COVID-19 safety measures but rather to include strippers in the development of workplace safety plans in a context of inconsistent managerial interest in their occupational health and safety: "We are trying to get the provincial government to realize that we, as workers, are knowledgeable about workplace risks and how to manage them, and that they should respect us enough to consult us" (Work Safe Twerk Safe, 2020, n.p.). When the matter was finally heard, it was dismissed as moot because the regulation being challenged was no longer in force (Work Safe Twerk Safe, 2022; *Work Safe Twerk Safe v Ontario*, 2021b). Nevertheless, it is worth noting that neither decision considers the morality of stripping, and, indeed, the first decision recognizes strippers' concerns as a matter of public interest (*Work Safe Twerk Safe v Ontario*, 2021a).

While the above-mentioned cases are important examples of worker resistance to managerial neglect and labour rights violations, it is important to remember, as this book has argued about strip club third parties, that managers are people, who can be caring or apathetic or exploitative, and whose decisions and actions are informed by broader socio-economic factors. In other words, important details about working conditions come to light when we look beyond simplistic characterizations of sex industry management as bad – and the management of "ordinary" work as *not* bad. A symptom of the latter is how the dominant focus on "street crime" continues to overshadow corporate crime, which includes neglect leading to workplace injury and death (Bittle,

2012), and other unfair practices that do not even meet the threshold of crime, such as forcing workers to work sixty-hour weeks, paying below a living wage, or evading compensating those injured on the job (Snider, 2001). Thus, just as strip club third parties fail to consider the effects of their decisions on workers when they perpetuate discriminatory hiring practices based on staid conceptions of feminine beauty or rely only on their own understandings of acceptable workplace interactions instead of dancers' comfort or boundaries, mainstream organizational leaders also callously perpetuate an inequitable status quo – for example, when app-based online gig platforms take advantage of loopholes in labour regulation to misclassify workers, restaurant managers pressure servers to dress sexily, or military superiors refuse to respond to sexual violence in the armed forces. The scrutiny to which we subject business operators in the sex industry and elsewhere, and how we hold them accountable, should be informed by workers' articulations and experiences of the conditions they provide, empirical study of what they actually do, and good managerial practices in comparable occupations. Through such a labour lens, it is also possible to see that strippers are part of and contribute to workers' struggles for fair treatment and working conditions.

Appendix

Methodology

Although this book is informed by institutional ethnography (IE), the data on which it draws were collected through individual and focus-group interviews, and not field observation, which is also usually included in IE. The two projects through which the data were collected were a large cross-sectoral project on sex industry third parties, and my doctoral dissertation, which expanded data collection in the erotic dance sector. Both included research interviews, which were undertaken for practical and methodological reasons – among them, a concern to compare worker and management accounts of each other, with an eye toward verification and the identification of disparate views. To this end, interviewing third parties and strippers separately, and in a space removed from the workplace, minimized the possibility of their feeling inhibited about discussing workplace issues, grievances, or dissatisfaction with each other. To be inclusive of diverse and previously unidentified social actors employing, working with, or working for sex workers, both projects defined "third parties" as people with experience organizing, supervising, managing, or coordinating people working in the sex, adult, or exotic dance industries.

The first, and larger, project, Rethinking Management in the Adult and Sex Industry (hereinafter the Management Project), was conducted by a research team of professors, graduate students, sex workers, and sex worker rights advocates (see Bruckert & Parent, 2018; Bruckert & Law, 2013). It pertained to the work of third parties in eastern Canada in strip clubs; brothels, dungeons, and erotic massage parlours (incall locations); escort agencies (outcall businesses); and street-based sex work. The second project was my doctoral research, which focused on the erotic dance sector (Law, 2016). Both projects recruited participants through social media, activist listservs, personal and community networks, flyers, and snowball sampling. The Management Project additionally used newspaper advertisements and coverage, a project website, and paper mail to strip clubs. Both projects received ethics clearance through the University of Ottawa, where they were based. Throughout the research, participants' confidentiality was safeguarded with measures including the use of pseudonyms, not recording personal information, removing any identifying details from (otherwise verbatim) transcripts, and keeping the data stored in locked physical, and/or encrypted or password-protected virtual, locations.

The Management Project comprised individual interviews with third parties and focus groups with sex workers (including strippers) who had worked with third parties. The interviews were semi-structured (Barribal & While, 1994, p. 330), in order to allow for the consistency of an interview guide as well as space for elaboration and for respondents to identify and talk about complex and sensitive issues. The focus groups (Berg, 2009; Patton, 2002), which endeavoured to gather workers' perspectives on working with third parties, were a means to facilitate dynamic group discussions in which participants could brainstorm, interact, and converse, allowing the researchers to gauge commonalities and diversity of opinion. Individual interviews lasted from approximately forty-five minutes to four hours, and each focus group lasted approximately two hours. To alleviate some of the difficulties associated with recruiting sex industry workers – including stigma and feeling like an object of too much salacious scrutiny (Maggie's, n.d.) – and to show respect, participants were offered honorariums of $100 for individual interviews or $75 for focus groups. Interviews for both projects were conducted between 2011 and 2014. Participants were asked about their work experience as, or working for or with, third parties from the year 2000 to the time of the interviews, a date range chosen for its continuity of industry practices and legal responses. The Management Project erotic dance–sector interviews – including two focus groups with a total of eight strippers, and eleven individual interviews with strip club third parties – were conducted only in Toronto and Ottawa due to recruitment difficulties in Quebec and the Maritimes.

Endeavouring to gather more data on strip club management, my doctoral research used virtually the same recruitment materials and interview guide as the larger project, adjusted to reflect the language of the erotic dance sector. This interview guide touched on third parties' roles and responsibilities; their relationships with dancers and other staff; organizational policies and practices; risks and risk management; laws and regulations; stigma and the impact of work on private life; work history; and opinions of the sex industry. To supplement the information gathered in the Management Project focus groups, I then interviewed women who had worked regularly as strippers (at least twice per week for at least one year) in strip clubs in Ottawa and/or Toronto, as of the year 2000. The publicity materials for both third parties and strippers used the term *exotic dance* industry, as it is the more popular term; however, like other academic studies, this book generally employs the word *erotic dance*, in recognition that *exotic* is othering. The interview guide for dancers touched on issues similar to those in the third-parties individual interview guide, adjusted to dancers' perspective, and also elaborated on some issues arising from the focus groups.

In the research for my dissertation, saturation (Munn & Bruckert, 2013) was reached after four third-party interviews in addition to those in the Management Project, as it was clear that they were eliciting little new information and had much in common with previously collected data. Moreover, with only seventeen strip clubs in Toronto and nine in Ottawa at the time, a total of fifteen third-party interviews seemed like a representative sample. My interviews with individual dancers provided more detail than the focus groups; still, similarities became increasingly apparent after about five individual interviews, and I conducted only two more. Together, interview data from a total of thirty participants adequately reflected the social processes and structures on which I was focusing (see Munn & Bruckert, 2013, p. 185–6). It is further worth noting that this book and the dissertation on which it is based focused on strip clubs featuring, and third parties working with, women. This focus is, in part, because only two third parties working at establishments featuring other gender presentations participated in the Management Project (a trans strip event and a male strip club, respectively – these interviews were excluded), and only women strippers participated in both projects, and also because there are too few establishments featuring other genders to mitigate confidentiality and comparability issues.

To bolster analytical rigour and minimize distortion of participants' intended meanings, the analysis process began with team coding with my supervisor and the principal investigator of the larger project, Dr Chris Bruckert. Deductive codes were adapted from the literature, the interview guides, and the codes we had developed for the incall/outcall sector interviews; inductive codes arose from the interview data. Dancer and third-party interviews were coded in two separate NVivo (qualitative analysis software) files to facilitate comparison as well as the development of codes specific to each. Since I was coding while collecting the last few interviews, I noted concerns to attend to in the horizontal analysis, and coded and recoded as new trends emerged, refining my theoretical framework as needed.

Like any research method, interviews have limitations. In addition to being a contextually bound, collaborative effort by the researcher and the respondent that does not necessarily accurately reflect events (Fontana & Frey, 2005), interviews are also limited by a lack of control over who chooses to participate. As Sanders (2006) notes, people working for (or, in this research, as) unscrupulous employers may be more reluctant to participate than those who work at more reputable establishments. However, in comparing participants' accounts, I was able to glean both good and bad management practices in the erotic dance sector.

Notes

Introduction

1 Studies examining the management of strip clubs include Althorp (2013), Bouclin (2004, 2006, 2009), Bruckert, Parent, & Robitaille (2003), J. Lewis (2000), J. Lewis & Shaver (2006), and Maticka-Tyndale (2004). Studies that include interview or ethnographic data from managerial individuals include Barton (2006), Brooks (2010), Bruckert (2002), Colosi (2010a; 2010b), Egan(2004), Frank (2002a), Lavin (2013), J. Lewis (2006), Lilleston et al. (2012), Murphy (2003), Price (2008), Price-Glynn (2010), and Ross (2009).
2 The no-touching bylaw in particular has proven difficult to enforce (MLS, 2012): police officers interpreted it in different ways, and have also been unable to produce sufficient evidence of intent to allow physical contact, resulting in charges being dismissed (e.g., *Toronto v Zanzibar*, 2007). In cases where convictions have resulted, punishment has been minimal: a strip club operator charged with permitting physical contact was fined $250 for breaking a Vaughan bylaw with a maximum penalty of $25,000 (*R v Mijatovic*, 2008), and, under a similar charge, a Barrie strip club bartender was ordered to pay a fine of $700 for contravening a bylaw that had a maximum penalty of $5,000 (*Bravakis v Barrie*, 2005).
3 Notable exceptions include a few clubs in Japan and Turkey that describe themselves as Western-style, and a few Mexican tourist destinations offering lap dancing. Hostess bars in Hong Kong and Thailand more closely resemble erotic massage parlours or incall agencies in Canada. While there is lap dancing in other Western countries such as France, English-language academic scholarship about erotic dance hails largely from the United States, Canada, the United Kingdom, and Australia.
4 Although scholars such as West and Zimmerman (1987) and Butler (1990) have theorized gender as an ongoing, socially mediated process undertaken across social spaces and institutions, Goffman (1959) is more useful for

examining workplace performances of gender because he acknowledges the specificity and instrumentality of occupational roles, in which performers are conforming to or subverting normative expectations within the confines of the concrete space of a business.

Chapter 1

1 Although there is anecdotal evidence of dancers moving to the position of waitress or bartender (see Bruckert, 2002), the only opportunity for dancers to advance to a third-party position noted in the erotic dance literature is to the position of housemother (see Price-Glynn, 2010), a role that existed only at one club in this study. However, in Ontario, the move does not appear to be a promotion. According to some dancers who had worked at a club where such a role existed, a "housemom" works in the dancers' change room, offering them help and supplies (e.g., costume repair, takeout, beauty products) in exchange for tips. One focus-group participant described this role as "more of a cleaning lady," contrasting it to housemoms she had worked with in the United States, who were "sort of like unspoken referees a little – or supervisors – but they're kind of like just somebody you can go to instead of the manager, like, instead of the men" (Leigh, dancer). The latter description is supported in studies of American strip clubs, where the housemother appears to be relatively common and more important than in Ontario (see Murphy, 2003; Price, 2008; Price-Glynn, 2010). Because the housemom inhabits an exclusively supporting role that appears to be marginal in Ontario's erotic dance sector, and no one occupying the role participated in this study, this particular occupation is not included in this book.
2 These two income ranges are not related; rather, dancers were given a choice between estimating their income earned per year or per day. Some chose a per night estimation to account for inconsistent schedules from week to week or month to month, while others preferred calculating their yearly income.
3 More or less channelling this salacious question into a research question, several studies focus precisely on why women elect to become strippers (e.g., Dressel & Petersen, 1982a; Forsyth & Deshotels, 1998; Skipper & McCaghy, 1970; Sweet & Tewksbury, 2000). Bruckert (2014) reflects on the implications and ethics of this fascination in her auto-ethnographic chapter on activism and research as an academic and former sex worker.

Chapter 2

1 Recent studies detailing the central role of Eurocentric beauty norms in strip club practices in Canada and the United States include Bouclin (2006),

Brooks (1997, 2010), Bruckert & Frigon (2003), Deshotels et al. (2012), Maticka-Tyndale (2004), and Price-Glynn (2010). Ross (2000), and Ross and Greenwell (2005) provide historical accounts of racialization, racial discrimination, and resistance in western Canadian strip clubs.

2 Unlike the female strip clubs in this book, a male strip club featured in another data set (see Law, 2021) reported that applicants had to audition. Additionally, community activists have noted recent hiring changes at female strip clubs in Ontario, some of which have begun asking for auditions or for applicants to submit their photos over the internet (Work Safe Twerk Safe, personal communication, 6 October 2022).

3 Given that their operating costs may be higher (because of rent, for example), incall agencies may charge a larger cut of sex workers' rates (40 to 50 per cent), while outcall agencies, which have to pay drivers but sometimes demand additional separate fees from sex workers to do so, take between 20 and 50 per cent of hourly service rates (Bruckert & Law, 2013). As with hair stylists, sex workers may earn tips in addition to the rates set by the agency; unlike hair stylists, tips are sometimes actually fees charged by sex workers for additional or specialized services (as with "extras" at strip clubs).

4 Exceptionally, three participants mentioned establishments where dancers were required to pay 10 (on credit cards only), 15, and 50 per cent, respectively, of their lap dance earnings to the club. These three clubs more closely resemble the US clubs studied by DeMichele and Tewskbury (2004) and Egan (2004) than they do other Ontario clubs.

Chapter 3

1 Wilful ignorance has indeed proven effective in court. Perhaps most famously, in *R v Mara*, only club owner Mara was granted leave to appeal to the Supreme Court of Canada; the judges concluded that, unlike manager East, who "was entirely responsible for the activity of the dancers at the tavern" (*R v Mara*, 1997, para. 48), Mara was not directly present as a third party to the activities in question, and could thus credibly claim to be unaware of their inappropriateness.

2 Dancers' responses in the city of Toronto's 2012 adult entertainment bylaw review survey demonstrate diverse perspectives in regard to lap dancing and the physical contact it involves. Their responses ranged from "dancers are comfortable enough to say whether they want contact or not, we are not animals or children" to "touching leads directly to prostitution" (City of Toronto, 2012, pp. 41–3). At the same time, many acknowledged that touching is common in lap dancing and important to their financial well-being (City of Toronto, 2012).

3 This discretion contrasts with establishments in Baltimore studied by Lilleston et al. (2012), where customers could pay a club-affiliated third party to leave with a dancer. Neither the literature nor participants in this study suggest that such a practice, which Lilleston et al. (2012) describe as a "buyout," occurs in Ontario. Discretion around leaving with customers for the purpose of providing sexual services also contrasts somewhat with Ross and Greenwell's (2005) finding that dancers in the mid-twentieth century who combined stripping with prostitution kept the latter discreet to minimize stigma from their colleagues. Although discretion remains important, contemporary dancers appear concerned primarily about fair competition.

4 As with other contemporary surveillance scholars, Andrejevic (2005) focuses mainly on technological means of surveillance. As I have argued elsewhere (see Law & Bruckert, 2016), in strip clubs, in-person surveillance remains an important tool of managerial discipline. However because third parties are unable to see everything that is happening in the club, surveillance at strip clubs is better explained through the metaphor of a web than Foucault's panopticon (Foucault 1977/1995). In this web, the sight lines of lateral or peer surveillance fill gaps in managerial surveillance (directed along alternate lines of sight), while simultaneously protecting dancers' collective financial interests (Law & Bruckert, 2016).

Chapter 4

1 The notion of the "party" environment expands on characterizations by Frank (2003), Ross (2000), and other scholars (e.g., Bradley-Engen & Ulmer, 2009; Brooks, 2010; Bruckert, 2002; DeMichele & Tewksbury, 2004; Ross & Greenwell, 2005) of the strip club as an environment shaped by (mostly white, heterosexual, affluent) men's shared definitions of female beauty and sexuality (Ross, 2000), and in which customers can engage in stereotypically masculine behaviours that are largely unacceptable in other social contexts (Frank, 2003).

2 Scholars who make the former argument include Deshotels et al. (2012), Pasko (2002), Pilcher (2009), Price (Price, 2008; Price-Glynn 2010), Spivey (2005), Trautner (2005), and Wood (2000). Scholars who nuance the issue of social hierarchies and privilege by highlighting their co-existence with, and the complexities of, resistance include Bruckert (2002), Frank (2002a, 2003), Liepe-Levinson (2002), Murphy (2003), Raguparan (2017), Sanders (2005), and Wolkowitz (2006).

3 Studies focusing on male erotic dance include DeMarco (2007), Dressel & Petersen (1982a; 1982b), Escoffier (2007), Kaufman (2009), Margolis and Arnold (1983), Montemurro (2001), Montemurro et al. (2003), Pilcher (2011), Scull (2013), C. Smith (2002), and Tewksbury (1994). Studies comparing

women's and men's stripping include Bernard et al. (2003); Liepe-Levinson (2002), Pilcher (2009), and Ronai and Cross (1998).

Chapter 5

1 Though strip clubs may seem an unlikely target of anti-prostitution/anti-trafficking campaigns, Weitzer argues that prostitution prohibitionists have expanded the focus of their activism over time, such that they "now associate sex trafficking with all sexual commerce – prostitution, pornography and strip clubs. Fusing trafficking with other commercial sex practices arguably makes it easier to condemn and criminalize them – which is precisely the prohibitionists' ultimate objective" (2012, p. 1357). He problematizes the lack of credible evidence among prohibitionist academics (e.g., Hughes, 1999; Jeffreys, 2008) who claim that women and girls are trafficked to work in strip clubs.
2 As of 2013, Toronto's bylaws specify that "All private rooms, booths or cubicles must have no more than three sides or have one side constructed of a transparent material ... [to ensure] a clear view of its interior" (Bylaw 243-2013: 11). Similarly, Ottawa's layout requirements were amended in 2004; they aimed to remove visual obstructions obscuring lap dances (*Adult Entertainment Association of Canada v Ottawa*, 2007: para. 7; Ottawa Bylaw 2002-189; Ottawa Bylaw L6-2000).

Chapter 6

1 As Bouclin (2004; 2006) has aptly observed, the introduction of lap dancing in the 1990s caused significant division between dancers who had begun working in the table-dancing era and perceived touching as akin to prostitution, and dancers who instead saw lap dancing as an opportunity to make more money (see also Bruckert & Parent, 2007; DERA, 2002).
2 Pheterson describes the "whore stigma" as "a mark of shame or disease on an unchaste woman" (1998, p. 231). Pheterson conceptualizes unchastity as comprising two dimensions: impurity and defilement. She characterizes impurity as an attribute associated with identity (e.g., dirty, adulterated) and often ascribed with racializing implications, and uses defilement to refer to conduct, specifically female sexual experience or a reputation thereof.

Conclusion

1 See *Toronto Municipal Code*, 2019, 545, s. 396(a)(1) and *Ottawa Bylaw No. 2002-189*, 11, s. 24(1)(a), and *Toronto Municipal Code*, 2019, 545, s. 396(a)(2) and *Ottawa Bylaw No. 2002-189*, 11, s. 24(1)(b), respectively.

2 As Bouclin (2009) documents, there were several groups by-and-for erotic dancers in Ontario between the late 1970s and early 2000s. In chronological order, these groups included the Canadian Association of Burlesque Entertainers (the Toronto group that was the complainant in *Canadian Labour Congress (Canadian Association of Burlesque Entertainers, Local Union No. 1689) v Algonquin Tavern*, 1981), the Association for Burlesque Entertainers (a Toronto group that advocated for anti–lap dancing bylaws in the mid-1990s), the Exotic Dancers Alliance (Toronto), and Dancers for Equal Rights (Ottawa). Two more groups, Strippers' United Association (Toronto) and the Exotic Dancers' Rights Association of Canada (Toronto and Ottawa), were short lived, forming and folding in the mid- and late 2000s, respectively (Gall, 2016). Currently, Work Safe Twerk Safe, which launched in 2019 and is based in Toronto, is the only stripper group in Canada.

3 An improved relationship with police may not make pursuing a sexual assault complaint through the criminal justice process any better than it is for non-sex-working women; indeed, Canadian scholars have extensively critiqued police, judges, and defence lawyers for disrespecting, retraumatizing, and viciously attacking the character and credibility of women sexual assault complainants (Craig, 2016; DuBois, 2012). However, fully decriminalizing sex work would remove barriers to third parties in strip clubs and other sex industry businesses calling the police, and therefore facilitate the physical removal of violent customers from the premises as well as the initial charging of clients for sexual assault.

References

Abel, G.M., Fitzgerald, L.J., & Brunton, C. (2009). The impact of decriminalisation on the number of sex workers in New Zealand. *Journal of Social Policy, 38*(3), 515–31. https://doi.org/10.1017/S0047279409003080

Acker, J. (2009). From glass ceilings to inequality regimes. *Sociologie du travail, 51*, 199–217. https://doi.org/10.4000/sdt.16407

AEAC (Adult Entertainment Association of Canada). (2013). http://www.adultentertainmentassociation.ca/ (site discontinued)

Althorp, J. (2013). *Beyond the stage: A gaze into the working lives of exotic stage dancers in Western Canada.* [Unpublished master's thesis, Simon Fraser University].

Andrejevic, M. (2005). The work of watching one another: Lateral surveillance, risk, and governance. *Surveillance and Society, 2*(4), 479–97. https://doi.org/10.24908/ss.v2i4.3359

Ashforth, B.E., Kreiner, G.E., Clark, M.A., & Fugate, M. (2007). Normalizing dirty work: Managerial tactics for countering occupational taint. *Academy of Management Journal, 50*(1), 149–74. https://doi.org/10.5465/amj.2007.24162092

Ball, K. (2010). Workplace surveillance: An overview. *Labor History, 51*(1), 87–106. https://doi.org/10.1080/00236561003654776

Barriball, K.L., & While, A. (1994). Collecting data using a semi-structured interview: A discussion paper. *Journal of Advanced Nursing, 19*, 328–35. https://doi.org/10.1111/j.1365-2648.1994.tb01088.x

Barry, K. (1995). Pimping: The world's oldest profession. *On the Issues, 4*(3), 42–9.

Barton, B. (2006). *Stripped: Inside the lives of exotic dancers.* New York: New York University Press.

Basford, T., Offermann, L., & Behrend, T. (2014). Do you see what I see? Perceptions of gender microaggressions in the workplace. *Psychology of Women Quarterly, 38*(3), 340–9. https://doi.org/10.1177/0361684313511420

Bastarache, M. (2020). *Broken dreams, broken lives: The devastating effects of sexual harassment on women in the RCMP*. Ottawa: Merlo Davidson. https://www.rcmp-grc.gc.ca/wam/media/4773/original/8032a32ad5dd014db5b135ce3753934d.pdf

Beer, S. (2018). Action, advocacy, and allies: Building a movement for sex worker rights. In E.M. Durisin, E. van der Meulen, & C. Bruckert (Eds.), *Red light labour: Sex work, regulation, agency and resistance* (pp. 329–39). Vancouver: UBC Press.

Benoit, C., & Unsworth, R. (2022). COVID-19, stigma, and the ongoing marginalization of sex workers and their support organizations. *Archives of Sexual Behavior, 51*(1), 331–42. https://doi.org/10.1007/s10508-021-02124-3

Benson, J. (2012). Myths about pimps: Conflicting images of hypermasculine pimps in US American hip-hop and bisexual pimps in the novels of Donald Goines and Iceberg Slim. *Journal of Bisexuality, 12*, 429–41. https://doi.org/10.1080/15299716.2012.702627

Berg, B.L. (2009). *Qualitative research methods for the social sciences* (7th ed.). Boston: Allyn & Bacon.

Berg, H., & Penley, C. (2016). Creative precarity in the adult film industry. In M. Curtin & K. Sanson (Eds.), *Precarious creativity: Global media, local labor* (pp. 159–71). Oakland: University of California Press.

Bernard, C., DeGabrielle, C., Cartier, L., Monk-Turner, E., Phill, C., Sherwood, J., & Tyree, T. (2003). Exotic dancers: gender differences in societal reaction, subcultural ties, and conventional support. *Journal of Criminal Justice and Popular Culture, 10*(1), 1–11.

Bittle, S. (2012). *Still dying for a living: Corporate criminal liability after the Westray mine disaster*. Vancouver: UBC Press.

Blowdryer, J. (2009). Lap dancing is my business! In D.H. Sterry & R.J. Martin Jr. (Eds.), *Hos, hookers, call girls and rent boys: Professionals writing on life, love, money, and sex* (pp. 175–8). Berkeley, CA: Soft Skull Press.

Bolton, S.C., & Houlihan, M. (2010). Bermuda revisited? Management power and powerlessness in the worker-manager-customer triangle. *Work and Occupations, 37*(3), 378–403. https://doi.org/10.1177/0730888410375678

Bouclin, S. (2004). *Organizing resistance: The case of erotic dancers*. [Unpublished master's thesis, University of Ottawa].

Bouclin, S. (2006). Dancers empowering (some) dancers: The intersections of race, class and gender in organizing erotic labourers. *Race, Gender and Class, 13*(3/4), 98–130. http://www.jstor.org/stable/41675175

Bouclin, S. (2009). Bad girls like good contracts: Ontario erotic dancers' collective resistance. In E. Faulkner & G. MacDonald (Eds.), *Victim no more: Women's resistance to law, culture and power* (pp. 46–60). Winnipeg: Fernwood Publishing.

Boyle, K.M. (2015). Social psychological processes that facilitate sexual assault within the fraternity party subculture. *Sociology Compass, 9*(5), 386–99. https://doi.org/10.1111/soc4.12261

Bradley, M.S. (2007). Girlfriends, wives, and strippers: Managing stigma in exotic dancer romantic relationships. *Deviant Behavior, 28*(4), 379–406. https://doi.org/10.1080/01639620701233308

Bradley-Engen, M.S., & Hobbs, C.M. (2010). To love, honor, and strip: An investigation of exotic dancer romantic relationships. In M.H. Ditmore, A. Levy, & A. Willman (Eds.), *Sex work matters: Exploring money, power, and intimacy in the sex industry* (pp. 67–84). New York: Zed Books.

Bradley-Engen, M.S., & Ulmer, J.T. (2009). Social worlds of stripping: The processual orders of exotic dance. *Sociological Quarterly, 50*, 29–60. https://doi.org/10.1111/j.1533-8525.2008.01132.x

Brents, B.G., & Hausbeck, K. (2005). Violence and legalized brothel prostitution in Nevada: Examining safety, risk, and prostitution policy. *Journal of Interpersonal Violence, 20*(3), 270–95. https://doi.org/10.1177/0886260504270333

Brents, B., & Jackson, C.A. (2013). Gender, emotional labour and interactive body work: Negotiating flesh and fantasy in sex workers' labour practices. In C. Wolkowitz, R.L. Cohen, T. Sanders, & K. Hardy (Eds.), *Body/sex/work: Intimate, embodied and sexualized labour* (pp. 77–92). New York: Palgrave Macmillan.

Brents, B.G., & Sanders, T. (2010). Mainstreaming the sex industry: Economic inclusion and social ambivalence. *Journal of Law and Society, 37*(1), 40–60. https://doi.org/10.1111/j.1467-6478.2010.00494.x

Brewis, J., & Linstead, S. (2000). *Sex, work and sex work: Eroticizing organization*. London: Routledge.

Brooks, S. (1997). Dancing toward freedom. In J. Nagel (Ed.), *Whores and other feminists* (pp. 252–5). New York: Routledge.

Brooks, S. (2010). Hypersexualization and the dark body: Race and inequality among Black and Latina women in the exotic dance industry. *Sexuality Research and Social Policy, 7*, 70–80. https://doi.org/10.1007/s13178-010-0010-5

Brown, J.A. (2005). Class and feminine excess: The strange case of Anna Nicole Smith. *Feminist Review, 81*, 74–94. https://doi.org/10.1057/palgrave.fr.9400240

Bruckert, C. (2002). *Taking it off, putting it on: Women in the strip trade*. Toronto: Women's Press.

Bruckert, C. (2012). The mark of "disreputable" labour: Workin' it – Sex workers negotiate stigma. In S. Hannem & C. Bruckert (Eds.), *Stigma revisited: Negotiations, resistance and implications of the mark* (pp. 55–78). Ottawa: University of Ottawa Press.

Bruckert, C. (2014). Activist academic whore: Negotiating the fractured otherness abyss. In J. M. Kilty, S. Fabian, & M. Felices-Luna (Eds.), *Demarginalizing voices: Commitment, emotion, and action in qualitative research* (306–25). Vancouver: UBC Press.

Bruckert, C., & Dufresne, M. (2002). Re-configuring the margins: Tracing the regulatory context of Ottawa strip clubs, 1974–2000. *Canadian Journal of Law and Society*, 17(1), 69–87. https://doi.org/10.1017/S0829320100007006

Bruckert, C., & Frigon, S. (2003). "Making a spectacle of herself": On women's bodies in the skin trades. *Atlantis*, 28(1), 48–62.

Bruckert, C., & Hannem, S. (2013a). Rethinking the prostitution debates: Transcending structural stigma in systemic responses to sex work. *Canadian Journal of Law and Society*, 28(1), 43–63. https://doi.org/10.1017/cls.2012.2

Bruckert, C., & Hannem, S. (2013b). To serve and protect? Structural stigma, social profiling, and the abuse of police power in Ottawa. In E. van der Meulen, E. Durisin, & V. Love (Eds.), *Selling sex: Experience, advocacy and research on sex work in Canada* (pp. 297–313). Vancouver: UBC Press.

Bruckert, C., & Law, T. (2013). *Beyond pimps, procurers and parasites: Mapping third parties in the incall/outcall sex industry*. Ottawa: Rethinking Management in the Adult and Sex Industry Project.

Bruckert, C., & Law, T. (2018a). The business of sex business: Third parties in the incall/outcall sector. In C. Bruckert & C. Parent (Eds.), *Getting past "the pimp": Management in the sex industry* (pp. 73–100). Toronto: University of Toronto Press.

Bruckert, C., & Law, T. (2018b). *Women and gendered violence in Canada: An intersectional approach*. Toronto: University of Toronto Press.

Bruckert, C., & Parent, C. (2007). La danse érotique comme métier à l'ère de la vente de soi. *Cahiers de recherche sociologique*, 43, 95–107. https://doi.org/10.7202/1002481ar

Bruckert, C., & Parent, C. (Eds.) (2018). *Getting past "the pimp": Management in the sex industry*. Toronto: University of Toronto Press.

Bruckert, C., Parent, C., & Robitaille, P. (2003). *Erotic service/erotic dance establishments: Two types of marginalized labour*. Ottawa: University of Ottawa, Department of Criminology.

Burawoy, M. 1979. *Manufacturing consent: Changes in the labor process under monopoly capitalism*. Chicago: University of Chicago Press.

Butler, J. (1990). *Gender trouble and the subversion of identity*. New York: Routledge.

Campbell, H., & Chinnery, S. (2018). *What works? Preventing and responding to sexual harassment in the workplace*. Canberra: CARE Australia.

Canada. (2017). *Harassment and sexual violence in the workplace: Public consultations*. Ottawa: Employment and Social Development Canada.

Caradonna, A. (2018, 7 November). From brothels to independence: The neoliberalisation of (sex) work. *Open Democracy*. https://www.opendemocracy.net/en/beyond-trafficking-and-slavery/from-brothels-to-independence-neoliberalisation-of-sex-work/

Carrigan, T., Connell, B., & Lee, J. (1985). Toward a new sociology of masculinity. *Theory and Society, 14*(5), 551–604. https://doi.org/10.1007/BF00160017

Castel, R. (2003). *From manual workers to wage laborers: The transformation of the social question* (R. Boyd, Trans. & Ed.). New Brunswick, NJ: Transaction Publishers.

CASWLR. (2022). *CASWLR v Canada: Our challenge to sex work-specific criminal offences*. Canadian Alliance for Sex Work Law Reform. http://sexworklawreform.com/wp-content/uploads/2022/09/Infosheet-ENG.pdf

Cawley, J. (2004). The impact of obesity on wages. *Journal of Human Resources, 39*(2), 451–74. https://doi.org/10.2307/3559022

CBS News. (2014). New York City strippers win $10 million in back wages. https://www.cbsnews.com/news/new-york-city-strippers-win-10-million-in-back-wages/

Centola, D., Becker, J., Brackbill, D., & Baronchelli, A. (2018). Experimental evidence for tipping points in social convention. *Science, 360*(6393), 1116–19. https://doi.org/10.1126/science.aas8827

Chapkis, W. (2000). Power and control in the commercial sex trade. In R. Weitzer (Ed.), *Sex for sale: Prostitution, pornography, and the sex industry* (pp. 181–201). New York: Routledge.

Chateauvert, M. (2013). *Sex workers unite: A history of the movement from Stonewall to Slutwalk*. Boston: Beacon Press.

Chu, S.K.H., & Clamen, J. (2022, 4 October). Chu and Clamen: Canada must change the law and respect sex workers' rights. *Ottawa Citizen*.

City of Toronto, Licensing and Standards Committee. (2012, 12 October). *Review of Adult Entertainment Parlour Regulations: Amendments to Toronto Municipal Code Chapter 545*. https://www.toronto.ca/legdocs/mmis/2012/ls/bgrd/backgroundfile-50917.pdf

Coe, I.R., Wiley, R., & Bekker, L.G. (2019). Organisational best practices towards gender equality in science and medicine. *The Lancet, 393*(10171), 587–93. https://doi.org/10.1016/S0140-6736(18)33188-X

Colosi, R. (2010a). *Dirty dancing? An ethnography of lap-dancing*. New York: Willan Publishing.

Colosi, R. (2010b). "Just get pissed and enjoy yourself": Understanding lap-dancing as "anti-work." In K. Hardy, S. Kingston, & T. Sanders (Eds.), *New sociologies of sex work* (pp. 181–96). Burlington, VT: Ashgate Publishing.

Comack, E., & Balfour, G. (2004). *The power to criminalize: Violence, inequality and the law*. Halifax: Fernwood Publishing.

Connell, R.W., & Messerschmidt, J.W. (2005). Hegemonic masculinity: Rethinking the concept. *Gender and Society*, *19*(6), 829–59. https://doi.org/10.1177/0891243205278639

Couto, A. (2006). Clothing exotic dancers with collective bargaining rights. *Ottawa Law Review*, *38*(1), 37–66. https://rdo-olr.org/clothing-exotic-dancers-with-collective-bargaining-rights/

Craig, E. (2016). The inhospitable court. *University of Toronto Law Journal*, *66*(2), 197–243. https://doi.org/10.3138/UTLJ.3398

Crenshaw, K. (1989). Demarginalizing the intersection of race and sex: A Black feminist critique of antidiscrimination doctrine, feminist theory and antiracist politics. *University of Chicago Legal Forum*, *1*, 139–67.

Crenshaw, K. (1991). Mapping the margins: Intersectionality, identity politics, and violence against women of color. *Stanford Law Review*, *43*(6), 1241–99. https://doi.org/10.2307/1229039

Crocker, D., & Kalemba, V. (1999). The incidence and impact of women's experiences of sexual harassment in Canadian workplaces. *Canadian Review of Sociology* 36(4): 541–58. https://doi.org/10.1111/j.1755-618X.1999.tb00963.x

CUPE. (2005). *Sex work: Why it's a union issue*. Canadian Union of Public Employees.

CUPW. (2020, 25 August). CUPW and Foodora Canada reach settlement for workers. Ottawa: Canadian Union of Postal Workers. https://www.cupw.ca/sites/default/files/08-25-20_Media%20Release_NR_CUPW%20and%20Foodora%20Canada%20reach%20settlement%20for%20workers_PDF_E.pdf

Czekalla, R. (2014). *Enhanced adult services study*. Toronto: Municipal Policy Consultants.

Day, S. (2008). Prostitution: Violating the human rights of poor women. Ottawa: Action ontarienne contre la violence faite aux femmes. http://www.socialrightscura.ca/documents/publications/shelagh/Prostitution.pdf

Deachman, B. (2019, 11 March). "A nice dive": Glue Pot Pub set to say goodbye. *Ottawa Citizen*. https://ottawacitizen.com/business/local-business/a-nice-dive-glue-pot-pub-set-to-say-goodbye

DeMarco, J.R. (2007). Power and control in gay strip clubs. *Journal of Homosexuality*, *53*(1–2), 111–27. https://doi.org/10.1300/J082v53n01_05

DeMichele, M.T., & Tewksbury, R. (2004). Sociological explorations in site-specific social control: The role of the strip club bouncer. *Deviant Behavior*, *25*, 537–58. https://doi.org/10.1080/01639620490484068

DERA. (2002). *Current issues concerning exotic dancers in Ontario*. Ottawa: Dancers Equal Rights Association.

Dennis, J.D. (2008). Women are victims, men make choices: The invisibility of men and boys in the global sex trade. *Gender Issues*, *25*, 11–25. https://doi.org/10.1007/s12147-008-9051-y

Deschamps, M. (2015). *External review into sexual misconduct and sexual harassment in the Canadian Armed Forces*. Ottawa: National Defence and the Canadian Armed Forces. https://www.canada.ca/en/department-national-defence/corporate/reports-publications/sexual-misbehaviour/external-review-2015.html

Deshotels, T.H., Tinney, M., & Forsyth, C.J. (2012). McSexy: Exotic dancing and institutional power. *Deviant Behavior, 33*(2), 140–8. https://doi.org/10.1080/01639625.2011.573370

DeVault, M., & McCoy, L. (2006). Institutional ethnography: Using interviews to investigate ruling relations. In D.E. Smith (Ed.), *Institutional ethnography as practice*, 15–44. Lanham, MD: Rowman & Littlefield.

Devers, C., Dewett, T., Mishina, Y., & Belsito, C. (2009). A general theory of organizational stigma. *Organization Science, 20*(1), 154–71. https://doi.org/10.1287/orsc.1080.0367

Dmitrieva, K. (2017, 6 December). It's closing time for Toronto's strip clubs. *Bloomberg Businessweek*. https://www.bloomberg.com/news/articles/2017-12-12/it-s-closing-time-for-toronto-s-strip-clubs

Dressel, P.L., & Petersen, D.M. (1982a). Becoming a male stripper: Recruitment, socialization, and ideological development. *Work and Occupations, 9*(3), 387–406. https://doi.org/10.1177/0730888482009003007

Dressel, P.L., & Petersen, D.M. (1982b). Gender roles, sexuality, and the male strip show: The structuring of sexual opportunity. *Sociological Focus, 15*(2), 151–62.

Dua, E. (2009). On the effectiveness of anti-racist policies in Canadian universities: Issues of implementation of policies by senior administration. In F. Henry & C. Tator (Eds.), *Racism in the Canadian university: Demanding social justice, inclusion, and equity* (pp. 160–95). Toronto: University of Toronto Press.

DuBois, T. (2012). Police investigation of sexual assault complaints: How far have we come since Jane Doe? In E.A. Sheehy (Ed.), *Sexual assault in Canada: Law, legal practice and women's activism* (pp. 191–210). Ottawa: University of Ottawa Press.

Dworkin, A. (1985). Against the male flood: Censorship, pornography, and equality. *Harvard Women's Law Journal, 8*, 1–29.

Ebaugh, H.R.F. (1988). *Becoming an ex: The process of role exit*. Chicago: University of Chicago Press.

Egan, R.D. (2004). Eyeing the scene: The uses and (re)uses of surveillance cameras in an exotic dance club. *Critical Sociology, 30*(2), 299–319. https://doi.org/10.1163/156916304323072125

Egan, R.D. (2006a). *Dancing for dollars and paying for love: The relationships between exotic dancers and their regulars*. New York: Palgrave Macmillan.

Egan, R.D. (2006b). Resistance under the black light: Exploring the use of music in two exotic dance clubs. *Journal of Contemporary Ethnography, 35*(2), 201–19. https://doi.org/10.1177/0891241605283570

Entwistle, J., Frankling, C., Lee, N., & Walsh, A. (2019). Fashion diversity. *Fashion Theory*, *23*(2), 309–23. https://doi.org/10.1080/1362704X.2019.1567065

Erickson, K. (2010). Talk, touch and intolerance: Sexual harassment in an overtly sexualized work culture. In C. Williams & K. Delinger (Eds.), *Research in the sociology of work 20: Gender and sexuality in the workplace* (pp. 179–202). Bingley, UK: Emerald Group Publishing.

Escoffier, J. (2007). Porn star/stripper/escort: Economic and sexual dynamics in a sex work career. In T. Morrison & B. Whitehead (Eds.), *Male sex work: A business doing pleasure* (pp. 173–200). Philadelphia: Haworth Press.

Farley, M. (2003). Prostitution and the invisibility of harm. *Women and Therapy*, *26*(3–4), 247–80. https://doi.org/10.1300/J015v26n03_06

Farley, M. (2004). "Bad for the body, bad for the heart": Prostitution harms women even if legalized or decriminalized. *Violence against Women*, *10*(10), 1087–125. https://doi.org/10.1177/1077801204268607

Fischer, C.B. (1996). Employee rights in sex work: The struggle for dancers' rights as employees. *Law and Inequality: A Journal of Theory and Practice*, *14*(2), 521–54.

Flanagan, C. 2019. The problem with HR. *The Atlantic*. https://www.theatlantic.com/magazine/archive/2019/07/hr-workplace-harrassment-metoo/590644/

Fogel, C.A., & Quinlan, A. (2011). Dancing naked: Precarious labour in the contemporary female strip trade. *Canadian Social Science*, *7*(5), 1–6. https://doi.org/10.3968/j.css.1923669720110705.349

Fontana, A., & Frey, J. (2005). The interview: From neutral stance to political involvement. In N. Denzin & Y. Lincoln (Eds.), *Handbook of qualitative research* (3rd ed.). Thousand Oaks, CA: SAGE Publications.

Forsyth, C.J., & Deshotels, T.H. (1998). A deviant process: The sojourn of the stripper. *Sociological Spectrum*, *18*(1), 77–92. https://doi.org/10.1080/02732173.1998.9982185

Foucault, M. (1995). *Discipline and punish* (A. Sheridan, Trans.; 2nd ed.). New York: Vintage Books. (Original work published 1977).

Frank, K. (2002a). *G-strings and sympathy: Strip club regulars and male desire*. Durham, NC: Duke University Press.

Frank, K. (2002b). Stripping, starving, and the politics of ambiguous pleasure. In M.L. Johnson (Ed.), *Jane sexes it up: True confessions of feminist desire* (pp. 171–206). New York: Four Walls Eight Windows.

Frank, K. (2003). "Just trying to relax": Masculinity, masculinizing practices, and strip club regulars. *Journal of Sex Research*, *40*(1), 61–75. https://doi.org/10.1080/00224490309552167

Frank, K. (2005). Exploring the motivations and fantasies of strip club customers in relation to legal regulations. *Archives of Sexual Behavior*, *34*(5), 487–504. https://doi.org/10.1007/s10508-005-6275-8

Frank, K. (2007). Thinking critically about strip club research. *Sexualities, 10*(4), 501–17. https://doi.org/10.1177/1363460707080989

Fuckförbundet. (2019). *Twenty years of failing sex workers: A community report on the impact of the 1999 Swedish Sex Purchase Act*. Gothenburg, SE: Fuckförbundet Community för Sexarbetare.

Fudge, J., Tucker, E., & Vosko, L. (2003). Employee or independent contractor? Charting the legal significance of the distinction in Canada. *Canadian Labour and Employment Law Journal, 10*(2), 193–230.

Gall, G. (2016). *Sex worker unionization: Global developments, challenges and possibilities*. New York: Palgrave Macmillan.

Gallagher, D.G., & Sverke, M. (2005). Contingent employment contracts: Are existing employment theories still relevant? *Economic and Industrial Democracy, 26*(2), 181–203. https://doi.org/10.1177/0143831X05051513

Giles, D. (2014, 2 January). New stripping laws now in place in Saskatchewan. Global News. http://globalnews.ca/news/1058448/new-stripping-laws-now-in-place-in-saskatchewan/

Gillies, K., Lam, E., Law, T., Reece, R., Sterling, S., & van der Meulen, E. (2019). Understanding the work in sex work: Canadian contexts. In L. Nichols (Ed.), *Working women in Canada: An intersectional approach* (pp. 359–80). Toronto: Women's Press.

Godenzi, A., Schwartz, M.D., & DeKeseredy, W.S. (2001). Toward a gendered social bond/male peer support theory of university woman abuse. *Critical Criminology, 10*(1), 1–16. https://doi.org/10.1023/A:1013105118592

Goffman, E. (1959). *The presentation of self in everyday life*. New York: Anchor Books.

Goffman, E. (1961). *Asylums: Essays on the social situation of mental patients and other inmates*. New York: Anchor Books.

Goffman, E. (1963). *Stigma: Notes on the management of spoiled identity*. New York: Simon & Schuster.

Goldstein, P.J. (1983). Occupational mobility in the world of prostitution: Becoming a madam. *Deviant Behavior, 4*(3), 267–79.

Gowland, M. (2020, 16 December). "A game changer": Virtual strip clubs are here to stay. *The Pigeon*. https://the-pigeon.ca/2020/12/16/strap-house-sexworkers/

Green, T.K. (2005). Work culture and discrimination. *California Law Review, 93*(3), 623–84.

Guadagno, R., & Cialdini, R. (2007). Gender differences in impression management in organizations: A qualitative review. *Sex Roles, 56*, 483–94. https://doi.org/10.1007/s11199-007-9187-3

Hacking, I. (2004). Between Michel Foucault and Erving Goffman: Between discourse in the abstract and face-to-face interaction. *Economy and Society, 33*(3), 277–302. https://doi.org/10.1080/0308514042000225671

Hadjisolomou, A. (2019). Front-line service managers' misbehaviour and disengagement: The elephant in the store? *Employee Relations, 41*(5), 1015–32. https://doi.org/10.1108/ER-06-2018-0176

Hafen, S. (2004). Organizational gossip: A revolving door of regulation and resistance. *Southern Journal of Communication, 69*(3), 223–40. https://doi.org/10.1080/10417940409373294

Hallgrimsdottir, H.K., Phillips, R., & Benoit, C. (2006). Fallen women and rescued girls: Social stigma and media narratives of the sex industry in Victoria, B.C., from 1980 to 2005. *Canadian Review of Sociology and Anthropology, 43*(3), 265–80. https://doi.org/10.1111/j.1755-618X.2006.tb02224.x

Hallgrimsdottir, H.K., Phillips, R., Benoit, C., & Walby, K. (2008). Sporting girls, streetwalkers, and inmates of houses of ill repute: Media narratives and the historical mutability of prostitution stigmas. *Sociological Perspectives, 51*(1), 119–38. https://doi.org/10.1525/sop.2008.51.1.119

Ham, J. (2011). *What's the cost of a rumour? A guide to sorting out the myths and facts about sporting events and trafficking.* Bangkok: Global Alliance Against Trafficking in Women. https://www.gaatw.org/publications/WhatstheCostofaRumour.11.15.2011.pdf

Handy, C. (1993). *Understanding organizations* (4th ed.). London: Penguin Books.

Hanlon, A. (2014, 6 February). The business of bare: Inside Ralph's Place. *The Coast.* https://www.thecoast.ca/halifax/the-business-of-bare-inside-ralphs-place/Content?oid=4254930

Hannem, S. (2012). Theorizing stigma and the politics of resistance: Symbolic and structural stigma in everyday life. In S. Hannem & C. Bruckert (Eds.), *Stigma revisited: Implications of the mark* (pp. 10–28). Ottawa: University of Ottawa Press.

Hannem, S., & Bruckert, C. (Eds.) (2012). *Stigma revisited: Implications of the mark.* Ottawa: University of Ottawa Press.

Hardy, K., & Sanders, T. (2015). The political economy of "lap dancing": Contested careers and women's work in the stripping industry. *Work, Employment and Society, 29*(1), 119–36. https://doi.org/10.1177/0950017014554969

Hayes, M. (2018, 4 September). The last dance: Why the Canadian strip club is a dying institution. *Globe and Mail.* https://www.theglobeandmail.com/canada/article-the-last-dance-why-the-canadian-strip-club-is-a-dying-institution/

Healy, C., Wi-Hongi, A.H.I., & Hati, C. (2017). It's work, it's working: The integration of sex workers and sex work in Aotearoa/New Zealand. *Women's Studies Journal, 31*(2), 50–60. http://www.wsanz.org.nz/journal/docs/WSJNZ312HealyWiHongiHati50-60.pdf

Hersch, J. (2008). Profiling the new immigrant worker: The effects of skin color and height. *Journal of Labor Economics, 26*(2), 345–86. https://doi.org/10.1086/587428

Heyl, B.S. (1977). The madam as teacher: The training of house prostitutes. *Social Problems, 24*, 545–55. https://doi.org/10.2307/800124

Heyl, B.S. (1979). *The madam as entrepreneur: Career management in house prostitution*. New Brunswick, NJ: Transaction Books.

Hill Collins, P. (2000). *Black feminist thought* (2nd ed.). New York: Routledge.

Hobbs, D., Hadfield, P., Lister, S., & Winlow, S. (2005). *Bouncers: Violence and governance in the night-time economy*. Oxford: Oxford University Press.

Hochschild, A. (1983). *The managed heart: Commercialization of human feeling*. Berkeley and Los Angeles: University of California Press.

Hodson, R. (1991). The active worker: Compliance and autonomy at the workplace. *Journal of Contemporary Ethnography, 20*(1), 47–78. https://doi.org/10.1177/089124191020001003

Hodson, R. (1999). Organizational anomie and worker consent. *Work and Occupations, 26*(3), 292–323. https://doi.org/10.1177/0730888499026003002

Holsopple, K. (1998). *Strip club testimony*. Minneapolis: Freedom and Justice Center for Prostitution Resources.

Hubbard, P. (2009). Opposing striptopia: The embattled spaces of adult entertainment. *Sexualities, 12*(6), 721–45. https://doi.org/10.1177/1363460709346111

Hubbard, P., & Colosi, R. (2012). Sex, crime and the city: Municipal law and the regulation of sexual entertainment. *Social and Legal Studies*. https://doi.org/10.1177/0964663912459292

Hudson, B., & Okhuysen, G. (2009). Not with a ten-foot pole: Core stigma, stigma transfer, and improbable persistence of men's bathhouses. *Organization Science, 20*(1), 134–53. https://doi.org/10.1287/orsc.1080.0368

Hughes, D. (1999). *Pimps and predators on the Internet: Globalizing the sexual exploitation of women and children*. Kingston: Coalition Against Trafficking in Women.

Hunt, A. (1997). Moral regulation and making-up the new person: Putting Gramsci to work. *Theoretical Criminology, 1*(3), 275–301. https://doi.org/10.1177/1362480697001003001

Hunt, A. (2003). Risk and moralization in everyday life. In R.V. Ericson & A. Doyle (Eds.), *Risk and morality* (pp. 165–92). Toronto: University of Toronto Press.

Hunter, B. (2017, 17 December). Last dance: With Caddy's closing, another Toronto strip club bites the dust. *Toronto Sun*. https://torontosun.com/news/local-news/last-dance-with-caddys-closing-another-toronto-strip-club-bites-the-dust

Ikeda, N., & Rosser, E. (2010). "You be vigilant! Don't rape!" Reclaiming space and security at York University. *Canadian Woman Studies, 28*(1), 37–45. https://cws.journals.yorku.ca/index.php/cws/article/view/30778

Ilcan, S., Oliver, M., & O'Connor, D. (2007). Spaces of governance: Gender and public sector restructuring in Canada. *Gender, Place and Culture, 14*(1), 75–92. https://doi.org/10.1080/09663690601122333

Jackson, C.A. (2011). Revealing contemporary constructions of femininity: Expression and sexuality in strip club legislation. *Sexualities, 14*(3), 354–69. https://doi.org/10.1177/1363460711400964

Jahic, G., & Finckenauer, J.O. (2005). Representations and misrepresentations of human trafficking. *Trends in Organized Crime, 8*(3), 24–40. https://doi.org/10.1007/s12117-005-1035-7

Jeffrey, L.A., & MacDonald, G. (2006a). "It's the money, honey": The economy of sex work in the Maritimes. *Canadian Review of Sociology and Anthropology, 43*(3), 313–27. https://doi.org/10.1111/j.1755-618X.2006.tb02227.x

Jeffrey, L.A., & MacDonald, G. (2006b). *Sex workers in the Maritimes talk back.* Vancouver: UBC Press.

Jeffreys, S. (2008). Keeping women down and out: The strip club boom and the reinforcement of male dominance. *Signs: Journal of Women in Culture and Society, 34*(1), 151–73. https://doi.org/10.1086/588501

Jeffries, S., & Lynch, M. (2007). Female striptease in the sunshine state: A description of Queensland's live adult entertainment industry and its regulation. *Queensland University of Technology Law and Justice Journal, 7*(2), 234–54. https://doi.org/10.5204/qutlr.v7i2.134

Jeon, S., Liu, H., & Ostrovsky, Y. (2019). *Measuring the gig economy in Canada using administrative data.* Ottawa: Statistics Canada. https://www150.statcan.gc.ca/n1/en/pub/11f0019m/11f0019m2019025-eng.pdf?st=tSKxtNhy

Jones, E.E., Farina, A., Hastorf, A.H., Markus, H., Miller, D.T., Scott, R.A., & French, R. (1984). *Social stigma: The psychology of marked relationships.* New York: Freeman.

Kandel, J. (2012). Strippers win $13 million settlement in wage dispute. https://www.nbclosangeles.com/news/local/Strippers-Win-13-Million-Settlement-Wages-Dispute-179336841.html

Kassam, A. (2020). Canada: 550 people exposed to Covid-19 at Toronto strip club. *The Guardian.* https://www.theguardian.com/world/2020/aug/16/canada-toronto-strip-club-brass-rail-tavern-covid-19

Kaufman, M.R. (2009). "It's just a fantasy for a couple of hours": Ethnography of a nude male show bar. *Deviant Behavior, 30*(5), 407–33. https://doi.org/10.1080/01639620802296220

Kearney, G.P., Corman, M.K., Gormley, G.J., Hart, N.D., Johnston, J.L., & Smith, D.E. (2018). Institutional ethnography: A sociology of discovery – In conversation with Dorothy Smith. *Social Theory and Health, 16*(3), 292–306. https://doi.org/10.1057/s41285-018-0077-2

Kimmel, M. (2013). *Angry white men: American masculinity at the end of an era.* New York: Nation Books.

Kimmel, M.S., & Mahler, M. (2003). Adolescent masculinity, homophobia, and violence: Random school shootings, 1982–2001. *American Behavioral Scientist, 46*(10), 1439–58. https://doi.org/10.1177/0002764203046010010

Knights, D. (2004). Michel Foucault. In S. Linstead (Ed.), *Organization theory and postmodern thought* (pp. 14–34). London: SAGE Publications.

Knights, D., & Willmott, H. (1987). Organizational culture as management strategy: A critique and illustration from the financial services industry. *International Studies of Management and Organization, 17*(3), 40–63. https://doi.org/10.1080/00208825.1987.11656461

Kolanko, D. (2017, 19 January). Exit stage left: The decline of strip clubs in Canada. *The 10 and 3*. http://www.the10and3.com/exit-stage-left-the-decline-of-strip-clubs-in-canada/

Kraus, C. (2007). Trick. In A. Oakley (Ed.), *Working sex: Sex workers write about a changing industry* (pp. 41–51). Emeryville, CA: Seal Press.

Krishnan, M. (2020, 30 September). Strippers say the Covid-19 ban on strip clubs is discrimination. *Vice*. https://www.vice.com/en/article/4ayzjm/strippers-say-doug-fords-covid-19-ban-on-strip-clubs-is-discrimination

Lam, E. (2020). Pandemic sex workers' resilience: COVID-19 crisis met with rapid responses by sex worker communities. *International Social Work, 63*(6), 777–81. https://doi.org/10.1177/0020872820962202

Lam, E., & Lepp, A. (2019). Butterfly: Resisting the harms of anti-trafficking policies and fostering peer-based organising in Canada. *Anti-Trafficking Review, 12*, 91–107.

Lambrinos, T. (2014, 9 July). Testimony to the House of Commons Standing Committee on Justice and Human Rights (Session 38). http://www.ourcommons.ca/DocumentViewer/en/41-2/JUST/meeting-38/evidence

Lavin, M.F. (2013). Rule-making and rule-breaking: Strip club social control regarding alcohol and other drugs. *Deviant Behavior, 34*, 361–83. https://doi.org/10.1080/01639625.2012.735611

Law, T. (2013). Transitioning out of sex work: Exploring sex workers' experiences and perspectives. In E. Durisin, E. van der Meulen, & V. Love (Eds.), *Selling sex: Experience, advocacy, and research on sex work in Canada* (pp. 101–10). Vancouver: UBC Press.

Law, T. (2015). Licensed or licentious? Examining regulatory discussions of stripping in Ontario. *Canadian Journal of Law and Society, 30*(1), 31–50. https://doi.org/10.1017/cls.2014.25

Law, T. (2016). *Managing the "party": Third parties and the organization of labour in Ontario strip clubs* [Unpublished doctoral dissertation, University of Ottawa].

Law, T. (2020). His reputation precedes him: Examining the construction and management of the pimp in strip clubs. *Deviant Behavior, 41*(1), 103–17. https://doi.org/10.1080/01639625.2018.1519140

Law, T. (2021). A different kind of risky business: Men who manage men in the sex industry. *Sexualities, 24*(7), 941–56. https://doi.org/10.1177/13634607211026312

Law, T., & Bruckert, C. (2016). The surveillance web: Surveillance, risk and resistance in Ontario strip clubs. In E. van der Meulen & R. Heynen (Eds.), *Expanding the gaze: Gender and the politics of surveillance* (pp. 240–63). Toronto: University of Toronto Press.

Law, T., & Raguparan, M. (2019). "It's a puzzle you have to do every night": Performing creative problem solving at work in the indoor Canadian sex industry. *Work, Employment and Society, 34*(3), 424–40. https://doi.org/10.1177/0950017019878325

Lawrence, S. (2015). Expert-tease: Advocacy, ideology and experience in *Bedford* and Bill C-36. *Canadian Journal of Law and Society/La revue Canadienne droit et société, 30*(1), 5–7. https://doi.org/10.1017/cls.2015.3

LeBlanc, H. (2014). *A study on sexual harassment in the federal workplace*. Ottawa: House of Commons. https://www.ourcommons.ca/Content/Committee/412/FEWO/Reports/RP6376948/feworp02/feworp02-e.pdf

LeBlanc, M., & Barling, J. (2004). Understanding the many faces of workplace violence. In S. Fox & P. Spector (Eds.), *Counterproductive work behavior: Investigating actors and targets* (pp. 41–63). Washington, DC: APA Publishing.

Leidholdt, D. (1993). Prostitution: A violation of women's human rights. *Cardozo Women's Law Journal, 1*, 133–47.

Leigh, C. (1997). Inventing sex work. In J. Nagle (Ed.), *Whores and other feminists* (pp. 225–31). New York: Routledge.

LeRoy, M.H. (2017). Bare minimum: Stripping pay for independent contractors in the share economy. *William and Mary Journal of Race, Gender, and Social Justice, 23*(2), 249–70.

Lerum, K. (2004). Sexuality, power and camaraderie in service work. *Gender and Society, 18*(6), 756–76. https://doi.org/10.1177/0891243204269398

Lewis, J. (2000). Controlling lap dancing: Law, morality and sex work. In R. Weitzer (Ed.), *Sex for sale: Prostitution, pornography and the sex industry* (pp. 203–16). New York: Routledge.

Lewis, J. (2006). "I'll scratch your back if you'll scratch mine": The role of reciprocity, power and autonomy in the strip club. *Canadian Review of Sociology and Anthropology, 43*(3), 297–311. https://doi.org/10.1111/j.1755-618X.2006.tb02226.x

Lewis, J., & Shaver, F. (2006). *Safety, security and the well-being of sex workers: A report to the House of Commons Subcommittee on Solicitation Laws*. Windsor, ON: Sex Trade Advocacy and Research (STAR).

Lewis, P., Thornhill, A., & Saunders, M. (2003). *Employee relations: Understanding the employment relationship*. Essex, UK: Pearson Education.

Liepe-Levinson, K. (2002). *Strip show: Performances of gender and desire.* New York: Routledge.

Lilleston, P., Reuben, J., & Sherman, S. (2012). "This is our sanctuary": Perceptions of safety among exotic dancers in Baltimore, Maryland. *Health and Place, 18,* 561–7. https://doi.org/10.1016/j.healthplace.2012.01.009

Link, B., & Phelan, J. (2001). Conceptualizing stigma. *Annual Review of Sociology, 27,* 363–85. https://doi.org/10.1146/annurev.soc.27.1.363

Lister, B.M. (2015). "Yeah, they've started to get a bit fucking cocky" ... Culture, economic change and shifting power relations within the Scottish lap-dancing industry. *Graduate Journal of Social Science, 11*(2), 38–54. https://eprints.leedsbeckett.ac.uk/id/eprint/1453/

Liu, X., & Sierminska, E. (2014). Evaluating the effect of beauty on labor market outcomes: A review of the literature. *Luxembourg Institute of Socio-Economic Research (LISER) Working Paper Series, 11.*

Longmore, M. (1998). Symbolic interactionism and the study of sexuality. *Journal of Sex Research, 35*(1), 44–57. https://doi.org/10.1080/00224499809551916

Lorenz, K., & Ullman, S.E. (2016). Alcohol and sexual assault victimization: Research findings and future directions. *Aggression and Violent Behavior, 31,* 82–94. https://doi.org/10.1016/j.avb.2016.08.001

Lowman, J. (2000). Violence and the outlaw status of (street) prostitution in Canada. *Violence against Women, 6*(9), 987–1011. https://doi.org/10.1177/10778010022182245

Lowman, J., & Atchison, C. (2006). Men who buy sex: A survey in the Greater Vancouver Regional District. *Canadian Review of Sociology/Revue canadienne de sociologie, 43*(3), 281–96. https://doi.org/10.1111/j.1755-618X.2006.tb02225.x

Lyons, Dan. (2017, 1 April). Jerks and the start-ups they ruin. *New York Times.* https://mobile.nytimes.com/2017/04/01/opinion/sunday/jerks-and-the-start-ups-they-ruin.html

Machat, S., Shannon, K., Braschel, M., Moreheart, S., & Goldenberg, S.M. (2019). Sex workers' experiences and occupational conditions post-implementation of end-demand criminalization in Metro Vancouver, Canada. *Canadian Journal of Public Health, 110*(5), 575–83. https://doi.org/10.17269/s41997-019-00226-z

MacKinnon, C.A. (1987). *Feminism unmodified: Discourses on life and law.* Cambridge, MA: Harvard University Press.

Maggie's. (n.d.). A note to researchers, students, reporters and artists who are not sex workers. Toronto: Maggie's. http://maggiestoronto.ca/uploads/File/A-note-to-researchers.pdf

Margolis, M., and Arnold, M. (1983). Turning the tables? Male strippers and the gender hierarchy in America. In B. Miller (Ed.), *Sex and gender hierarchies* (pp. 334–50). New York: Cambridge University Press.

Maticka-Tyndale, E. (2004). *Exotic dancing in Ontario: Health and safety.* Windsor, ON: Sex Trade Advocacy and Research (STAR).

Maticka-Tyndale, E., Lewis, J., Clark, J.P., Zubick, J., & Young, S. (2000). Exotic dancing and health. *Women & Health, 31*(1), 87–108. https://doi.org/10.1300/J013v31n01_06

Maynard, R. (2015). Fighting wrongs with wrongs? How Canadian anti-trafficking crusades have failed sex workers, migrants, and Indigenous communities. *Atlantis: Critical Studies in Gender, Culture and Social Justice, 37*(2), 40–56. https://journals.msvu.ca/index.php/atlantis/article/view/3041

McDonald, P. (2012). Workplace sexual harassment 30 years on: A review of the literature. *International Journal of Management Reviews, 14*, 1–17. https://doi.org/10.1111/j.1468-2370.2011.00300.x

McInlay, A. (2010). Performativity and the politics of identity: Putting Butler to work. *Critical Perspectives on Accounting, 21*, 232–42. https://doi.org/10.1016/j.cpa.2008.01.011

Melnychuk, M. (2019, 7 February). Stripping off the table at Regina 151's current location as owner tries to get club re-opened. *Regina Leader-Post.* https://leaderpost.com/news/local-news/stripping-off-the-table-at-regina-151s-current-location-as-owner-tries-to-get-club-re-opened

Mensah, N.M. (2018). The representation of the "pimp": A barrier to understanding the work of third parties in the adult Canadian sex industry. In C. Bruckert & C. Parent (Eds.), *Getting past "the pimp": Management in the sex industry* (pp. 19–35). Toronto: University of Toronto Press.

Mercer, J. (2003). Homosexual prototypes: Repetition and the construction of the generic in the iconography of gay pornography. *Paragraph, 26*(1–2), 280–90. https://doi.org/10.3366/para.2003.26.1-2.280

Michau, L., Horn, J., Bank, A., Dutt, M., & Zimmerman, C. (2015). Prevention of violence against women and girls: Lessons from practice. *The Lancet, 385*(9978), 1672–84. https://doi.org/10.1016/S0140-6736(14)61797-9

Miller-Young, M. (2014). *A taste for brown sugar: Black women in pornography.* Durham, NC: Duke University Press.

Montemurro, B. (2001). Strippers and screamers: The emergence of social control in a noninstitutionalized setting. *Journal of Contemporary Ethnography, 30*(3), 275–304. https://doi.org/10.1177/089124101030003001

Montemurro, B., Bloom, C. & Madell, K. (2003). Ladies night out: A typology of women patrons of a male strip club. *Deviant Behavior, 24*(4), 333–52. https://doi.org/10.1080/713840221

Mumby, D.K. (2005). Theorizing resistance in organization studies: A dialectical approach. *Management Communication Quarterly, 19*(1), 19–44. https://doi.org/10.1177/0893318905276558

Munn, M., & Bruckert, C. (2013). *On the outside: From lengthy imprisonment to lasting freedom.* Vancouver: UBC Press.

Murphy, A.G. (2003). The dialectical gaze. *Journal of Contemporary Ethnography*, *32*(3), 305–35. https://doi.org/10.1177/0891241603032003003

Noack, A., & Vosko, L. (2011). Precarious jobs in Ontario: Mapping dimensions of labour market insecurity by workers' social location and context. Law Commission of Ontario.

O'Connell Davidson, J. (2006). Will the real sex slave please stand up? *Feminist Review*, *83*, 4–22. https://doi.org/10.1057/palgrave.fr.9400278

O'Doherty, T. (2007). *Off-street commercial sex: An exploratory study*. [Unpublished doctoral dissertation, Simon Fraser University].

Ontario Federation of Labour. (2016). *Precarious work engagement final survey report*. Toronto: Stratcom. https://www.whsc.on.ca/Files/Other/2017-4-6_E-lert_OFL-Precarious-Work-Final-Report

Ontario Human Rights Commission. (2017). Not on the menu: Inquiry report on sexualized dress codes in Ontario's restaurants. Toronto: Ontario Human Rights Commission. http://www.ohrc.on.ca/en/not-menu-ohrc-inquiry-report-sexualized-and-gender-based-dress-codes-restaurants

Pasko, L. (2002). Naked power: The practice of stripping as a confidence game. *Sexualities*, *5*(1), 49–66. https://doi.org/10.1177/1363460702005001003

Patton, M.Q. (2002). *Qualitative research and evaluation methods* (3rd ed.). Thousand Oaks, CA: SAGE Publications.

Pheterson, G. (1998). The social consequences of unchastity. In F. Delacoste & P. Alexander (Eds.), *Sex work: Writings by women in the sex industry* (pp. 231–46). San Francisco: Cleis Press. (Original work published 1987).

Pilcher, K. (2009). Empowering, degrading or a "mutually exploitative" exchange for women? Characterising the power relations of the strip club. *Journal of International Women's Studies*, *10*(3), 73–83. https://vc.bridgew.edu/jiws/vol10/iss3/7/

Pilcher, K. (2011). A "sexy space" for women? Heterosexual women's experiences of a male strip show venue. *Leisure Studies*, *30*(2), 217–35. https://doi.org/10.1080/02614367.2010.512048

Pinel, E.C. (1999). Stigma consciousness: The psychological legacy of social stereotypes. *Journal of Personality and Social Psychology*, *76*(1), 114–28. https://doi.org/10.1037/0022-3514.76.1.114

Pinel, E.C. (2004). "You're just saying that because I'm a woman": Stigma consciousness and attributions of discrimination. *Self and Identity*, *3*, 39–51. https://doi.org/10.1080/13576500342000031

Prasad, P., & Prasad, A. (2000). Stretching the iron cage: The constitution and implications of routine workplace organization. *Organization Science*, *11*(4), 387–403. https://doi.org/10.1287/orsc.11.4.387.14597

Price, K. (2008). "Keeping the dancers in check": The gendered organization of stripping work at the Lion's Den. *Gender and Society*, *22*(3), 367–89. https://doi.org/10.1177/0891243208316518

Price-Glynn, K. (2010). *Strip club: Gender, power and sex work*. New York: New York University Press.

Purcell, J., & Graham, K. (2005). A typology of Toronto nightclubs at the turn of the millennium. *Contemporary Drug Problems*, 32(1), 131–67. https://doi.org/10.1177/009145090503200109

Raguparan, M. (2017). "If I'm gonna hack capitalism": Racialized and Indigenous Canadian sex workers' experiences within the neo-liberal market economy. *Women's Studies International Forum*, 60: 69–76. https://doi.org/10.1016/j.wsif.2016.12.003

Rambo, C., Presley, S.R., & Mynatt, D. (2006). Claiming the bodies of exotic dancers: The problematic discourse of commodification. In D. Waskul & P. Vannini (Eds.), *Body/embodiment: Symbolic interaction and the sociology of the body* (pp. 213–28). Burlington VT: Ashgate Publishing.

Raymond, J.G. (2003). Ten reasons for not legalizing prostitution and a legal response to the demand for prostitution. In M. Farley (Ed.), *Prostitution, trafficking and traumatic stress* (pp. 315–32). Binghamton, NY: Haworth Maltreatment & Trauma Press.

Reed, S. (1997). All stripped off. In J. Nagel (Ed.), *Whores and other feminists* (pp. 179–88). New York: Routledge.

Reger, J. (2014). Micro-cohorts, feminist discourse, and the emergence of the Toronto SlutWalk. *Feminist Formations*, 26(1), 49–69. https://doi.org/10.1353/ff.2014.0005

Rigakos, G. (2008). *Nightclub: Bouncers, risk, and the spectacle of consumption*. Montreal and Kingston: McGill-Queen's University Press.

Ronai, C., & Cross, R. (1998). Dancing with identity: Narrative resistance strategies of male and female stripteasers. *Deviant Behavior*, 19(2), 99–119. https://doi.org/10.1080/01639625.1998.9968078

Roscigno, V., & Hodson, R. (2004). The organizational and social foundations of worker resistance. *American Sociological Review*, 69(1), 14–39. https://doi.org/10.1177/000312240406900103

Ross, B.L. (2000). Bumping and grinding on the line: Making nudity pay. *Labour*, 46, 221–50. https://www.erudit.org/en/journals/llt/2000-v46-llt_46/llt46art06/

Ross, B.L. (2009). *Burlesque west: Showgirls, sex, and sin in postwar Vancouver*. Toronto: University of Toronto Press.

Ross, B.L., & Greenwell, K. (2005). Spectacular striptease: Performing the sexual and racial other in Vancouver, B.C., 1945–1975. *Journal of Women's History*, 17(1), 137–64. https://doi.org/10.1353/jowh.2005.0012

Rubin, G. (1992). Thinking sex: Notes for a radical theory of the politics of sexuality. In C.S. Vance (Ed.), *Pleasure and danger: Exploring female sexuality* (pp. 267–319). London: Pandora Press.

Rudman, L.A. (1998). Self-promotion as a risk factor for women: The costs and benefits of counterstereotypical impression management. *Journal of*

Personality and Social Psychology, 74(3), 629–45. https://doi.org/10.1037/0022-3514.74.3.629

Sanday, P.R. (1992). *Fraternity gang rape: Sex, brotherhood, and privilege on campus.* New York: NYU Press.

Sanders, T. (2005). "It's just acting": Sex workers' strategies for capitalizing on sexuality. *Gender, Work & Organization, 12*(4), 319–42. https://doi.org/10.1111/j.1468-0432.2005.00276.x

Sanders, T. (2006). Sexing up the subject: Methodological nuances in researching the female sex industry. *Sexualities, 9*(4), 449–68. https://doi.org/10.1177/1363460706068044

Sanders, T., Cohen, R.L., & Hardy, K. (2013). Hairdressing/undressing: Comparing labour relations in self-employed body work. In C. Wolkowitz, R.L. Cohen, T. Sanders, & K. Hardy (Eds.), *Body/sex/work: Intimate, embodied and sexualized labour* (pp. 110–25). New York: Palgrave Macmillan.

Scambler, G. (2007). Sex work stigma: Opportunist migrants in London. *Sociology, 41*(6), 1079–96. https://doi.org/10.1177/0038038507082316

Schneider, M., & Hirsch, J.S. (2018). Comprehensive sexuality education as a primary prevention strategy for sexual violence perpetration. *Trauma, Violence, and Abuse, 21*(3), 439–55. https://doi.org/10.1177/1524838018772855

Scott, J. (1985). *Weapons of the weak: Everyday forms of peasant resistance.* New Haven, CT: Yale University Press.

Scull, M.T. (2013). Reinforcing gender roles at the male strip show: A qualitative analysis of men who dance for women (MDW). *Deviant Behavior, 34*(7), 557–78. https://doi.org/10.1080/01639625.2012.748624

Sex Workers United Against Violence, Allan, S., Bennett, D., Chettiar, J., Jackson, G., Krüsi, A., Pacey, K., Porth, K., Price, M., Shannon, K., & Taylor, C. (2014). *My work should not cost me my life: The case against criminalizing the purchase of sex in Canada.* Vancouver: Sex Workers United Against Violence.

Showden, C.R. (2011). *Choices women make: Agency in domestic violence, assisted reproduction, and sex work.* Minneapolis: University of Minnesota Press.

Shteir, R. (2004). *Striptease: The untold history of the girlie show.* New York: Oxford University Press.

SIECCAN. (2019). *Canadian guidelines for sexual health education.* Toronto: Sex Information and Education Council of Canada. http://sieccan.org/wp-content/uploads/2021/02/SIECCAN-Canadian-Guidelines-for-Sexual-Health-Education-1.pdf

Simon, W., & Gagnon, J.H. (1986). Sexual scripts: Permanence and change. *Archives of Sexual Behavior, 15*(2), 97–120. https://doi.org/10.1007/BF01542219

Singh, K. (2020). This is how sex workers are using streaming services during the pandemic. *Flare.* https://www.flare.com/sex-and-relationships/sex-workers-only-fans-canada/

Skipper, J.K., & McCaghy, C.H. (1970). Stripteasers: The anatomy and career contingencies of a deviant occupation. *Social Problems, 17*(3), 391–405. https://doi.org/10.2307/799557

Smart, C. (1989). *Feminism and the power of law*. London: Routledge.

Smith, C. (2002). Shiny chests and heaving G-strings: A night out with the Chippendales. *Sexualities, 5*(1), 67–89. https://doi.org/10.1177/1363460702005001004

Smith, D.E. (2005). *Institutional ethnography: A sociology for people*. Lanham, MD: Rowman Altamira.

Smith, M.D., Grov, C., Seal, D.W., Bernhardt, N., & McCall, P. (2015). Social-emotional aspects of male escorting: Experiences of men working for an agency. *Archives of Sexual Behavior, 44*(4), 1047–58. https://doi.org/10.1007/s10508-014-0344-9

Smith, M.D., & Seal, D.W. (2008). Motivational influences on the safer sex behavior of agency-based male sex workers. *Archives of Sexual Behavior, 37*(5), 845–53. https://doi.org/10.1007/s10508-008-9341-1

Snider, L. (2001). Abusing corporate power: The death of a concept. In S.C. Boyd, D.E. Chunn, & R. Menzies (Eds.), *(Ab)using power: The Canadian experience* (pp. 112–27). Winnipeg: Fernwood Publishing.

Spivey, S.E. (2005). Distancing and solidarity as resistance to sexual objectification in a nude dancing bar. *Deviant Behavior, 26*(5), 417–37. https://doi.org/10.1080/016396290931731

Spradley, J., & Mann, B. (1975). *The cocktail waitress: Woman's work in a man's world*. New York: McGraw-Hill.

Statistics Canada. (2020). Table 14-10-0335-02: Proportion of men and women in occupations, annual. https://www150.statcan.gc.ca/t1/tbl1/en/tv.action?pid=1410033502

Stecy-Hildebrand, N., Fuller, S., & Burns, A. (2018). "Bad" jobs in a "good" sector: Examining the employment outcomes of temporary work in the Canadian public sector. *Work, Employment and Society, 33*(4), 560–79. https://doi.org/10.1177/0950017018758217

Stella. (2013). *Language matters: Talking about sex work*. Montreal: Stella. https://www.nswp.org/sites/default/files/StellaInfoSheetLanguageMatters.pdf

Sterry, D.H., & Martin, Jr., R.J. (Eds.). (2009). *Hos, hookers, call girls and rent boys: Professionals writing on life, love, money, and sex*. Brooklyn: Soft Skull Press.

Sue, D.W., Capodilupo, C., Torino, G., Bucceri, J., Holder, A., Nadal, K., & Esquilin, M. (2007). Racial microaggressions in everyday life: Implications for clinical practice. *American Psychologist, 62*(4), 271–86. https://doi.org/10.1037/0003-066X.62.4.271

Sweet, N., & Tewksbury, R. (2000). "What's a nice girl like you doing in a place like this?" Pathways to a career in stripping. *Sociological Spectrum, 20*(3), 325–43. https://doi.org/10.1080/027321700405072

Taylor, L.C. (2008, 5 September). Stripper ban called "unconstitutional." *Toronto Star*. https://www.thestar.com/news/gta/2008/09/05/stripper_ban_called_unconstitutional.html

Teitel, E. (2015, 31 May). The last true strip club in Saskatchewan. *Maclean's*. https://www.macleans.ca/news/canada/the-last-true-strip-club-in-saskatchewan/

Tewksbury, R. (1994). A dramaturgical analysis of male strippers. *Journal of Men's Studies*, 2(4), 325–42. https://doi.org/10.3149/jms.0204.325

Thompson, W.E., & Harred, J.L. (1992). Topless dancers: Managing stigma in a deviant occupation. *Deviant Behavior*, 13(3), 291–311. https://doi.org/10.1080/01639625.1992.9967914

Tracey, L. (1997). *Growing up naked: My years in bump and grind*. Vancouver: Douglas & McIntyre.

Trautner, M.N. (2005). Doing gender, doing class: The performance of sexuality in exotic dance clubs. *Gender and Society*, 19(6), 771–88. https://doi.org/10.1177/0891243205277253

Trautner, M.N., & Collett, J.L. (2010). Students who strip: The benefits of alternate identities for managing stigma. *Symbolic Interaction*, 33(2), 257–79. https://doi.org/10.1525/si.2010.33.2.257

Turner, S.M. (2006). Mapping institutions as work and texts. In D.E. Smith (Ed.), *Institutional ethnography as practice* (pp. 139–61). Lanham, MD: Rowman & Littlefield.

Valverde, M. (1989). Beyond gender dangers and private pleasures: Theory and ethics in the sex debates. *Feminist Studies* 15(2), 237–54. https://doi.org/10.2307/3177786

Van Wijk, E., & Mascini, P. (2019). The responsibilization of entrepreneurs in legalized local prostitution in the Netherlands. *Regulation and Governance*, 16(3), 875–91. https://doi.org/10.1111/rego.12273

Vance, C.S. (1992). Pleasure and danger: Towards a politics of sexuality. In C.S. Vance (Ed.), *Pleasure and danger: Exploring female sexuality* (pp. 1–28). London: Pandora Press.

Villeneuve, P. (2017, 15 May). One of Toronto's most notorious strip clubs is closing. *blogTO*. https://www.blogto.com/city/2017/05/house-lancaster-strip-club-closing-toronto/

Vosko, L. (2010). *Managing the margins: Gender, citizenship, and the international regulation of precarious employment*. Oxford: Oxford University Press.

Vosko, L., & Clark, L.F. (2009). Canada: Gendered precariousness and social reproduction. In L. Vosko, M. MacDonald, & I. Campbell (Eds.), *Gender and the contours of precarious employment* (pp. 26–42). New York: Routledge.

Vosko, L.F., Tucker, E., Gellatly, M., & Thomas, M.P. (2011). New approaches to enforcement and compliance with labour regulatory standards: The case of Ontario, Canada. Comparative Research in Law and Political Economy, Research Paper No. 31.

Vosko, L.F., Zukewich, N., & Cranford, C. (2003). Precarious jobs: A new typology of employment. *Perspectives in Labour and Income*, 4(10).

Weitzer, R. (2012). Sex trafficking and the sex industry: The need for evidence-based theory and legislation. *Journal of Criminal Law and Criminology*, 101(4), 1337–69.

West, C., & Zimmerman, D.H. (1987). Doing gender. *Gender & Society*, 1(2), 125–51. https://doi.org/10.1177/0891243287001002

Westcott, M., Baird, M., & Cooper, R. (2006). Reworking work: Dependency and choice in the employment relationship. *Labour and Industry*, 17(1), 5–17. https://doi.org/10.1080/10301763.2006.10669336

Whitehead, S.M. (2002). *Men and masculinities*. Cambridge: Polity Press.

Williams, C., & Connell, C. (2016). The invisible consequences of aesthetic labour in upscale retail stores. In M.G. Crain, W.R. Poster, & M.A. Cherry (Eds.), *Invisible labor: Hidden work in the contemporary world* (pp. 193–213). Oakland: University of California Press.

Willis, P.E. (1977). *Learning to labor: How working class kids get working class jobs*. New York: Columbia University Press.

Willmott, H. (1997). Rethinking management and managerial work: Capitalism, control and subjectivity. *Human Relations*, 50(11), 1329–59. https://doi.org/10.1177/001872679705001101

Wingfield, A.H., & Skeete, R. (2016). Maintaining hierarchies in predominantly white organizations: A theory of racial tasks as invisible labor. In M.G. Crain, W.R. Poster, & M.A. Cherry (Eds.), *Invisible Labor: Hidden Work in the Contemporary World* (pp. 47–68). Oakland: University of California Press.

Wolkowitz, C. (2006). *Bodies at work*. Thousand Oaks, CA: SAGE Publications.

Wood, E.A. (2000). Working in the fantasy factory: The attention hypothesis and the enacting of masculine power in strip clubs. *Journal of Contemporary Ethnography*, 29(1), 5–31. https://doi.org/10.1177/089124100129023800

Work Safe Twerk Safe. (2020, 21 November). Donate to our GoFundMe! Funds go towards our legal action. https://worksafetwerksafe.com/2020/11/21/donate-to-our-gofundme-funds-go-towards-our-legal-action/

Work Safe Twerk Safe. (2021, 27 February). Legal action update 4: Our first win! https://worksafetwerksafe.com/2021/02/27/legal-action-update-4-our-first-win/

Work Safe Twerk Safe. (2022, 12 May). Last and final legal update. https://worksafetwerksafe.com/2022/05/12/last-and-final-judicial-review-update/

Zaveri, M. (2019, 15 December). Black women now hold crowns in 5 major beauty pageants. *New York Times*. https://www.nytimes.com/2019/12/15/style/black-women-win-beauty-pageants.html

Cases Cited

Adult Entertainment Association of Canada v Ottawa (City), [2007] ONCA 389.
Alexandre c R, [2009] QCCS 16.
Bravakis v Barrie, [2005] ONCJ 398.
Canadian Labour Congress (Canadian Association of Burlesque Entertainers, Local Union No. 1689) v Algonquin Tavern, 1981 CanLII 812 (ON LRB).
Canada (Attorney General) v Bedford, [2013] 3 SCR 1101.
Canadian Union of Postal Workers v Foodora Inc., 2020 CanLII 25122 (ON LRB).
Locomotion Tavern v Ontario, [2010] ONSC 1184.
Milk and Bread Drivers, Dairy Employees, Caterers and Allied Employees, Local 647, affiliated with the International Brotherhood of Teamsters v Canada Bread Company Limited, [2017] ON LRB 62172.
Ontario Adult Entertainment Bar Association v Metropolitan Toronto, [1995] ONSC 10668.
Ontario Adult Entertainment Bar Association v Metropolitan Toronto, [1997] ONCA 14486.
Peck v Chomyc Hotels, [1989] AB QB 3306.
R v Anwar, [2020] ONCJ 103.
R v Mara, [1997] 2 SCR 630.
R v Mijatovic, [2008] ONCJ 179.
R v Pelletier, [1999] 3 SCR 863.
Roberts v Club Expose, [1993] ON HRT 547.
Terry, Nuno, Cosper, Pelaez, Morgan, Charest, et al. v Sapphire Gentlemen's Club, [2014] NV SC 59214.
Toronto v Zanzibar Tavern Inc., [2007] ONCJ 401.
Varma v G.B. Allright Enterprises Inc., [1988] BC HRT 8913, 9 CHRR 5290.
Work Safe Twerk Safe v Ontario, [2021] ONSC 1100 (2021a).
Work Safe Twerk Safe v Ontario, [2021] ONSC 6736 (2021b).

Legislation Cited

Allow States and Victims to Fight Online Sex Trafficking Act of 2017, 1st session, 115th Congress.
Criminal Code of Canada, R.S.C. 1985, c. C-46.
Employment Standards Act, 2000, S.O. 2000, c. 41.
Human Rights Code, R.S.O. 1990, c. H.19.
Occupational Health and Safety Act, R.S.O. 1990, c. O.1.
Ottawa Bylaw No. L6 2000, Schedule 27, Relating to Adult Entertainment Parlours.
Ottawa Bylaw No. 2002-189, Schedule 11 – Adult Entertainment Parlours. https://ottawa.ca/en/business/business-assistance-and-growth

/permits-licences-and-applications-laws-and-garbage/laws-businesses
/licensing-law-no-2002-189/businesses-regulated-licensing-law-no
-2002-189#adult-entertainment-parlours-schedule-no-11

Protection of Communities and Exploited Persons Act, S.C. 2014, c. 25.

Stop Enabling Sex Traffickers Act of 2017, 2nd session, 115th Congress.

Toronto Bylaw No. 243-2013, To Amend City of Toronto Municipal Code Chapter 545, Licensing, Respecting Adult Entertainment Parlours.

Toronto Municipal Code, 2019, c. 545, Licensing https://www.toronto.ca
/legdocs/municode/1184_545.pdf

Index

abuse of dancers, 22
Adult Entertainment Association of Canada (AEAC), 24–5, 122, 123
adult entertainment bylaw, Toronto, 136, 155n2 (ch. 3), 157n2 (ch. 5)
aesthetic requirements for dancers, 25, 28, 39, 40. *See also* racialization of dancers
agents, 29, 42–3
alcohol consumption, 21, 77, 96, 98, 104, 105, 137
Althorp, J., 3, 48
Ashforth, B.E., 119
assault, risk of, 103, 104
associates, third parties as, 30
Association for Burlesque Entertainers, 158n2

back regions, 11, 54, 55, 56, 70
Baird, M., 115
bartenders: gender disparity, 27; misbehaviour, 51; path to work at strip club, 17–18; responsibilities of, 27–8; stigmatic assumptions about, 119, 120; treatment of dancers, 80; verbal strategies, 103; work schedule, 22
Barton, B., 132
Basford, T., 91

beauty: Eurocentric ideal of, 38, 60, 154n1 (ch. 2); pageant, 133; racialized notions of, 9, 77, 133
Berg, B.L., 44
Black men, stereotypical image of, 76, 99, 120
Black queer performers, 141
Black women: beauty norms and, 63; discrimination against, 38, 133
Bolton, S.C., 50, 52, 57
Bouclin, S., 3, 37, 48, 157n1 (ch. 6), 158n2
bouncers: arrangement of stag parties, 30, 31; background of, 14, 76; career after leaving sex industry, 23; customers' perception of, 116–17; dancers' perception of, 113; demographics of, 14; job satisfaction of, 21; misbehaviour of, 51; night work, 22; non-violent strategies of, 27; path to work at strip club, 18, 19, 20; perception of, 74, 75–6; responsibilities of, 26–7, 76, 89–90; risk of physical assault, 103, 104; romantic partnerships, 119; scholarly studies of, 4, 103; security duties, 99, 103; services to dancers, 30, 68–9. *See also* enforcement of rules

Boyle, K.M., 97
Bradley-Engen, M.S., 3, 119
Brents, B.G., 94
"bro culture," 91
brothels, 42–3, 143, 144
Bruckert, C., 4, 28, 79, 99, 101, 121, 142, 143, 151
Butler, J., 153n4
bylaws: adult entertainment, 136, 155n2 (ch. 3), 157n2 (ch. 5); private room, 157n2 (ch. 5); touching-related, 123, 137, 142, 153n2

CABE v Algonquin Tavern, 36, 37, 43, 134, 144–5
Canada Labour Code, 90
Canada v Bedford, 93, 145, 146
Canadian Alliance for Sex Work Law Reform (CASWLR), 146
Canadian Association of Burlesque Entertainers (CABE), 36, 158n2
Canadian Union of Postal Workers v Foodora Inc., 145
Castel, R., 115, 123
champagne rooms, 35, 56, 60, 100. *See also* VIP rooms
change rooms, 48, 56–7
club owners, 24–5
contracts for dancers, 40
Cooper, R., 115
COVID-19 pandemic, impact of, 140, 147
Crenshaw, K., 9
Criminal Code, 5, 6, 33, 136, 137, 142, 143
critical management studies (CMS), 10
"culture fit," 91
customers of strip clubs: alcohol and drug use by, 98; behaviour of, 76–7, 78, 101–2, 156n1; collection of payment from, 81, 100–1; normative judgments about, 97; perceptions of, 95–6, 97–8; racial and social profiling of, 99, 100; risks assessment by, 131; screening of, 98–9; threat of legal actions against, 112; treatment of dancers, 59, 77, 127

Dancers for Equal Rights, 158n2
DeMichele, M.T., 4, 26, 27, 51, 83, 117, 155n4
disciplinary actions against dancers, 82–3
DJ booth, 1, 56
DJs: background of, 15, 18–19; clothing-related expectations, 74, 75; conflict with managers, 23; criticism of club owners, 22; job satisfaction of, 20, 21; misbehaviour of, 51; path to work at strip club, 18, 19, 20, 24; pay structures, 66; professionalism of, 74–5, 85; relations with dancers, 29, 66–7; responsibilities of, 14, 28–9, 108; romantic partnerships of, 119; social skills of, 23; stereotypes about, 118–19; work relations with dancers, 21, 29, 41, 65–7, 74–5, 80–2
dramaturgical approach, 9, 54
drivers, 30–1, 117, 144
drug consumption, 22, 77, 98, 104–6

economy of favours, 65–8, 69–70
education: peer (among dancers), 138; sexual, 139; of third parties, 14, 17, 92, 137–8
Egan, R.D., 3, 4, 65, 155n4
employment relationship, 45–50
Employment Standards Act, 135
enforcement of rules: by bouncers, 22, 45–6, 106; by third parties 46, 70–1, 107, 137

Erickson, K., 87, 90
erotic dancers: attitudes/expectation about, 81–2, 83, 86–7, 126–7, 131–2; boundary communication, 110, 111; celebrities as, 2; class and attitude of, 81–4; collective actions of, 44–5, 47–8; competition among, 63, 64, 82, 141; demographics, 8; emancipation of, 126; financial security of, 100, 112; immigration restrictions, 25; interviews of, 150–1; legal claims of, 43, 44, 146–7; negotiating strategies, 83; owners' service to, 25; pathways into work as, 16, 154n3; payment disputes, 81; price-fixing, 64–5; professionalism of, 93, 131; protection of, 113, 128; relationships with managers, 69; relative freedom of, 49–50; responsibilization of, 109–10, 113, 139; retirement of, 132, 154n1; scholarly study of, 7–8; screening practices of, 79, 110; second persona of, 75, 86; self-governance of, 57–9, 113; self-promotion of, 83; supplemental services to, 29; termination of employment of, 47; verbal strategies, 110–11. *See also* third party–dancer relations
erotic dance sector: best practices, 130–3; challenges of, 4; changes in, 140, 141–2; data collection about, 149; history of in Ontario, 4–5; labour practices in Ontario, 142–3; legitimacy of, 121; managerial power and control in, 10; moral justification of, 123; organizational relations and practices, 3, 6, 53; as provision of fantasy, 121; scholarly study of, 4, 74, 149–52
erotic massage parlours, 2, 5, 43, 122, 144

escort agencies, 144
exotic dancers, 7, 151
Exotic Dancers Alliance, 158n2
Exotic Dancers' Rights Association of Canada, 158n2
exploitation of dancers, 44–5
exploiter/exploited normative trope, 94, 120, 129, 142, 143, 146
extra services, 8–9, 22, 62–3, 64, 136

female "bossiness" trope, 83
female sex workers: normative scripts of, 73–4
flirtatiousness, as expectation of dancers, 85–7
Foodora (food delivery service), 145
Frank, K., 33, 35, 76, 105
fraternity parties, 97
friendliness versus professionalism, 85
front region, 11, 55–6, 57, 72, 73, 74, 76–8, 88
Fudge, J., 37

gender and sexual scripts, manipulation of, 83–4
gendered labour relations, 9, 91, 153n4
gendered violence, 139
gig workers, 141
"girls": framing of dancers as, 79, 80; good girl/bad girl trope, 122, 129
Goffman, E., 9, 11, 54–5, 95, 116, 121, 153n4
gossip campaigns, 64
Greenwell, K., 38, 156n3

Hadjisolomou, A., 51
hairstylists, 37, 48, 155n3
Hallgrimsdottir, H.K., 1
Hannem, S., 99, 121, 142, 143
harassment, 77. *See also* sexual harassment

Hardy, K., 141
Hausbeck, K., 94
health and safety standards, 136, 137
hiring practices, 37–8, 40, 132, 148, 155n2
Hobbs, C.M., 3, 76, 103, 119
Hodson, R., 93
Houlihan, M., 50, 52, 57
house fees, 36, 41, 42, 43, 68, 134, 155n4
housemother, 154n1
Hubbard, P., 6
human and labour rights of dancers, 132–3

incall/outcall agencies: police involvement, 107–8; scheduling requirements, 43; service fees, 43; wages in, 42–3, 155n3; working conditions, 49–50
income: of dancers, 16, 35, 65, 67, 154n2, 155n3; of managers, 15; of third parties, 15, 31, 52
independent contractors: dancers as, 36, 37, 52, 53, 71, 134, 135, 144–5; versus employees, 36, 37
institutional ethnography, 7, 149
intersectionality, 9

labour-protection mechanisms for exotic dancers, 2, 11, 93, 134–5, 138, 147–8
lap dancing: dancers' attitude to, 5, 157n1 (ch. 6); earnings from, 67; fees, 140; introduction of, 6, 35–6, 153n3, 157n1 (ch. 6); monitoring of, 60, 104; physical contact and, 4–6, 61, 106, 123; provision of sexual services, 106; regulations of, 4, 5, 123, 155n2 (ch. 3); stigmatic assumptions about, 5, 122; studies of, 4–5

Lavin, M.F., 3, 51, 60
Lawrence, S., 145
legal risks, 104–8
Leigh, Carol, 3, 34
LeRoy, M.H., 36
Lerum, K., 132
Lewis, J., 3, 4, 37
Lewis, P., 37
licensing: adult entertainment, 40, 92, 136; of dancers, 40
Lilleston, P., 156n3
Link, B., 115
liquor, 4, 43, 100, 137
lookism, 133

Maggie's with Strapped TO, 141
mainstream workplaces: discrimination and harassment in, 90–3; marginalization and exclusion in, 91; micro-aggressions in, 91; sexually overt work culture in, 87–8
male aggressive behaviour, 97
male sex workers, 74
managers: clothing-related expectations, 74; dancer's perception of, 113; female, 14, 134; job perception, 26; occupational roles, 75; path to work at strip club, 17, 19, 20; perceptions of customers, 95; popular perception of, 33; professional image of, 74, 75; relationships with staff, 25, 41; responsibilities of, 14, 25–6, 33, 34, 39; romantic partnerships, 119; rule enforcement, 45–7, 48, 51, 106–7; scholarship on, 4, 34; sense of importance, 120; sex life, 21; skills of, 118; working relation between dancers and, 26, 29, 43, 45, 81, 127–8; workplace injuries, 103

Maticka-Tyndale, E., 3
#MeToo movement, 91
Michau, L., 139
micro-aggressions, 73, 78, 91, 93
Milk and Bread Drivers et al. v Canada Bread Company, 37
Murphy, A.G., 3
music guidelines at clubs, 99. *See also* DJs

New Zealand's sex industry, 143

Occupational Health and Safety Act, 135
occupational performance, 54, 57, 72–3, 76, 78, 135
Ontario Human Rights Commission (OHRC), 39
Ontario Labour Relations Board (OLRB), 36, 144
organizational culture, 72, 78, 86, 132, 134
Ottawa strip clubs: closing of, 140; house fees, 43; regulations of, 136, 137; rule enforcement in, 62; scheduling requirements, 41, 134; stage show rates, 67

parallel organizational structures, 11, 45, 52–3, 54, 58, 70–1, 128, 131, 135
"party" environment, 51, 72, 76–8, 87–8, 96, 98, 101, 104, 113, 132, 156n1
Peck v Chomyc Hotels, 147
Penley, C., 44
performance: of aggressive masculinity, 76, 101; creation of, 72–3; normative scripts of, 73–4; theory of, 54–5. *See also* occupational performance
Phelan, J., 115
Pheterson, G., 126, 157n2 (ch. 6)

physical contact in strip clubs, 4–6, 61, 62, 106, 123
pimps, 15, 22, 31, 34, 99, 102, 120–1
Pinel, E.C., 118
police, 92–3, 107, 111, 158n3; presence at strip clubs, 104, 107–8
power relations in strip clubs, 14–15, 47, 49, 53
Price, K., 28, 79
Price-Glynn, K., 41, 48
private room bylaw, 157n2 (ch.5)
procurer, 34
prostitution: attitudes of third parties to, 106, 123, 124; campaigns against, 141–2; lap dancing as, 5; laws, 15, 25, 94, 106, 145–6; moral objections to, 106, 116; popular framings of, 122; scholarship on, 3; versus stripping, 121, 122–3, 124–5
Protection of Communities and Exploited Persons Act (PCEPA), 25, 146

R v Mara, 5, 155n1
R v Pelletier, 5
racial discrimination, 91, 92
racialization of dancers, 38, 40, 77–8, 83, 133, 154n1
regulation: in Ontario, 6, 24, 137, 143–4; of sex industry, 142–3, 145–6; of strip clubs, 5, 6, 24, 136–9
restaurants, 16, 25, 39, 90
Rethinking Management in the Adult and Sex Industry Project, 7, 120, 149–51
Rigakos, 103, 107
risk-mitigation strategies, 95–8, 103, 104, 108–12, 113–14
Roberts v Club Expose, 146
Roscigno, V., 93
Ross, B.L., 38, 156n3

rules: enforcement of, 22, 45–7, 48, 51, 62, 70–1, 106–7, 137; lap dancing, 4, 123; non-adherence to, 46–7, 53, 59, 61–2, 82
ruling relations, 33, 34

safety, 11–12, 49, 98, 113
Sanders, T., 141, 152
Sapphire Gentlemen's Club, 44
scheduling, 28, 41–2, 134, 155n4
security at strip clubs, 94–114; DJs' involvement in, 108; as gendered endeavour, 101; methods of provision of, 94, 95, 102–3, 104, 109, 113, 131; police involvement in, 107; preventive policies, 11–12, 100
self-employed informal labour, 141
service sector: aesthetic requirements in, 39–40; separation between third parties and workers in, 50
sex industry: aesthetic requirements in, 40; association with violence, 3, 94–5; in comparative perspective, 142–3; competition in, 40; decriminalization of, 93, 141, 142, 143; feminists' view of, 3; hierarchical divisions in, 31; labour framework, 3–4; legalization of, 143–4, 158n3; migrants and, 146; normative scripts in, 73–4; partial criminalization of, 146; regional variations of, 4, 8; scholarly studies of, 3–4, 6–9; socio-legal context, 4–6; workplace relationships, 9
sex trafficking, 15–16, 146, 157n1 (ch. 5)
sex work, 3, 34, 115, 143
sexual assault, 109, 158n3
sexual exploitation, 94
sexual harassment: in mainstream workplaces, 90–1, 98; prevention of, 92, 138–9; risk of, 94; strip club culture and, 73, 92; underreporting of, 90, 91
sexually overt work culture, 87, 88, 90
Shaver, F., 3
signage in clubs, 60–1
Skeete, R., 91
Smith, Dorothy, 33
Stella (sex worker rights organization), 79
stereotypes: about dancers, 120, 125; about DJs, 118–19; about sex industry, 1–2, 13, 120–1; third parties and, 32, 33, 118–19, 121
stigma: bartenders and, 119, 120; bouncers and, 116–17, 124; as cultural object, 115–16; dancers and, 12, 89, 116, 12, 124, 126, 128; DJs and, 117, 119; effects of, 12, 115, 128, 129, 147; impact on romantic partnerships, 119–20; interpersonal determinants, 116; intersection with classism and sexism, 124–5; justification of, 121; management of, 117–18, 128–9, 133; pervasiveness of, 116, 129; reinforcement of, 121–2, 123, 124–5, 133; relationship between stratification and, 123; third parties and, 12, 116–22, 128, 133
stigma consciousness, 118, 120
stratification, 121, 123, 133
strip clubs: aesthetic guidelines, 39; bad practices, 133–5; best practices, 130–3; "buyout" practices, 156n3; change rooms, 48; cleanliness, 49; as communities, 130; contemporary

trends, 139–43; decline of, 140, 141; employment relationships, 1, 10–11, 14, 131–2, 134; equipment, 48; financial disputes at, 107; front and back regions of, 55–6; lawsuits against, 44–5; local social norms, 5–6; versus mainstream workplaces, 90–2; management of, 1, 22, 34, 132, 156n4; marketing of, 44; media representation of, 2; organizational culture in, 51, 72; owners' groups, 123–4; parallel structures of, 11, 49, 55, 70–1, 131, 135; proliferation of, 43–4; rule enforcement, 62; scholarship on, 25; screening practices, 98–9, 101, 110, 113, 132; thefts in, 48; violation of criminal law in, 137–8
strippers. *See* erotic dancers
Strippers' United Association, 158n2
stripping, 6, 33; versus prostitution, 122–3. *See also* erotic dancers
surveillance: of dancers, 60, 63–4; lateral (peer), 63–4, 70; as tool of managerial discipline, 156n4; by third parties, 29, 89; of VIP areas, 60, 107, 114, 124

table dancing, 35
Tewksbury, R., 4, 26, 27, 51, 83, 117, 155n4
third parties: affiliated and unaffiliated, 10, 30; background of, 13, 17; benefits and drawbacks of being, 20–2; and club owners, 123–4; definition of, 4, 34, 149; demographics of, 8, 13–16; fee-for-service arrangements, 31; gender disparity in, 134; intervention in payment disputes, 107; interviews of, 151; job satisfaction, 20, 32, 135; lifestyle, 21; misbehaviour of, 50–2, 78, 87; in neoliberal capitalist workplace relations, 34–5; night shifts, 22; objections to punitive regulations, 132; pathways into work as, 16–20, 57; personalities of, 32; preparation areas, 56; preventive actions by, 113; professionalism of, 84, 85, 92, 131; reasons for leaving the industry, 23; rejection of normative tropes, 74, 119, 129; responsibilization of dancers by, 109–10, 113; scholarship on, 73, 144; skills of, 23; tasks of, 4, 10, 11, 14, 23–4, 35, 37, 43, 131; types of, 29–30; work experience in unrelated jobs, 15, 18; *See also* bouncers; DJs; drivers; enforcement of rules; managers; third party–dancer relations
third party–dancer relations: collaboration in, 65; conflicts in, 144–5; flirtatiousness in, 85–7; friendliness in, 84, 85; inappropriate behaviour in, 87, 88, 90; paternalism and condescension in, 79–80; perceptions in, 21, 78, 79–80, 81, 89, 90, 125–6, 128, 129; power relations, 47, 49, 53; professionalism in, 72–3, 84, 85, 86; resentment in, 135; sexual interactions in, 78, 86–7; socio-economic trends and, 144; sympathy in, 127–8
tipping practices, 65–6, 67, 68–9, 70, 155nn3–4
Toronto Municipal Standards Complaints and Information Line, 138
Toronto strip clubs: closing of, 140, 141; house fees, 42, 43; lap dancing in, 6; scheduling requirements, 42, 44, 134

touching-related bylaw, 123, 137, 142, 153n2
trafficking of women in clubs, 142
training: of dancers, 57–9, 71; peer education, 138

unchastity, 157n2 (ch. 6)

Varma v G.B. Allright Enterprises, 146
violence: alcohol and, 96; client-initiated, 94, 95, 98; in clubs, 27, 95, 114; as conflict-resolution method, 102–3; against male sex workers, 74; risk of, 95, 103, 114; third parties and, 96; types of, 96
VIP rooms: dancers' perception of, 100; entry fee for, 27; location of, 56; safety and security, 101, 106, 110; surveillance of, 60, 107, 114, 124. *See also* champagne rooms

waitresses, 41, 70, 132
Weitzer, R., 142, 157n1 (ch. 5)
West, C., 153n4
Westcott, M., 115
"whore stigma," 124, 126, 129, 157n2 (ch. 6)
Willmott, H., 10, 34, 35, 120
Wingfield, A.H., 91
work organization in Ontario, 35–7
Work Safe Twerk Safe (WSTS), 7, 147, 158n2
Work Safe Twerk Safe v Ontario, 93
worker-manager-customer triangle, 50, 52
working conditions: of dancers, 35, 36, 48, 56–7, 128; of DJs, 35

Zimmerman, C., 153n4

Milton Keynes UK
Ingram Content Group UK Ltd.
UKHW031620150324
439587UK00005B/27